# French and West Indian:

## Martinique, Guadeloupe, and French Guiana Today

# French and West Indian:

## Martinique, Guadeloupe, and French Guiana Today

### Edited by

### Richard D.E Burton and Fred Reno

A. James Arnold, Series Editor
*New World Studies*

University Press of Virginia
Charlottesville and London

First published 1994 by The Macmillan Press Ltd
First published 1995 in the United States of
America by the University Press of Virginia
Box 3608 University Station
Charlottesville, VA 22903

Library of Congress Cataloging-in-Publication Data
French and West Indian : Martinique, Guadeloupe, and French Guiana
today / edited by Richard D.E. Burton and Fred Reno.
    p.    cm. — (New World studies)
'Most of the chapters in this collection first appeared in French
in Les Antilles-Guyane au rendez-vous de l'Europe . . . published by
Economica (Paris), 1994' — Acknowledgements.
Includes bibliographical references and index.
Contents: The French West Indies à l'heure de l'Europe : an
overview / Richard D.E. Burton and Fred Reno — Constitutional and
political change in the French Caribbean / Helen Hintjens —
Politics and society in Martinique / Fred Reno — Guadeloupean
consensus / Jean-Paul Eluther — Society, culture and politics in
French Guiana / Bridget Jones and Elie Stephenson — Dialectics of
descent and phenotypes in racial classification in Martinique /
Michel Giraud — The Declaration of the Treaty of Maastricht on the
ultra-peripheral regions of the Community : an assessment / Emmanuel
Jos — The French Antilles and the wider Caribbean / Maurice Burac —
West Indians in France / Alain Anselin — Women from Guadeloupe
and Martinique / Arlette Gautier — The idea of difference in
contemporary French West Indian thought : Négritude, Antillanité,
Créolité / Richard D.E. Burton — French West Indian writing since
1970 / Beverley Ormerod.
    ISBN 0–8139–1565–1. — ISBN 0–8139–1566–X (pbk.)
    1. West Indies, French — Civilization — 20th century.  2. French
Guiana — Civilization — 20th century.  3. Blacks — France — Race
identity.  4. West Indies, French — Relations — France.  5. France —
Relations — West Indies, French.  6. French Guiana — Relations —
France.  7. France — Relations — French Guiana.  I. Burton, Richard
D. E., 1946– .  II. Reno, Fred.  III. Antilles-Guyane au rendez-
vous de l'Euope.  IV. Series.
F2151.F83   1995
972.97'6—dc20                                                94–39219
                                                                  CIP

Printed in Hong Kong
*Cover photo: Chris Huxley*

# Contents

                    Martinique
                    *Arlette Gautier*

**CHAPTER 10**       The idea of difference in contemporary   137
                    French West Indian thought: Négritude,
                    Antillanité, Créolité
                    *Richard D.E. Burton*

**CHAPTER 11**       French West Indian writing since 1970     167
                    *Beverley Ormerod*

                    Select bibliography                       188

                    Index                                     200

# Foreword

In what corner of the Western hemisphere does the majority population 1) claim primarily African descent; 2) carry a French passport; and 3) belong to the European Community? Only the French overseas departments of Guadeloupe and its dependencies (which include St Martin, shared with the Netherlands), Martinique, and French Guiana (on the Atlantic coast of the South American mainland) qualify. Richard D. E. Burton and Fred Reno have edited a volume that explores the anomalies of this situation in a remarkable example of interdisciplinary scholarship.

In 1981 Edouard Glissant told a wry anecdote that bespeaks the contradictions of France's New World departments: 'A Martinican political figure imagined as a bitter joke that in the year 2100, tourists would be invited by satellite advertisement to visit this island and gain firsthand knowledge of "what a colony was like in past centuries." '.[1] Glissant had in mind the political unwillingness of French West Indians to strike out on their own and to affirm their Americanness. The joke has, however, become a very complicated reality since ratification of the Maastricht accords. Guadeloupe, French Guiana, and Martinique are now not only French but European as well. In this respect they represent the limits of a New World cultural process that our series proposes to explore and describe.

At another level, there is no doubt that the process of creolization that characterizes the French West Indies invites comparison with other regions of the Americas. The juxtaposition of this title with Vera M. Kutzinski's *Sugar's Secrets: Race and the Erotics of Cuban Nationalism*, the first book in this series, is telling in this regard.[2] In the French West Indies, as in Cuba, the cultural construction of the mulatto woman is a battleground on which ideological wars are fought. Michel Giraud contributes the elements of a sociological analysis of the problem of racial classification, using evidence from Martinique (chapter 5). Arlette Gautier looks to literary, as well as sociological sources, in her examination of the status of women in the region (chapter 9). Some of her best information is taken from the documentary novel *Leonora* by Dany Bébel-Gisler, which has just been published by our CARAF BOOKS series.[3] Richard Burton skillfully uses data from politics, linguistics, and literature to complement Giraud's analysis and demonstrate how social groups have evolved into the unique political arrangement one finds in the region today (chapter 10).

The cover photo chosen for our edition is emblematic of the contradictions in French West Indian society. The statue of the nineteenth-century abolitionist Schoelcher, a member of the French legislature from Alsace during the Second Republic, stands in a prominent place in downtown Fort-de-France, Martinique. Subsequent generations have been invited to admire the noble Frenchman's paternal gesture in *giving* freedom to the slaves of the French West Indies in 1848. This monumental icon of republican ideology proclaims, apparently for all time, that freedom — and everything else — comes from France, whose generosity alone assures the prosperity and liberty of her children overseas. *French and West Indian: Martinique, Guadeloupe, and French Guiana Today* can be read as a teasing out, from varied methodological perspectives, of the tensions embodied in the ideological statement implicit in the monument to Schoelcher.

A. James Arnold

## Notes

1   Edouard Glissant, *Caribbean Discourse*, CARAF BOOKS (Charlottesville and London: Univ. Press of Virginia, 1989), p. 1.

2   Vera M. Kutzinski, *Sugar's Secrets: Race and the Erotics of Cuban Nationalism*, New World Studies (Charlottesville and London: Univ. Press of Virginia, 1993).

3   Dany Bébel-Gisler, *Leonora*, CARAF BOOKS (Charlottesville and London: Univ. Press of Virginia, 1994).

# Acknowledgements

Most of the chapters in this collection first appeared in French in *Les Antilles-Guyane au rendez-vous de l'Europe. Le Grand Tournant*, edited by Richard Burton and Fred Reno and published by Economica (Paris) in 1993: we are grateful to the director of Economica, Monsieur Jean Pavlevski, for permission to republish them here in translation. Chapter 10 first appeared in *New West Indian Guide* in 1993 (Vol. 67, No. 1 and 2), and we thank the managing editor, Gert Oostindie, for permission to reprint it here. Many of the ideas developed in the book were first debated at a conference on the French West Indies held at the Centre for Caribbean Studies at Warwick University in May 1990. Thanks are due to Alistair Hennessy who, as director of the Centre, organized the conference and, as editor of the present series, saw the need for the French West Indies to be represented in it; without generous financial assistance from the Nuffield Foundation the conference could not have taken place, nor would the book, which partly issued from it, have appeared in its present form. We are also grateful to Ralph Grillo, former Dean of the School of African and Asian Studies at Sussex University, who made funds available for the final preparation of the text, and to Margaret Ralph who word-processed most of the chapters. Finally, thanks are due to Shirley Hamber and Bill Lennox of Macmillan for their indispensable commitment to the project.

# The contributors

**Alain Anselin** teaches at the Lycée Professionnel de la Dillon in Fort-de-France, Martinique, and is the author of two major studies on French West Indians in France, *L'Emigration antillaise en France: du bantoustan au ghetto* (1979) and *L'Emigration antillaise en France: la Troisième Ile* (1990). He has also written widely on the history of precolonial Africa and India, and is a member of the editorial committee of the Martinican review *Carbet*.

**Maurice Burac** teaches geography at the Université des Antilles et de la Guyane in Martinique and is director of the university's Groupe de Recherche Géographie Développement Environnement. He is author of *Les Petites Antilles. Etude géographique des disparités de développement* (1989).

**Richard Burton** teaches French in the School of African and Asian Studies at Sussex University. He has published widely on French West Indian history, society and literature and is the author of the forthcoming *Famille, idéologie et pouvoir à la Martinique 1789-1992*. He has also written extensively on nineteenth-century French literature and has published two books on Baudelaire: *Baudelaire in 1859. A Study in the Sources of Poetic Creativity* (1988) and *Baudelaire and the Second Republic. Writing and Revolution* (1991).

**Jean-Paul Eluther** teaches at the Université des Antilles et de la Guyane in Guadeloupe and is personal assistant to the mayor of Pointe-à-Pitre. He has published widely on French West Indian politics and economy and is the author of *La Guadeloupe ambitieuse* (1990).

**Arlette Gautier** teaches at the Université de Nanterre in Paris and is the author of the seminal study on women and slavery *Les Soeurs de Solitude. La Condition féminine dans l'esclavage aux Antilles du 17ᵉ au 19ᵉ siècle* (1985). She has also published widely on contemporary French West Indian women and was the coordinator of a special number of *Nouvelles questions féministes* on the French West Indies in 1985.

**Michel Giraud** is a researcher for the Centre National de la Recherche Scientifique in Paris. Born in Guadeloupe, he was a founder member of the Institut Martiniquais d'Etudes and a regular contributor to its journal *Acoma* in the early 1970s. He is the author of *Races et classes à la Martinique. Les relations sociales entre enfants de différentes couleurs à l'école* (1979) and co-author (with Léon Gani and Danièle Manesse) of *L'Ecole aux Antilles. Langues et échec scolaire* (1992).

**Helen Hintjens** teaches politics at the University of Swansea and is co-editor, with Malyn Newitt, of *The Political Economy of Small Tropical Islands. The Importance of Being Small* (1992).

**Bridget Jones** teaches French at Roehampton Institute, having previously been senior lecturer in French at the University of the West Indies, Mona, Jamaica. She has published extensively on Caribbean writing in both French and English and is the translator of *Cathedral of the August Heat* (1987) by the Haitian novelist Pierre Clitandre.

**Emmanuel Jos** lectures in public law at the Université des Antilles et de la Guyane in Martinique, and is vice-president of the local Conseil Régional's Comité de la Culture, de l'Education et de l'Environnement. He has published widely on the relationship between the *départements d'outre-mer* and the European Community.

**Beverley Ormerod** was born in Jamaica and is senior lecturer in French at the University of Western Australia. She is the author of *An Introduction to the French Caribbean Novel* (1985) and, with Anne-Marie Nisbet, of *Négritude et antillanité: étude d'Une Tempête d'Aimé Césaire* (1982).

**Fred Reno** teaches political science at the Université de Rennes II. Of Martinican origin, he is director of the research laboratory Territoires et Pouvoir Local. He has published widely on West Indian politics and institutions and has written a thesis comparing constitutional developments in Martinique and Barbados.

**Elie Stephenson** was born in Cayenne (French Guiana) and has gained considerable local fame as a poet and playwright: he is the author of four collections of poetry and of the play *O Mayouri* (1988). He is currently teaching economics in France at the Lycée de Chartres, and has also made recordings as singer and guitarist with the French Guianese music group Les Neg' marrons.

# Introduction

## The French West Indies *à l'heure de l'Europe*: an overview

*Richard D.E. Burton*

Looked at from the perspective of Jamaica, Barbados, Trinidad or Guyana, the French Caribbean departments of Martinique, Guadeloupe and French Guiana can only appear as anomalies. Here are three 'territories' which, in defiance of the historical movement that brought almost the whole of the British Caribbean to at least nominal independence by the early 1970s, have remained tied, to all appearances willingly, to their 'mother-country' France and which have, if voting figures are any guide, decisively turned their back on the prospect of political independence for the foreseeable future. By remaining attached as overseas departments (*départements d'outre-mer*, DOM) to France, Martinique and Guadeloupe have, by common consent, achieved a standard of living far superior to that enjoyed not only in the neighbouring islands of Dominica and St Lucia but also – though here the divergence is less marked – in Barbados or Trinidad. For its part, mainland French Guiana, though less favoured than the island departments, appears as a haven of prosperity and stability when set beside the troubled political economies of the former British and Dutch Guianas. Social security and medical provisions in the DOM have no parallel in the Eastern Caribbean, wages are higher, the general infrastructure of roads and housing immeasurably superior: small wonder that, every year, hundreds, perhaps thousands, of St Lucians, Dominicans, Haitians and (in the case of French Guiana) Surinamese and Brazilians attempt to gain access to the French Antilles as illegal immigrants.

The Frenchness of the DOM is undeniable. It is not just the Monoprix and Unimags which have precipitated a widespread 'Europeanization' of consumer patterns over the last twenty-five years, not just the administrative and political superstructures, the French-style educational and social security systems, the *autoroutes* chock-a-block with Peugeots, Citroëns and Renaults as in some subtropical Languedoc or Provence, not just the *baguettes*, the day-old copies of *Le Monde* and *Libération*, the *mulâtresses* in the latest Paris fashions. Far deeper than such surface manifestations, the Frenchness of Martinique, Guadeloupe and French Guiana involves a mentality produced by more than 350 years of near-continuous occupation by France and, specifically, by the century and a half that has elapsed since the emancipation of French West Indian slaves in 1848. Coming ten years after emancipation in the British Caribbean, emancipation in the French colonies involved a crucial difference: the adult male ex-slaves became simultaneously free men *and* French citizens, voting, like the newly-enfranchised adult males of France itself, in the various elections of the French Second Republic (1848–51). That citizenship was abrogated by the right-wing régime of Napoleon III (1851–70) but restored by the Third Republic in the late 1870s. The identification of coloured (mulatto and black) French West Indians with the institutions and values of French Republicanism is the key to an understanding of contemporary Martinique, Guadeloupe and French Guiana.[1] If the Republic sought (though less wholeheartedly than is sometimes claimed) to assimilate its colonies politically and culturally into itself, so, for their part, the colonized sought quite desperately to be assimilated into the 'national family' where, losing all separate identity, they might enjoy complete equality of rights with French citizens of the *mère-patrie* and where, progressively, they might raise their standard of living to something approaching that of France itself. The acquisition of French schooling and, above all, of the French language itself was a crucial part of this project of individual and collective self-advancement, memorably captured in Euzhan Palcy's film *La Rue Cases-Nègres*. Dreading the power of the former white slaveholders – the infamous *békés* whose descendants still exercise enormous, though declining, economic, political and social power, especially in Martinique – coloured French West Indians looked to the white metropolitan Frenchman, his institutions, his language, his schools, to raise them progressively to the level of integral French citizens. Identification with the the *béké-France* was the obvious counter, from 1848 up to full departmentalization in 1946, to the still massive influence of the *békés-pays* (white Creoles). At every stage, the initiative for greater assimilation came not from France but from French West Indians themselves, particularly from the mulatto middle classes of the principal towns: Saint-Pierre and (after its destruction by volcanic eruption in 1902) Fort-de-France in Martinique, Pointe-à-Pitre and Basse-Terre in Guadeloupe, and Cayenne in French Guiana. Contrary to widespread anti-colonialist myth, it was French West Indians themselves, unprompted by governments in

Paris or colonial governors on the spot, who desperately sought to pay the 'blood tax' (*l'impôt du sang*) by enlisting in the French army in 1914 and 1939. How better to prove one's total Frenchness than willingly to die for *la mère-patrie*? From the 1870s onwards, French West Indians were thus involved in a curious and characteristic 'double bind' from which, more than a century later, they show no signs of emerging. In a peculiar way, coloured French West Indians have asserted their identity by denying it or, more precisely, they have asserted one identity (as French) by denying another (as West Indians). Social, political, economic and cultural advance were held to depend on a denial of difference: one became French to the precise extent that one abjured West Indian-ness or, to put it differently, the identification with the Other (France) required a prior negation of the (West Indian) self. Between 1848 and 1946, the vast majority of coloured French West Indians were more than prepared to sacrifice West Indian-ness for the sake of Frenchness. When legal and institutional Frenchness was achieved through departmentalization in 1946, a century-long process of self-advancement by self-negation was brought to a close, though it left unresolved, as we shall see, the question of French West Indians' 'double identity' as both French *and* West Indian. The West Indian-ness that had been denied for close to a century had not been suppressed, and would resurface with a vengeance in the decades following departmentalization.

The legal and political assimilation of France's *vieilles colonies* (Martinique, Guadeloupe, French Guiana and Réunion) in 1946 was, as Helen Hintjens shows in the opening chapter of this book, a logical culmination of a century and a half of colonial history going back to the French constitution of 1795 which had already declared France's overseas possessions to be a 'partie intégrante' of the motherland. Departmentalization was opposed in 1946 only by the *béké* minority and by a handful of prescient spirits who feared for the survival of the traditional economies and who regretted the loss of the limited, but nevertheless real, influence that local people could bring to bear on colonial governors and officials under the old régime. The whole decision-making process would, they feared, be initiated henceforth from Paris, and measures vital to the local societies would be implemented by Prefects far less sensitive to local needs and feelings than the colonial governors of old.

Both fears rapidly turned out to be real. Almost immediately after departmentalization, French manufactured goods – clothes, shoes, furniture, household implements – began to flood into the fledgeling overseas departments, displacing locally made goods and undermining the very real degree of economic self-sufficiency that had obtained under the former dispensation. Shortly afterwards, local agriculture, both export (sugar, bananas, pineapples) and subsistence, began the long downward curve that would dip still more sharply in the mid-1960s to produce the situation that exists today: a vestigial sugar industry unable to compete with metropolitan sugar beet; bananas and pineapples rendered uncompetitive by cheap alternative supplies from Central America and Africa; and a subsistence sector increasingly marginalized by a growing preference for imported foodstuffs. Scarcely 25 years after departmentalization, French West Indians were confronted by the effective erosion of the traditional economic base (agriculture, fishing, craft industries) and its replacement by a top-heavy service economy dependent on imported goods, themselves purchased by transfers of public and private funds from France. By the mid-1970s, the French West Indian departments were, so to speak, all superstructure and no base, rich by virtue of the funds which, for scarcely disinterested reasons, France continued to pour into them, totally impoverished when measured by the standards of what they actually produced. The viable productive economy of the colonial epoch had been supplanted by a skewed consumer economy, over which French West Indians had effectively no control even as they reaped its unevenly distributed benefits.

This loss of economic control was replicated at the political level. Although the DOM continued, as under the colonial régime, to send deputies and senators to the French Assembly, there was a growing feeling of peripheralization on the part of local élites who had once been able, through such institutions as the Chamber of Commerce, to exert considerable influence on the gubernatorial administration. Now, however, decisions were no longer taken locally by the governor and his aids but by ministries in Paris. Policies designed to fit French conditions were either applied automatically in the Caribbean departments or, in the case, for example, of social security arrangements or minimum wage legislation, after amendments had been made which effectively gave the DOM a second-class status. Whether they were included in or excluded from French legislation, French West Indians thought they were getting the worst of the departmental bargain. On the one hand, they wanted all the social and material benefits that assimilation was intended to bring and to that extent identified unreservedly with France. On the other hand, they – and particularly their élites – wished to preserve some measure of local control over local issues and to that extent sought to 'dissimilate' themselves from the metropole.

The urge to identify was countered by an urge to 'disidentify', the two cancelling each other out to produce a sense of unease and impotence which finally erupted, a dozen or so years after departmentalization, in the riots of December 1959 in Fort-de-France. Triggered off by a 'racial incident' involving a local (black) motorcyclist and a (white) car-driver recently arrived from Algeria, the riots were significantly directed not against local white Creoles but against metropolitans, whether soldiers, policemen, teachers or civil servants. Cars containing white people were systematically stopped and their occupants interrogated; if they replied in Creole (that is, if they were *békés*), they were left unharmed, if in French, insulted, threatened and, in some cases, molested.[2] The traditional ally of the coloured French West Indian against the *béké*, the metropolitan had, in scarcely more than a decade, become a popular scapegoat for the disruptions and disappointments of departmentalization.

The years 1958–64 are without doubt the fulcrum of recent French West Indian history. They marked the transition, first, from the traditional agriculture-based economy of the past to the massively tertiarized, consumer-oriented economy of the contemporary DOM. In both Martinique and Guadeloupe – particularly the former – sugar production entered into precipitate decline to be replaced, effectively, by nothing. Unemployment correspondingly mounted to over 25 per cent, and was 'solved' by a policy of outmigration, encouraged, organized and financed by France, that Alain Anselin describes in Chapter 7. By the late 1960s the principal French West Indian export had become ... French West Indians. As more and more metropolitans arrived in the DOM on short-term contracts and local birthrates began a sharp decline as the use of contraception spread, local politicians, notably Aimé Césaire in Martinique, began to speak balefully of the threat of 'genocide by substitution' that, allegedly, hung over the DOM. At the same time that the traditional economic and social base was eroded, so the traditional creole culture it sustained was subject to increasing dilution, fragmentation or exoticization. Dress, food, family structures, music and, not least, the Creole language itself were all exposed in their different ways to a marked 'Europeanization'.

To the (highly exaggerated) threat of demographic 'genocide' was added the much more pressing danger of 'cultural genocide', denounced by the Martinican writer Edouard Glissant in 1977.[3] At every level, French West Indian societies were, by 1970, characterized by an increasingly sharp divergence between super-structures and infrastructure. On the surface, the DOM were far more prosperous than their neighbours, but, when examined, that prosperity turned out to be based almost entirely on French government capital in the form either of social security payments or on the inflated salaries paid to government employees, including teachers: underneath there was, in effect, nothing. It was as though traditional creole society, economy and culture had withered in the space of a decade. Symptomatically, the titles of the most characteristic literary works of the late 1960s and early 1970s foregrounded unambiguously their authors' preoccupation with spiritual and cultural death: *Malemort* (Edouard Glissant, 1975), *Mère la mort* and *La Meurtritude* (Jeanne Hyvrard, 1976 and 1978),[4] *La Vie et la mort de Marcel Gonstran* (Vincent Placoly, 1971).

In the circumstances, it was inevitable that a nationalist movement seeking independence from France would emerge, but equally inevitable, perhaps, that its influence would remain limited, essentially, to the young, the middle class and the university-educated. The first signs of discontent with the politics of assimilation came in 1956 when Aimé Césaire, the most vocal supporter of departmentalization in 1946, split from the French Communist Party to form his own Parti Progressiste Martiniquais (PPM) in 1958. It was, however, significant that the new party committed itself to the acquisition not of independence from France but of autonomy, by which was meant a large measure of internal self-government within the context of a never fully spelt-out federal-style relationship with France which would, in effect, continue to foot the bill for a lifestyle that Martinique could never, on its own, sustain. It was not long before more radical voices began to make themselves heard. The first out-and-out independentist movements in the DOM had their origins in French West Indian student organizations in France itself. From this base they evolved, in the early 1960s, into the Organisation de la Jeunesse Anticolonialiste Martiniquaise (OJAM) and the Groupe d'Organisation Nationale de la Guadeloupe (GONG), both of them heavily impregnated with French *gauchisme* and both open to the charge – inevitably made by defenders of the status quo both in France and the DOM – of middle-class élitism, combined with an absence of ideas concerning how, if French economic support was withdrawn, the DOM could possibly sustain the high living standards to which their populations had by now become inured. By the late 1960s the anti-assimilationist left in the French West Indies was fatally split between a centre-left committed to autonomy and a mixed economy, and an ultra-left – itself split into a multiplicity of 'tendencies' – committed to independence and 'socialism'. Neither had a realistic economic or political project, and though autonomism in its different expressions (orthodox communist parties and some socialists in Martinique, Guadeloupe and French Guiana, the PPM in Martinique) had significant popular backing, the same could not be said of the various independentist groups which became ever more *groupusculaire* in form, mentality and conduct. In the face of this fragmented opposition, France and the local supporters of the status quo were never subject to serious challenge.

The failure of the anti-assimilationists to reach a mass constituency did not, however, mean that all was well with assimilationism. Even on the departmentalist right, disquiet was regularly expressed concerning the loss of local control to a remote political centre, and a sense of impotence had, by the late 1970s, spread across the entire political spectrum. In the circumstances, the victory of the French Socialist Party in 1981 brought solace not only to the autonomist centre-left but also – though they took time to recognize it – to the pro-assimilationist right as well. The socialist victory, and the implementation of regionalist policies that followed, precipitated a major realignment in French West Indian politics, particularly in Martinique, where the autonomist PPM, previously the principal oppositional force in the island, became virtually overnight the principal defender – and, as Fred Reno explains in Chapter 2 – beneficiary of the modified status quo. Following the socialist victory, Césaire unilaterally declared a 'moratorium' on further discussion of the island-department's status and, in the ensuing years, was able to project the regionalizing policies of the new government as the fulfilment of his own 25-year struggle for *autonomie* for Martinique. The fact that decentralization had itself been imposed by decree from the centre was an irony that he either failed to see or chose to ignore.

As a result of the constitutional changes of the early 1980s, the new Conseil Régional has in all three departments become the most important local assembly, and the influence of the Conseil Général, or departmental assembly, has correspondingly declined. Unlike metropolitan France, where a region is composed of a number of departments, each DOM is a region, or *région monodépartementale*, unto itself. In the mid-1980s it was proposed – logically enough, it would seem – to merge the Conseil Régional and Conseil Général into a single local assembly (*assembleé unique*) with responsibility for the running of each department-region's internal affairs. Had this measure been implemented, it would at last have given the DOM a constitutional status clearly distinct from that of a metropolitan department and, to that extent, could well have resolved the perennial French West Indian dilemma: how to be both part of, yet apart from, metropolitan France? But though the proposal had significant backing both locally and in France, it was declared to be unconstitutional by the French Conseil d'Etat (Supreme Court), and a major opportunity for reconciling the permanent French West Indian urge both to 'assimilate' and 'dissimilate' was, at least for the time being, lost.

A similar opportunity arose in 1990 when the French Interior Minister Pierre Joxe issued a plan concerning the future constitutional status of Corsica. Breaking with the whole Jacobin tradition of the identity of people and nation, the plan recognized 'the historical and cultural community which is the Corsican people, a constituent part of the French people' and guaranteed the 'preservation of its cultural identity and the defence of its special economic and social interests linked to its island status and respecting national unity'.[5] This epochmaking proposal naturally excited considerable interest amongst autonomists and independentists in the French West Indies, as well as alarming local departmentalists who saw in it, as they had already (and wrongly) seen in regionalization, a concealed threat of 'abandonment' by France. As it turned out, both hopes and fears came to nothing as, once again, the proposal was declared to be unconstitutional. Thus the problem of the status of the French West Indian departments remains and will do so as long as France, or its constitutional lawyers, remain unable to admit the existence of variations within the body politic of *la République une et indivisible*.

For all this, it is undeniable that regionalization has remedied some, at least, of the imbalances that had become apparent by the late 1970s, though, equally clearly, real power still resides in Paris rather than in Fort-de-France, Pointe-à-Pitre or Cayenne. As Jean-Paul Eluther explains in the case of Guadeloupe (Chapter 3), an uneasy consensus has formed around the question of regionalization, despite fears unleashed in the French West Indies of imminent engulfment by the *Grand Méchant Loup* of *L'Europe des Treize* in the wake of Maastricht.[6] In Guadeloupe the independentist *groupuscules* which were still active and influential in the mid-1980s have, in Eluther's assessment, been neutralized, though as we shall see, in Martinique a relatively new political formation, the Mouvement Indépendantiste Martiniquais (MIM) led by Alfred Marie-Jeanne, made significant headway on an out-and-out independentist ticket in the regional elections of 1990 and 1992 and, most recently, in the French legislative elections of March 1993. Thus, amidst the prevailing sense of stability, even of torpor, symptoms of discontent persist. We shall return to the question of present-day political trends later in this introduction.

# The character of the three Caribbean DOMs

So far we have spoken of the French West Indies as of one single homogeneous entity. However, beneath the super-structures of shared institutional forms, each of the three Caribbean DOMs has its own distinctive character shaped by important divergences of geography, history, economic activity, social and racial structure, culture and mentality. These divergences, taken together, mean that French West Indians are still far more likely to think of themselves primarily as 'Martiniquais', 'Guadeloupéens' or 'Guianese' and only secondarily as 'Antillais'. There is, in the first instance, the major cleavage, discussed by Bridget Jones and Elie Stephenson in Chapter 4, between the mainland department of French Guiana, on the one hand, and Martinique and Guadeloupe on the other. With only a third (100–120,000) of the population of Martinique or of Guadeloupe, but with a land mass a third of the size of France itself, French Guiana is still in many respects a 'frontier society' which, even today, has not fully escaped its negative image as a former penitentiary colony, with an insalubrious climate and impenetrable forested hinterland.

Despite its small population, French Guiana is the most ethnically and economically diverse of the three Caribbean DOMs. Historically, forestry, gold prospecting and subsistence agriculture have been at least as important as sugar. With legal and illegal immigration continuing, the population brings together in an improbable mix of Creoles (descendants of African slaves), 'Bush Negroes' (descendants of runaway slaves), Amerindians, Europeans, Asians (principally Chinese, Cambodians and Javanese), Syrians and Lebanese, and foreign nationals from Brazil, Surinam, Guyana, St Lucia and Haiti. Paradoxically, it is French Guiana, the least 'developed' of the three Caribbean DOMs, which, with its mineral resources and hydro-electric capacity, has the greatest potential as far as France is concerned.

For their part, Martinique and Guadeloupe, though cognate societies, show major, if more subtle, differences from each other, differences, first of all, in population structure. Whereas the population of Martinique consists, historically, of three principal strata – a white (*béké*) upper class, a mulatto middle class and an overwhelmingly black lower class, Guadeloupe has a much smaller and much less powerful *béké* élite often composed of minor branches of Martinican *béké* families, a less numerous mulatto middle class and, in addition to a preponderantly black lower class, a very substantial East Indian minority making up one in six of the total population, in contrast to the small East Indian minority (one in thirty) in the 'sister island'.[7] Furthermore, Guadeloupe has a small but significant population of 'poor whites' known as *Blancs Matignon*, to whom may be added the distinctive white populations of the outlying island dependencies of La Désirade and Saint-Barthélémy and the light-skinned inhabitants of the Iles des Saintes. It is often said that the population of Guadeloupe is, in general, 'more African', 'darker' or 'less mixed' than that of Martinique. Impressions will differ, but it is certainly true that the figure of the mulatto (and of the *mulâtresse*) bulk less large in the historical mythology of Guadeloupe than Martinique.

There are also significant differences between the economies and land structure of the two departments. Whereas, until recently, the bulk of agricultural land in Martinique remained under local (principally *béké*) ownership, metropolitan-based companies bought up most of Guadeloupe's sugar plantations in the later nineteenth century, instituting a set of capitalistic social and economic relations which contrasted significantly with the 'feudal' or 'patriarchal' values still vestigially current on the sugar plantations of Martinique. It is perhaps for this reason that labour relations in Guadeloupe have, in general, been more conflictual than in Martinique, and the general political climate perhaps relatively more radical from the time of Hégésippe Légitimus' Parti Nègre of the 1890s onwards. These and other factors combine to give Guadeloupe a rather different 'feel' from Martinique. The island is commonly held to be 'less French' than Martinique, and it may be these divergent degrees of assimilation that gave rise to the legendary, but now diminishing, contempt of Martinicans for Guadeloupeans, and vice versa.

Viewed from the outside, 'race relations' in the French Caribbean, discussed by Michel Giraud in Chapter 5, are very much more harmonious than in, say, Jamaica or Trinidad.[8] There is certainly some hostility on the part of local people towards metropolitans – known locally as *zoreilles* from the alleged tendency of their ears to pinken and peel under the tropical sun – who number some 10–15,000 in Martinique and Guadeloupe and who, thanks to the space station at Kourou, make up a rather more substantial proportion of the population of French Guiana. Inter-racial tensions are manifested on the roads and, occasionally, on beaches which metropolitans (and tourists) are said to have 'colonized', and the practice of topless bathing by metropolitan women is condemned – somewhat hypocritically, it has to be said! – by (male) French West Indian nationalists. There is also evidence of a growing hostility towards tourists in such Martinican resorts as Sainte-Anne (where the Club Méditerranée is located) and Sainte-Luce, though nothing, so far, to compare with what seems to have become routine in parts of the English-speaking Caribbean. In general, though, metropolitans and locals mix politely at work and socialize apart, though it is not at all uncommon to see mixed couples walking arm in arm on the streets of Fort-de-France or Pointe-à-Pitre. For most coloured French West Indians, the *békés* are quasi-mythical beings, more talked about than seen, and social relations between white Creoles and other categories of the local population remain a rarity, though it is sometimes said that *békés* are less racist than in the past – at least they now marry metropolitans![9]

In Guadeloupe, relations between the black majority and the East Indian minority are likewise devoid of the overt animosities of Trinidad and Guyana. However, black disparagement of *koulis* is far from unknown, and in recent years there have been signs of the beginnings of racial and cultural self-assertion on the part of some East Indians.

Beneath the civilities of everyday life, and despite the impact of Négritude – or Black Nationalist – derived notions of 'Black is Beautiful', there can be little doubt that a perceptible 'white bias' continues to operate in French West Indians' somatic and sexual preferences, though this is without question far less obsessive than when Frantz Fanon wrote his pioneering study *Peau noire masques blancs* (1952). To be light-skinned still confers definite social and sexual advantages in Martinique (especially) and Guadeloupe, and, despite the rise of a substantial black middle class since 1946, a high degree of correlation still obtains between class and colour. But racial disparities are perhaps less corrosive than the profound disparities between French West Indian men and women documented by Arlette Gautier in Chapter 9. Here the divide sometimes seems total, with men and women apparently inhabiting distinct culture spheres, the men exploiting women domestically and sexually, the women despising the men for their 'infidelity', 'irresponsibility' and failure to provide economically, emotionally or sexually. Against the very negative picture painted by Gautier should be set the emergence – hailed by some, disputed by others – of a 'new woman' in the French West Indies: highly educated, often French-born or a returning migrant from France, self-assertive and autonomous, occupying positions of responsibility in both private and public sectors. Such women – the *femmes-matadors*,[10] perhaps, of a regionalized, Europeanized French Caribbean – undoubtedly exist, but whether their presence significantly modifies the general subordination of their sex is, at present, greatly to be doubted.

To the 800,000 or so inhabitants of the DOMs themselves

(Martinique and Guadeloupe each approximately 350,000, French Guiana between 100–120,000) must be added the inhabitants of what Alain Anselin has called the 'third island':[11] the 400,000 people of French West Indian origin or descent currently resident in France, 80 per cent of them in Paris or the Parisian region. The economic and other factors that brought about the mass migration of the 1960s are discussed by Anselin in Chapter 8, together with the problems and circumstances of their 'insertion' into French society. The importance of the 'third island' for the DOMs cannot be overstated. Almost all French West Indian families have members living in France from whom they often receive financial support and with whom they exchange regular visits on a bilateral basis. The constant crossing of the Atlantic tends to undermine the distinction between 'France' and the West Indies and causes distances to collapse. In so doing, the already fragile sense of Martinique, Guadeloupe and French Guiana as separate physical and human entities is further eroded. French West Indians routinely say of X or Y that they are *'en métropole'* or *'hors du département'* as though they have gone up the road to post a letter and will be back in twenty minutes. 'French West Indians no longer migrate, they circulate,' Anselin has written elsewhere,[12] and their ceaseless comings and goings across the Atlantic play a major part in the progressive decreolization of the DOMs discussed in the section that follows. An increasingly prominent figure in local life is the so-called *Négropolitain(e)*, the returning or visiting immigrant who brings back to the Caribbean Parisian attitudes, aspirations, values and lifestyles, who speaks Creole with a Parisian accent or cannot speak Creole at all and who is received by locals with a mixture of envy, amusement and contempt, feelings which – envy apart – are reciprocated by the visitors or returnees themselves. As we shall see in our final section, the dispersal of French West Indian families both sides of the Atlantic has been a major obstacle to the development of nationalist movements, autonomist but above all independentist, in the contemporary French West Indies.

## Decreolization and Creole revivalism

The massive social, economic and demographic transformations of the 1960s necessarily had a deleterious effect on traditional cultural forms, and, by the end of the 1970s, it seemed to many observers, both local and foreign, that the French West Indies were well on the way towards irreversible and definitive decreolization.[13] Creole costume had abandoned everyday life for tourist hotels and the most expensive restaurants, carnival was moribund, creole cooking was being displaced by French-style eating habits and, perhaps most significantly, the Creole language itself was being infiltrated by the structures and lexicon of standard French to produce a hybrid linguistic form that was neither Creole nor French, but a kind of *français créolisé* or *créole francisé*. Since regionalization, however, this pervasive decreolization has been mitigated, if not arrested, by the self-conscious determination of many French West Indians to protect and promote their threatened cultural heritage. They have been helped in this by grants and support from the French Ministry of Culture, which have been applied locally by such bodies as the Direction Régionale d'Action Culturelle (DRAC) in each department and, in Fort-de-France, by the Service Municipal d'Action Culturelle (SERMAC), founded by the PPM and closely associated with the political, cultural and other ideas of Aimé Césaire. Through such means many threatened cultural forms have been preserved though at the cost, it must be said, of some exoticization and commodification. Modern French West Indians do not so much live the creole culture as observe it, tourists in their own countries, from outside. None the less, carnival has been revitalized, drama, dance and music have all received notable encouragement from such institutions as the annual Festival Culturel de Fort-de-France and, in general, some sense of national cultural identity has been constructed in the face of the multiple contemporary pressures towards homogenization. While it cannot be said that creole culture is exactly vibrant in the contemporary French West Indies, it does at least survive, though whether it will ever again thrive in the absence of a sustaining socio-economic base is, of course, greatly to be questioned.

One area, though, where the French West Indies have been notably active is in the field of literature and thought. The very intensity of the experience of decreolization and loss of identity in the 1960s precipitated an impressive amount of reflection and theorization discussed by Richard Burton in Chapter 10. In opposition to the concept of Négritude which dominated thinking about French West Indian identity in the 1940s and 1950s, two new theories – first Antillanité and, most recently, Créolité – have been forged to describe, account for and, hopefully, to reinforce a sense of local distinctiveness. However, as Burton shows, it has been enormously difficult for local intellectuals and others to 'think West Indian' when all their philosophical concepts – not to mention their language itself – are derived from the entity that most threatens their sense of identity, namely France itself.

In the field of literature, discussed by Beverley Ormerod in Chapter 11, there has been a discernible shift from poetry to the novel as the principal literary form, a growing recourse to Creole or to a blend of French and Creole as an expressive medium and, in general, a more optimistic and energetic tone after the predominantly pessimistic literary output of the late 1960s and 1970s. In Martinique, the revival has been led by the Créolité school of writers headed by Patrick Chamoiseau and Raphaël Confiant, and Guadeloupean literature has been remarkable above all for the large numbers of women writers that it has produced: Simone Schwarz-Bart, Maryse Condé, Lucie Julia and Myriam Warner-Vieyra amongst others. The work of Maryse Condé, in particular, has gained an international audience, and the awarding of the Prix Goncourt to Patrick Chamoiseau's novel *Texaco* in 1992 marked some kind of official consecration of French West Indian literature as a whole. Whether, however, it is a good thing for a literature written against the threat of Frenchification to be consecrated by the French literary establishment is a question too complex to be entered into here.

## Towards a French West Indian distinctiveness

Such considerations bring us back, finally and inevitably, to the question of the present status of France's Caribbean departments and of the attitude of Martinicans, Guadeloupeans and French Guianese towards first the departmentalization, then the regionalization and now, finally, after Maastricht, the 'Europeanization' of their respective *pays nataux*.[14] It must be said at the outset that there can be no objective answer to this second question. No opinion polls on the DOMs present status have been held, and election results are a notoriously poor guide to people's real feelings on the subject. Thus a vote for an autonomist or independentist candidate is by no means necessarily a vote for autonomy or independence, and there is the continuing problem of high abstention rates – 40 per cent to 50 per cent is 'average', and figures of 60 per cent, 70 per cent even 80 per cent are not unknown – in elections, either local or national (i.e. French), in the French West Indies. Secondly, subjective assessments depend notoriously on which local circles the observer frequents. Independentist, or at least nationalist, feeling is undoubtedly stronger amongst the university-educated middle classes than it is in other sectors of society, and it is, of course, to this milieu that the visiting foreign academic is most likely to gain access. Similarly, it seems likely – though reliable data are, as ever, notably lacking –

that nationalist feeling, where it exists, tends to be stronger amongst men than women, particularly amongst lower-class mothers who are, after all, the most directly dependent on French social security and other state benefits. Finally, there are also significant generational differences. Nationalist feeling tends to be strongest amongst those who came to maturity in the 1960s and 1970s: the French West Indies' equivalent, in other words, of the *génération 68* in France. Older people still retain something, at least, of the traditional French West Indian identification with *la mère-patrie*, while the attitude of those under 25 is more pragmatic and utilitarian. For them there is no emotional identification with France but a recognition that French citizenship confers certain definite concrete advantages, combined with a fear, undoubtedly orchestrated by local pro-assimilationist media, that an independent Martinique or Guadeloupe would 'become like Saint Lucia' or, still worse, Haiti.

The situation, then, is of the greatest complexity and resists easy generalization or quantification. On the one hand, there is undoubtedly a growing sense of French West Indian distinctiveness now that that distinctiveness is menaced not simply, as in the past, by Frenchification but by 'Europeanization'. At the lowest level, such feelings manifest themselves in fears concerning the acquisition of property in the French West Indies not just by metropolitans but by Germans, Dutch, Italians and Britons. There is also resentment at the way in which, in recent years, metropolitans have moved into sectors of commerce previously dominated by local entrepreneurs. More generally, there is genuine and, it has to be said, all too well-founded anxiety concerning the likely effects of 'Europe' on the local economies, fears discussed by Emmanuel Jos in Chapter 5. It is difficult to see, in particular, how the local banana industry can survive unprotected in the face of relentless competition from Central America and elsewhere. At the same time that they have become conscious of 'Europe' as a potentially disruptive force, French West Indians have also developed a sense of belonging, at least in part, to another broader entity, physically close but, until recently, psychologically remote: the Caribbean. As Maurice Burac shows in Chapter 6, concrete links with the non-Francophone Caribbean remain tenuous, but a sense of 'West Indian-ness' has emerged, at least amongst younger Martinicans and Guadeloupeans, thanks, in part, to school visits to Barbados and Trinidad and, more generally, to an enthusiasm for Caribbean music of all kinds. Few French West Indians, however, think of themselves as exclusively, or even primarily, as West Indians, but an increasing number postulate for themselves a kind of *double identity*, so that it is not at all uncommon to hear people – particularly young people – say, for example, 'I am a French citizen but of Martinican/Guadeloupean nationality'. This disconnection of citizenship and nationality may be a pointer to the future evolution of the status of the French West Indian departments. Turning to recent election results in the French West Indies, the picture is again complex and confusing. In Guadeloupe and French Guiana, the regional elections of March 1992, followed by the legislatives of March 1993, returned candidates broadly sympathetic to the status quo in its regionalist form. It is worth noting that amongst the successful candidates to the French Assembly in 1993 were two women, Lucette Michaux-Chevry (Guadeloupe) and Christiane Taubira-Delannon (French Guiana). In Martinique two events have dominated the political scene in recent years: first, the apparent decline of Césaire's Parti Progressiste Martiniquais which Césaire's retirement as deputy in 1993 (he continues, for the time being, to be mayor of Fort-de-France) is likely to accentuate, and, secondly, the rise of an explicitly independentist party, the Mouvement Indépendantiste Martiniquais (MIM) to a position of prominence on the Conseil Régional, and the emergence of its leader, Alfred Marie-Jeanne, as the most charismatic figure in local politics. The breakthrough for Marie-Jeanne and the MIM came in October 1990 when, in re-run regional elections, the party gained over 15,000 votes (16.5 per cent of those cast) and seven out of the 41 seats on the Conseil Régional. In the regular regional elections of March 1992, it increased its 'score' to 19,000 votes (16 per cent of the total cast, slightly more than the proportion [15.8 per cent] cast for the PPM) and nine seats, the remaining 32 seats being split equally between the pro-assimilationist right and the autonomist centre-left.[15] A year later, Marie-Jeanne, who had previously condemned all participation in 'French' elections, stood for the French National Assembly in the southern constituency and, though he failed to defeat the pro-assimilationist candidate, received enough votes (17,912 or 41.7 per cent of those cast) to be able to claim a 'moral victory' for his independentist cause.[16] In the rest of the department, Camille Darsières, the deputy leader of the PPM, retained the centre constituency held by Césaire since 1946, though with a reduced majority on a greatly reduced turn-out. In the two northern constituencies the sitting centre-left/autonomist deputies were decisively beaten by candidates of the right.

The common feature of all four results was the decline of the autonomist centre-left in its various manifestations, a decline which, as noted earlier, is likely to be accelerated by the withdrawal of Aimé Césaire from active politics and the widely-predicted disintegration of the PPM that may follow. How, though, should the electoral rise of the MIM be interpreted? Did the 17,912 people who voted for the party in the south vote for its programme or its leader who, in addition to his definite personal charisma, enjoys a reputation – rare, to say the least, in Martinique – of incorruptibility in his role as mayor of the southern town of Rivière-Pilote. Patronage, clientelism and – it is rumoured – coercion undoubtedly account for an unquantifiable proportion of the votes he received, and it is also undeniable that independentist candidates in other constituencies (MIM and others) gained only marginal support in the first round of the elections pending elimination from the second (3 per cent and 5.4 per cent in the two northern constituencies, a rather larger 12.8 per cent in the centre). But the MIM's advance, at both regional and legislative elections, means that it, its leader and its independentist platform have established themselves as an unbudgeable presence on the local political scene for the foreseeable future. The son of a French policeman and a Martinican domestic servant, Marie-Jeanne is, to all appearances, a nationalist pure and simple, difficult to situate in conventional terms of 'left' and 'right'. He is backed by a powerful trade union (the Confédération Syndicale des Travailleurs Martiniquais) which, with many supporters at the airport at Le Lamentin, in the docks at Fort-de-France and amongst the drivers of Martinique's innumerable *transports collectifs*, could, in theory, bring the island-department to a standstill. He and his associates are condemned by both traditional right and traditional centre-left, but also by the remnants of the independentist ultra-left and the influential local ecological movement, the Association pour la Sauvegarde du Patrimoine Martiniquais (ASSAUPAMAR), also committed to independence. Inevitably, there are rumours of strongarm methods, clandestine pacts with the *békés*, and of financial backing from the CIA.

The rise of the MIM – significant, however one interprets it – makes assessment of the current political situation in the French West Indies more than usually tentative. The autonomist centre-left has weakened, relatively speaking, in Martinique but remains strong in Guadeloupe and French Guiana. Even in Martinique, however, regionalization itself probably remains the preferred option of a majority of voters. The MIM apart, independentist parties in all three departments seem to have lost even the marginal support they enjoyed in the mid-1980s; the right has undoubtedly recaptured some lost ground in Martinique. The overwhelming impression, though, is one of paralysis as parties fissiparously multiply, leading to repeated deadlocks in all three Conseils Régionaux and, in Martinique, to an inability to transact even the most basic regional business. Now that

Césaire has at last withdrawn from active politics, there is no figure in the French West Indies of genuine stature to guide the DOMs through what may well be the greatest crisis – the impact of '1993' – in their recent history.

Such, then, very impressionistically, are the French West Indies *à l'heure de l'Europe*: more prosperous, certainly, than neighbouring independent countries, but owing that prosperity – which, it should be stressed, is very unevenly distributed – entirely to the influx of private and public capital from France; increasingly 'Europeanized' in their lifestyles but still clinging determinedly to what remains of their creole culture; anxious about what incorporation into 'Europe' will bring, but still more anxious about the consequences of severing the links of 350 years and more with France; more and more open to the rest of the Caribbean but also to the United States and Canada; enjoying a standard of living which – particularly through the proliferation of cars and the remorseless advance across the country of shopping precincts, secondary residences, hotels, golf-courses – is undoubtedly having a deleterious effect on their environment; conscious of being French, but also of being something else as well; and finally, self-assertive but, deep down, desperately unsure of who they are and of where they are heading. There being no signs whatsoever that France will 'abandon' its Caribbean possessions in the short, medium or long term, it seems that political independence, as the formerly independentist Union Populaire pour la Libération de la Guadeloupe (UPLG) put it in the regional elections of 1992, *n'est pas à l'ordre du jour.*[17] An *assemblée unique* in each department with, ideally, a 'super-regional' council embracing all three DOMs is, perhaps, the most realistic goal for those who, like the present writer, continue to feel that the present constitutional arrangements, regionalization notwithstanding, give French West Indians far too little control over the creation of their own destinies.

## Notes

1  For a summary of the politics and ideology of assimilationism, see Richard D.E. Burton, 'Between the particular and the universal: dilemmas of the Martinican intellectual,' in *Intellectuals in the Twentieth-Century Caribbean, Vol.II Unity in Variety: the Hispanic and Francophone Caribbean*, (ed.) Alistair Hennessy (Macmillan, 1992), pp. 186–210, esp. pp. 188–96.

2  On the 1959 riots, see the special number of *Le Naïf*, 'Décembre 59', December, 1989.

3  Edouard Glissant, 'Une société morbide et ses pulsions', *Le Monde diplomatique*, 279, June 1977, pp. 16–18. The article is reproduced in Glissant, *Le Discours antillais* (Seuil, 1981), pp. 166–78, the reference to 'cultural genocide' being on p. 173.

4  Jeanne Hyvrard is a metropolitan writer who lived in Martinique during the early 1970s. The titles of her novels treating Martinican life are mentioned for their symptomatic value.

5  For a summary, see the article by Robert Cottrell in *The Independent*, 15 November 1990.

6  The reference is to the smash hit of the Martinican carnival of 1990, 'Le Grand Méchant Loup' by Djo Desormo in which 'Europe' is represented as the Big Bad Wolf about to gobble up the French West Indian departments.

7  For a full discussion of the question of East Indians in the French Caribbean, see the special number of *Carbet*, 'L'Inde en nous', 9, December 1989.

8  For a full and relatively recent discussion of this subject, see Michel Giraud, *Races et classes à la Martinique*, Editions Anthropos, 1979.

9  On the *békés*, see Edith Beaudoux Kovats and Jean Benoist, 'Les Blancs Créoles de la Martinique', in *L'Archipel inachevé*, (ed.) Jean Benoist (Presses de l'Université de Montréal, 1972), pp. 109–32, and Jean-Luc Jamard, 'Les Békés sont des judokas ...', *Les Temps modernes*, pp. 441–2 (1983).

10  'Femmes-Matadors' was the name given to the beautiful, self-reliant 'killer women', usually *mûlatresses*, of traditional creole society.

11  Alain Anselin, *L'Emigration antillaise en France: la troisième Ile*, Karthala, 1990.

12  *Ibid.*, p. 266.

13  See the article by Glissant cited in note 3 above, and Richard D.E. Burton, *Assimilation or Independence? Prospects for Martinique*, Centre for Developing-Area Studies, McGill University, Montreal, 1978, esp. pp. 33–8.

14  For a full discussion of the multiple issues raised by regionalization, see the collective work *Questions sur l'administration des DOM. Décentraliser autre-mer?*, (ed.) Jean-Claude Fortier, Economica/Presses universitaires d'Aix-Marseille, 1989.

15  Results taken from *La France dans ses régions*, published by *Le Monde* in April 1992, pp. 131–2.

16  These and all subsequent figures taken from *Antilla*, 530 (2–8 April 1993), pp. 6–8.

17  *La France dans ses régions*, p. 131.

# CHAPTER 1 | Constitutional and political change in the French Caribbean

*Helen Hintjens*

Constitutional and political ...

> My experience in public office has taught me that it is precisely because the fate of the colonies is decided in Paris, on the basis of inadequate information, ... that there is now such an urgency in the demands of the colonies.... I am convinced that if assimilation gives the central government total responsibility for the destiny of the colonial peoples, it will end up by severing the very ties which unite them (the colonies) emotionally with the metropolis. (Paul Valentino, 1946)[1]
>
> ... indigenous separatist movements are all too often the result of a failure by the metropolis to keep its promises. (Aimé Césaire, 1947)[2]

change ...

> There are two tendencies in our [overseas] territories; on the one hand there are the autonomists, and on the other those who want to be fully French. The autonomists are the big landowners, and all those who profit from the people's misery and seek to maintain their own privileges. (Léon de Lepervanche, 1947)[3]

in the French Caribbean.

> ... we must have the courage, and the honesty, to admit to the people [of the DOM – départements d'outre-mer] that any status which departed from the departmental status would deprive them of most of the benefits which indeed they receive precisely because they belong to the French Community. (Olivier Stirn, 1977)[4]

The existence of the overseas departments and territories is just one of the reasons why France cannot be considered solely a European power in today's world. (Michel Debré, 1980)[5]

## Introduction

These quotations set the tone for much of what follows in this chapter. The main concern is to explore the changing interpretation of the political and constitutional status and development of the French Caribbean islands and French Guiana since 1946. The decision to integrate the colonies of Guadeloupe, Martinique, French Guiana and Réunion into the political and legal framework of the French state, was agreed in March 1946, even before the Constitution of the Fourth Republic had been agreed upon.[6] Almost 50 years later the status of these territories, as integral parts of the French Republic, but several thousand miles from the mainland, appears anomalous. Outside France, the equal status of the overseas departments with other parts of France is regarded as a 'legal fiction', or even as a hangover from the colonial era.

Is it fair to consider the departmental status as a hangover from a colonial era? Or is it, as supporters of the French presence claim, an original form of decolonization? How have various forms of decentralization and regionalization been used by the government to resolve centre-periphery tensions?

In the contemporary world, the idea of self-determination is almost automatically associated with the national state. In the French context, however, self-determination also meant the individual right of citizens to join the nation. Exceptionally, in the former French colonies of the Caribbean, the population was able to determine to join the French state, rather than remain colonial subjects.

## Historical background to the law of 1946

Perhaps the most distinctive feature of French nationalism is its Jacobinism. This emphasises 'the individual civic conscience, the collective will to form a state and national pride'.[7] It does not focus only on race, religion or even territorial contiguity. Can this help to explain why Guadeloupe, Martinique and French Guiana were integrated into the French Republic in the way that they were?

The roots of the law of 1946 can be traced as far back as the French Revolution. At that time, the Antilles, together with St

Domingue, were extremely profitable for France. In Guadeloupe a slave revolt in 1802 decapitated the plantation society's élite, whilst in Martinique the planters resisted the abolition of slavery during the revolutionary period. By 1946, however, both islands were in the same depressed condition, with their plantation economies in tatters. Tensions existed between the islands, with the mulatto élite in Guadeloupe suspicious of the *béké* planter class in Martinique, and their economic power.

After the war, with Vichy collaborators on the Right discredited, the *vieilles colonies* of Martinique, Guadeloupe and French Guiana (as well as Réunion in the Indian Ocean) elected communist and socialist deputies to the National Assembly. These politicians were almost unanimous in their demand for the immediate transformation of these territories into full French departments.

Nowhere was the impact of the assimilatory doctrine of Jacobin colonial tradition more profound than in the slave-based, plantation colonies of the Caribbean. The colonial theorist and administrator Jules Harmand, drew a distinction between colonies of domination and colonies of immigration. Assimilation was practised only in the colonies of immigration, which included Algeria and the *vieilles colonies* of the Caribbean. Cultural assimilation was most complete in the old plantation colonies, because of the pervasive erosion of any alternative cultures through slavery.

Colonial administration in Guadeloupe, Martinique and French Guiana was as unstable as the régimes of metropolitan France. In 1848 adult men were first granted the right to vote, in the same year that slavery was abolished. The next year the right to vote was withdrawn, and it was not restored until 1870. General councils were created in the Caribbean colonies in 1871, freedom of association was granted in 1901 and trade union rights in 1919. In spite of this inconsistency, the perception of the left in the *vieilles colonies* was that central government in Paris could intervene to liberate the impoverished inhabitants of the colonies.

The most influential strand of French Jacobin nationalism was the doctrine of radical egalitarianism, which in the Caribbean colonial context appeared to provide a way out of the sheer oppression and injustice of the plantation system – in short a means of liberation. It provided an antidote to the notion that it was

> natural that men should be graded in ranks or degrees and it seemed equally natural ... that the grading should take account of colour ... in general, the lighter the shade, the greater the expectation of wealth, salary and power.[8]

In the context, the attachment of the freed mulatto class, and later of the freed slaves, to the republican ideals of France is not difficult to understand. In Martinique the planter class exercised almost exclusive control over political representation. Through a network of patron-client relations the colonial élite exploited the dependence of small planters and labourers. Violence was common at election times. In Guadeloupe the role of the mulatto élite was much more ambiguous. From the start they were the keenest advocates of full assimilation into France, both for themselves and for the colony. The planter élite in Martinique, by contrast, was fiercely resistant to encroachments by the central administration in Paris on their autonomy.

There had been several proposals to transform the Caribbean colonies into fully-fledged departments of France before 1946. The first was in 1890, when the senators of Guadeloupe and Martinique first suggested the reform. Two later proposals were presented to the National Assembly, in 1915 and in 1919, by the deputies of the same islands.

## 1946 – Transformation of the Caribbean colonies into Départements

These deputies' main concern in asking for the status of French departments after the war, was to grant the same social and welfare rights to the inhabitants of the former colonies as had been granted in the 1930s and in the immediate post-war years to the metropolitan French population. In 1945, before the departmentalization proposal had been put before the Constituent National Assembly, Aimé Césaire, deputy of Martinique, argued passionately for a 'colonial solidarity fund' to repair the colonies' infrastructure and improve the health and well-being of the poor.[9] In 1946 it was seen as the French government's duty to provide the new departments with the administrative and financial means to ensure equal treatment in social policy. As Paul Valentino, socialist deputy of Guadeloupe, remarked,

> The main concern of the proponents of the law was to promptly obtain the benefits of social and labour laws for the workers of the colonies.[10]

During the war, when the islands were for some time completely cut off from the outside world, their dependent colonial economies withered on the vine, resulting in near-starvation conditions. Liberal economic policies between the wars had further eroded the economic prosperity of the French Caribbean territories, and there were demands for greater intervention to support the price and to increase the quantity of sugar imported from Martinique and Guadeloupe. More specifically, it was hoped that all future legislation would come into operation in the overseas departments at the same time as in the metropolis. This would ensure that conditions improved dramatically for the poor. The overseas deputies also demanded the immediate nationalization and subsidization of the ailing sugar industries of the French Caribbean.

A certain amount of flattery was used by some of the overseas deputies in order to gain support for the proposal to departmentalize the colonies. Aimé Césaire pointed out the advantages for France of being legitimately present in the former *vieilles colonies*, when he said,

> At a time when doubts are being cast on the cohesion of the so-called Empire, at a time when there are rumours of dissidence from abroad, this request for integration, coming as it does in the present international climate, takes on tremendous significance.[11]

The most immediate concern for the Gaullists was to prevent the spread of the United States' sphere of influence to include Martinique, Guadeloupe and French Guiana. After the war, the time seemed right to a number of deputies to assert that France's presence in the Caribbean region was legitimate and permanent. As one Gaullist deputy put it:

> It is desirable that France should be represented on the other side of the Atlantic, not by colonies, but by territories which are entirely French.[12]

French Guiana was particularly important in this respect, as the only remaining French territory on the entire American mainland.[13] However, the military aspect of the French presence in the Caribbean only became important after De Gaulle came to power in 1958.

Most of the representatives of the former *vieilles colonies* who supported the proposal for departmental status to be granted, felt that the historical ties, and the extent of linguistic and cultural assimilation already attained in these colonies, fully justified the integration proposal.[14] The law was seen as the best means for ending colonial inequalities. This would happen not through separation, but through admission to the 'French family'. As Raymond Betts explains

By giving the colonies the same institutions as metropolitan France, assimilation little by little removes the distances which separate the diverse parts of the French territory, and finally realises their intimate union through the application of a common legislation.[15]

At the time of the debates, the traditional aspect of the law was emphasised, rather than its radical character. In these, the oldest parts of the Empire, so went the argument, only reactionaries would be against granting full citizenship on an equal basis. The quote from Léon de Lepervanche at the start of this chapter, illustrates this argument.

The proposal from the overseas deputies was unanimously approved by the Constituent National Assembly. The only doubts expressed during the debates concerned the cost of the implementation of the law for the French treasury,[16] and the long-term implications for the new departments' sense of responsibility for their own affairs, as more and more of the decisions affecting their futures would be made in Paris.[17] Such doubts were dismissed as unworthy of the generous spirit of the moment.[18]

The law of 1946 was in line with the long-term assimilatory trend of colonial history in the French Caribbean. However, it would not have been adopted after 1946. Immediately after the war, the right was discredited because of its alliance with Vichy during the war, and the experience of occupation had temporarily weakened the top administration in Paris. The National Assembly was completely dominated by the left, including the Communist Party, and by the Gaullists. One year later, the communists had left government, and the law would probably not have been accepted.

## Delayed implementation of the law of 1946

During the debates in the Constituent National Assembly in 1946, the Minister for the Colonies warned that there was no administrative infrastructure in place in the overseas departments. He did not question the principles behind the law, but expected it to take years rather than months to implement. Soon there was a fiscal crisis in France, with a heavy burden of indebtedness and hyperinflation. The three months originally specified in the law was inadequate – for example in Alsace and Lorraine, legal integration into the French Republic had taken ten years.

In the event, the implementation of the law of departmentalization was delayed for two years. Furthermore, whereas the original text had stipulated that new legislation would be automatically extended to the overseas departments, unless specified to the contrary, this was no longer the case. The reason was Article 73 of the Constitution, which allowed for legislation to be adapted to suit the 'particular conditions and requirements' of the overseas departments. Administration by decree, so hated during the colonial era, continued in this way throughout the Fourth Republic.[19] The *notables* still had access to the central administration in Paris. They could influence the *Préfet*, who was the local representative in the DOM of central government. The concern of the planters, expressed in a series of newspaper articles which appeared in the national press in 1948, was to keep labour costs down. There had indeed been spectacular increases in the minimum wage levels, which by 1956 were as high as those in the mainland (Antilles – 110 French francs (FF), metropolis – 92–116 FF).[21] Had this minimum wage been respected, then sugar production in the French Caribbean might have collapsed. In reality this was not a danger since the minimum legal wage was rarely paid.

The law of 1946 had created expectation of immediate improvements in economic and social conditions in the overseas departments of the Caribbean. Almost overnight, the standard of living in metropolitan France became the 'norm'. Local decisions depended more than ever on authorisation from Ministries in Paris. Paul Valentino had warned that in his experience this kind of centralization was harmful for the French Caribbean islands and French Guiana.

> My experience in public office has taught me that it is precisely because the fate of the colonies is decided in Paris, on the basis of inadequate information, ... that there is no such urgency in the demands of the colonies ... I am convinced that if assimilation gives the central government total responsibility for the destiny of the colonial peoples, it will end up by severing the very ties which unite them (the colonies) emotionally with the metropolis.[22]

This was prescient, since the same argument resurfaced years later, when the left started to oppose integration, and demanded instead the right of self-determination for the overseas departments. This was linked to a demand for *autonomie démocratique et populaire*. In the late 1950s, therefore, the left in the overseas departments started clearly to distance itself from the orthodox Jacobin line of the French Communist Party.

The left's new position was clear in Aimé Césaire's letter to Maurice Thorez, Secretary-General of the French Communist Party, in which Césaire stated that the colonial liberation struggle could never be secondary to the class struggle. For the PPM, the centre-periphery conflict took priority over the conflict between left and right.

By the time of the Fifth Republic there had been an apparent switch between left and right on the constitutional status issue. By 1958, it was the communists asking for greater autonomy from metropolitan France, and the right demanding greater centralization and continued departmentalization. Why did this turnaround take place?

There was a messianic quality to the expectations of the deputies of the overseas departments, which almost ensured that their constituents would be disappointed. As one speaker in the National Assembly commented, the government was being expected to perform miracles.[23] Of course, the manna which was to fall from the state into the laps of the French Caribbean people did not materialize. After only two weeks, the Caribbean deputies began to complain bitterly of delay, accusing the central authorities of bad will. Three years later, Léopold Bissol, deputy for French Guiana, painted a dismal picture of the deteriorating relationship between the overseas departments and metropolitan France.

> Things are getting worse and worse in the new departments. They are left with the impression that the metropolis has taken them to her bosom in order to suffocate them.[24]

A series of strikes by civil servants in the late 1940s and early 1950s centred on the demand that local civil servants be treated identically with civil servants of metropolitan origin and working in the overseas departments.

Furthermore, by the early 1950s, the autonomist current of the right had accepted that the departmental status was there to stay. As a result, the local right in the DOM started to seek accommodation within the existing constitutional arrangements rather than trying to change these arrangements themselves.[25]

## *From the* Union Française *to the* Communauté

In the first post-war government, the PCF. ministers legislatively abolished the French colonial empire, and put the *Union Française* in its place. There was a strong consensus in favour of equality, and the ending of colonial domination, as expressed in the wording of the Preamble to the Constitution, which stated:

the *Union Française* is composed of nations and peoples ...
France intends to lead those over whom it has taken
charge to freely and democratically administer their own
affairs.

Yet, any suggestion of autonomy or independence had been rejected
at the end of the Second World War at the Brazzaville Conference in
1944. As Alfred Grosser observes, this Constitution was ambiguous,
since it 'juxtaposed the federal idea of equal entities and the assimilationist idea of equal individuals'.[26] Perhaps only in the small former
plantation colonies of the Caribbean and the Indian Ocean did
assimilation finally win the day.

By the early 1960s the ideal of colonisation through individual
emancipation was almost everywhere swept aside in favour of
national anti-colonial liberation. We have seen that this switch also
took place in the French Caribbean departments, two years before
the transformation of the *Union Française* into the *Communauté* in
1958. As integral parts of the French Republic, the DOM (unlike the
overseas territories, or TOM) had no separate right of political self-
determination under the Constitution of the new Republic. This
argument (which was also used by Jacques Soustelle to support
*Algérie Française*) has not convinced opponents of French policies in
the Caribbean DOM. According to them, the French state had abandoned its historical role as an emancipatory and anti-colonial force,
and reverted since the 1950s to its 'capitalist, undemocratic and colonialist' self.[27]

For the political opponents of departmentalization, decolonization through accession to sovereignty was seen as a universal process,
which would eventually also affect the DOM. For most of the population, however, the greater fear was that the central authorities in
Paris would decide to 'abandon' the overseas departments to their
fate, and set them adrift into independence. The coming to power of
General De Gaulle ensured that this abandon would not occur. On
the contrary, from the start, De Gaulle understood the need to distinguish the position in the DOM from that in Algeria and in the former colonies. Whereas the TOM had the right of separate
self-determination, the DOM did not.[28]

The task for the new régime in Paris was both to reward the
faithfulness of the DOM electorate, and to build on the existing legacy of French *présence*. At the same time, strategic interests in the
Caribbean region became more important, especially the space base
at Kourou in French Guiana, because of the assertion by the new
régime of France's *indépendance* from the two superpower blocs.

De Gaulle understood that in order for support for departmentalization to be strengthened, improvements would have to be made in conditions, in the way in which elections were organised, and in the administrative and legislative systems in the DOM. The General's clear commitment to the overseas departments once again raised expectations of improvements in conditions. In 1958 there was an 81 per cent 'yes' vote for the new Constitution, compared with 77 per cent in metropolitan France.[29]

## A change of approach – from the Fourth to the Fifth Republic

The difficulty for central government in Paris was to enable the overseas departments to 'catch up' with the French mainland. A legacy of plantation colonialism, physical remoteness from the rest of France and very different climatic conditions made this a very difficult task. An immediate priority was to restore the infrastructure, and to create an administrative infrastructure from scratch. This took time – it was 1951 before local offices of technical ministries became operative in the French Caribbean departments.

Administrative changes were introduced which were to improve the effectiveness of policy. Under the Fourth Republic, the powers of the *Préfet* were strengthened, giving him overall responsibility for defence and security, and a central role in economic affairs. Poor coordination between the DOM and Paris remained a problem, even so, and resulted in a jumble of laws, derogations and decrees being in force.

A permanent inter-ministerial co-ordinating committee was set up in 1954, under a so-called 'super-*Préfet*', the IGAME (L'Inspecteur Général de l'Administration en Mission Extraordinaire dans les DOM). This became a permanent post under the Fifth Republic, with each government appointing either a delegate Minister, a full Minister, or a Secretary of State for the DOM-TOM attached to the Ministry of the Interior.

At the start of the Fifth Republic it was explicitly acknowledged that active intervention was needed to improve conditions in the overseas departments and to reduce the social unrest which characterized the French Caribbean in particular. Uniform treatment did not in itself bring about equality between the DOM and metropolitan France. Under the terms of Article 73 of the Constitution, active steps were taken to adapt and reform the administrative and political system in the DOM to suit socio-economic needs and conditions.

In 1960 a number of administrative reforms were introduced in the overseas departments on an experimental basis, four years before being introduced in the French mainland. Firstly, the *Préfet* was given additional powers, enabling him to improve communication between the central ministries in Paris and local administration in the overseas departments. The *Préfet* also had 'secondary accountability' for the departmental budget, and worked closely with the newly-created local planning commissions in each DOM. At the same time, to assess the effectiveness of the French state's planning policies, a branch of the national statistics office was opened in each of the four DOM in the early 1960s. Another reform strengthened the role of the *Conseil Général*, the locally elected council. This was all part and parcel of the regionalization of administration and planning. However, according to commentators, the effect of these reforms was simply to devolve power onto the *Préfet* in each department, rather than to decentralize administrative power.[30]

The same approach, of adapting in order to align, was introduced in social policy. Some real improvements were needed in order to counter the political unrest emerging in the French Caribbean. A special social fund was created, which provided the same overall level of benefits to the population, but distributed these benefits in a different way. Most of the funds were used to finance preventive measures such as primary health care, education, public housing and sanitation measures.

In political life also, the new régime was determined to make a break with the Fourth Republic. The most pressing political problem in the overseas departments was the violence and intimidation which were almost routine at election time.[31] After 1960, overt forms of fraud and bullying of voters were discouraged, and complaints were taken more seriously. At the same time, overt coercion was often replaced with preferential or denied access to welfare benefits and employment, according to how people voted.

In the meantime, the communist parties were branded 'separatist' and were quite fiercely repressed. Perhaps the harshest measure was the ordinance of 15 October 1960 (known as the 'vile ordinance'). This authorized the *Préfet* to order the removal to the mainland of any civil servant (including teachers), whose activities were considered to represent 'a threat to public order'. The ordinance was used in Algeria and against opponents of the departmental status in Guadeloupe, Martinique and Réunion. Altogether twenty-six people were affected. In 1972 the ordinance was finally revoked after several people affected by it staged a protracted hunger strike.

# The paradox of consensus over the departmental status

Opponents of present constitutional arrangements in the DOM accuse the French state of pursuing colonialist policies. Yet the communist parties of these territories do not wish to sever the connection with France. As André Oraison remarks, they are the only communist parties in the world which 'ask for autonomy within the framework of a former colonial power'.[32]

The communist parties in the French Caribbean territories demand autonomy, but wish for the DOM to receive financial support from the French state at an even higher level than at present. According to the communists, this would provide some form of compensation for several hundred years of French colonialism. The position of the French state, however, has consistently been that if Martinique, Guadeloupe or French Guiana cease to be French departments, they will lose all rights to official financial support.

During the 1960s, the debate on self-determination for the DOM focused on the constitutionality of such a claim. It was concluded by French lawyers that the overseas departments did not have the separate right to self-determination, since this would mean granting that right to each and every French department. The communist parties, on the other hand, claimed that under Article 72 new constitutional arrangements could be introduced, as indeed had been the case in Corsica.

The paradox is that virtually no political groupings in the French Caribbean want full sovereignty without a continuing attachment to France. Even the pro-independence parties, such as the UPLG (Union pour la Libération de la Guadeloupe) want France to maintain its financial support to any independent state created in Guadeloupe. What the nationalist political parties and movements have been asking for since the 1960s is the decentralization of power to the Caribbean. The debate in local politics, therefore, is less about constitutional and political status, as it may appear, and more about the use to which the present political institutions are put, and the degree of autonomy from the central administration in Paris. This does not include demands for financial and technical autonomy; far from it.

The issue of self-determination resurfaced in the 1980s with the election of a socialist government in France. Yves Meny has observed that the socialists' decentralization reforms were carried out with the conviction that decentralization or regionalization reinforces rather than diminishes national unity.[33]

At the same time, Michel Debré warned that 'decentralization is one of five ways to kill the state'.[34] By 1981 the proponents of centralization were the old guard of the Jacobin, Gaullist right. On the left, everyone (or almost everyone) had been converted to the merits of granting regions greater autonomy, and a certain *'droit à la différence'* culturally as well.

The decentralization proposals of the early 1980s were intended to undercut centrifugal pressures in the overseas departments, and in this they largely seem to have succeeded.[35] To the extent that they have succeeded in damping down and diverting opposition to the constitutional status of the French Caribbean, the reforms have been accepted by the right as well.

Thus in the 1990s as in the 1940s, the constitutional and political oppositions and changes cannot be reduced to a simple tension between right and left. This is because, in these region-departments, as in Corsica for instance, centre-periphery conflict remains a crucial variable in understanding local politics.

## Notes

1  Paul Valentino, *Débats de l'Assemblée Nationale (DAN)*, Journal Officiel de la République Française, La Documentation Française, 14 March 1946.
2  Aimé Césaire, *DAN*, 10 July 1947.
3  De Lepervanche, *DAN*, 10 July 1947.
4  Olivier Stirn, *DAN*, 3 November 1977.
5  Michel Debré, *DAN*, 28 October 1980.
6  The full title of the law is 'Projet de loi tendant au classement comme département français de la Guadeloupe, de la Martinique, de la Réunion et de la Guyane', proposal made by Aimé Césaire (deputy Martinique), Léopold Bissol (French Guiana) and Raymond Vergès (Réunion). The proposal became law No. 46-451, AN(C) Décrets et Lois (Constituent National Assembly Decrees and Laws), 19.3.1946, p. 2294.
7  J.F. Bluntschli, *The Theory of the State*, The Clarendon Press, 1885, p. 95.
8  Philip Mason, *Patterns of Dominance*, Oxford University Press, 1971, p. 277.
9  Aimé Césaire, *Débats de l'Assemblée Nationale Constituante (DAN(C))*, October 1945, p. 544.
10  Paul Valentino, *DAN(C)*, 14 March 1946, p. 757.
11  Aimé Césaire, *DAN(C)*, 12 March 1946, p. 659.
12  Juglas, *DAN(C)*, 14 March 1946, p. 755.
13  Gaston Monnerville, *DAN(C)*, 14 March 1946, p. 754.
14  Léonde Lepervanche, *DAN(C)*, 12 March 1946, p. 665.
15  Raymond Betts, *Assimilation and Association in French Colonial Theory*, Columbia University Press, 1961, p. 8.

16 Moutet, *DAN(C)*, 14 March 1946, pp. 756–7.
17 Valentino, *DAN(C)*, 14 March 1946, p. 760.
18 Césaire, *DAN(C)*, 12 March 1946, p. 662.
19 Victor Sablé, *La Transformation des Iles d'Amérique en départements français,* Larose 1955, p. 172.
20 Léopold Bissol, *DAN*, 4 July 1949, p. 4146.
21 Robert Mestre, 'Le Problème des salaires', *Marchés coloniaux du monde*, 14 July 1956, p. 1947.
22 See note 1.
23 Juglas, *DAN(C)*, 14 March 1946, p. 756.
24 Léopold Bissol, *DAN*, 4 July 1949, p. 4146.
25 Gaumont, *DAN*, 3 August 1954, p. 3814.
26 Alfred Grosser, *Affaires extérieures. La politique de la France 1944–1984*, Flammarion, 1984, pp. 44–5.
27 Girard, *DAN*, 4 February 1949, p. 356.
28 Jean-Claude Maestre, 'L'Indivisibilité de la République Française et l'exercice du droit à l'autodétermination', *Revue du droit public et de la science politique en France et à l'étranger*, April–May 1976, pp. 431–61.
29 Sylvie Jacquemart, *La Question départementale outre-mer*, Presses universitaires de France, 1983, pp. 115–6.
30 See Pierre Bauchet, *L'Expérience française de planification*, Editions du Seuil, 1962, p. 153 and Jacquemart, *op. cit.*, p. 200.
31 Jacquemart, *op. cit.*, p. 206.
32 André Oraison, *Le Parti Communiste Réunionnais et l'Autonomie démocratique et populaire*, Centre universitaire de la Réunion, 1978, p. 113.
33 Yves Meny, 'Decentralisation in Socialist France: the Politics of Pragmatism', *West European Politics*, 7, 1 (January 1984), p. 66.
34 Michel Debré, *DAN*, 10 January 1981, pp. 326–7.
35 See Fred Constant, 'Politique et décentralisation aux Antilles Françaises', paper presented to International Colloquium on the Geopolitics of the Eastern Caribbean Region, Oxford University, 1988.

# CHAPTER 2 | Politics and society in Martinique

*Fred Reno*

Relating the two concepts of politics and society in Martinique inevitably requires an analysis of power relations in terms of its organization and functioning. To place this relationship in a framework of dependency does not necessarily signify that we adhere to the well known conclusions of 'dependency theorists'. These, using the centre-periphery paradigm to study the politico-economic exchanges on a world scale, deduce in the majority of cases, the domination by a centre represented by an international bourgeoisie, over a periphery which is atomized and subjugated, the latter represented by the developing countries.[1]

If these works allow for the illustration of the weight of external factors on the functioning of the periphery, they neglect the importance of 'internal' variables. For example, they do not always take account of the reality of a dependence sometimes sustained internally by diverse social actors including those who, in the logic of the theorists and economists of the dependency theory, should oppose it.[2] These limits of economic determinism are also verified at a strictly internal level by the functioning of the society.

In effect, contrary to a watered-down Marxist theory, we do not consider power as a simple reflection of socio-economic relations.[3] The rediscovery of the specificity of politics has made it possible to measure at what degree the state can be autonomous with respect to social classes. This approach is more pertinent when applied to the French politico-administrative model which is historically more interventionist than those of many Western European countries.[4] Using considerable resources, France has managed to install itself and rule over the peripheral society. However, to affirm the autonomy of the political centre and its administration does not exclude the recognition of a relative autonomy of the peripheral society in its own capacity of self-regulation and especially in the production of local political phenomena.

In this chapter we will attempt to translate these different aspects, by presenting the structures and mechanisms of the working of the politico-administrative model of Martinique, for a public which knows little of the reality of the French overseas departments, while taking the precaution of not abusing the institutional approach. We highlight, therefore, the principal actors of the model, in particular the civil servants and the élite, occasionally referring to organizational sociology. The principal interest of this study of politics and society, within a framework of a non-sovereign recipient society managed by the French politico-administrative model is, therefore, to show how the local population and élite accept the power structures, values and personnel from France. In so doing, we avoid reducing, on the one hand, the political relationship to 'the action of the centre', and on the other, the political and social relations to the domination of the periphery by the centre.

Exported to Martinique, the French politico-administrative model acquires its own dynamism, even if it borrows its principal constituent elements from metropolitan administrative bodies. The image which will allow us best to understand the working of this model is that of the ingestion of food, a stage, which in nutritional terms precedes digestion, followed by its rejection or non-digestion. Neither rejected, nor completely digested, this model seems to be ingested as a necessary requirement by a population, who directly or indirectly, receive it as a resource. But the society is not content just to receive external political structures but secretes its own power phenomena. The political system associated with the name of Aimé Césaire is an example of this, made more significant by the real power it exerts on local society.

## The French politico-administrative model

The French politico-administrative model was introduced to Martinique as a result of colonization. Considering the historical conditions of its establishment allows us to understand its contemporary importance. One of the particularities of Caribbean societies, in comparison with other colonized territories, was their lack of prior institutional structures at the time of colonization. This was a characteristic of the region as a whole, where the administrative structures exported by the metropolitan centres were established in territories uninhabited or emptied of their populations,[5] a characteristic which can be compared to that of African or Asian colonies where the indigenous culture and people were more resistant to colonialism. In these countries, the introduction of external models was rather a superimposition onto the structures which already existed within the colonised societies. Thus in the Caribbean and specifically in Martinique, the French administration model did not have to negotiate its establishment with a hostile environment.[6] Instead, its influence was easily dispersed throughout the territory, as it penetrated a society which it helped to create and then controlled. Later, the metropolitan institutions which had been established in the island were slightly modified by both post-war reforms and the increasing role played by the coloured population.

However these reforms are hardly significant. In reality the Martinican environment has ingested successive administrative reforms without initiating or contesting their application. The relationship between France and Martinique has often been stimulated by the metropole. For instance, the application of Overseas Common Law, followed by France conceding to allow room for adaptation of this common law to overseas specificities,[7] measures which the periphery considered to be a factor of social development. The recent reforms are inspired by the same logic, a logic which ought not to be reduced to a simple juridical assimilation or a colonial domination of the overseas territories by the French state. The administration of the overseas collectivities, although inspired largely by French common law, can be distinguished from that of metropolitan constituencies.

In Martinique today the local government hierarchy comprises three levels. In the commune, the mayor is the executive at the head of the debating assembly or municipal council. In the '*département*' as in the commune (following the 1982 reforms of decentralization), the executive is elected. Prior to this it was nominated by the president of the general council. Finally the regional council, the new territorial collectivity created by the laws of decentralization, also has an elected executive at the head of its assembly. Admittedly, although similar administrative divisions exist in metropolitan France, these do not have the same organizational structure. In the metropole, the influence of these collectivities changes according to ever-increasing concentric circles; that is, from the commune, to the department, to the region, to the state. In Martinique, this image taken from geometry is inaccurate to the extent that certain circles cover the same surface area without sharing the same centre. Although difficult to conceive of this situation in geometric terms, it is apparent in the local administration of the DOMs, where the departmental circle and the regional circle have the same territorial surface, both possessing executives, assemblies and distinct domains of juridical competence.

This singular case would not need to be mentioned, if it was not a source of conflict between the two councils directing the same territory, which run the risk of confusing their prerogatives. Under the Fifth Republic other examples limited the idea of juridical assimilation of French overseas collectivities. The first structural indication of a difference was the establishment of a central administration of the overseas territories, under the direction of the Minister of the Colonies. As the intermediary between the periphery and the French political centre, this illustrates that the managing of overseas affairs merits special treatment as compared to that accorded to the other departments and metropolitan regions.[8] The absence of juridical assimilation can be verified also when we consider the powers of the *département* and the region of Martinique. The *'Octroi de Mer'*, a consumption tax on certain products, does not exist in metropolitan departments. Managed conjointly by the departmental and regional councils since the laws of decentralization, this tax contributes significantly to the working budgets of the communes and constitutes for them an important resource.[9]

Constitutionally it is Article 73 of the French fundamental law of 1958 which formally recognizes that the overseas collectivities present differences which justify an adaptation of their legislative system and their administrative organization. Combined with a decree of 26 April 1960, this article of the constitution allows those elected locally to transmit to the political centre proposals of laws for adaptation. Although the laws of decentralization of the 1980s align Martinique with the common law, they also confirm the right of Martinique to contest the application of all suggested French legislation. In so doing, the laws of decentralization enhance in particular the possibility for the creation of agencies for regional development, as well as allowing a larger use of opportunity and local decision-making. If the majority of the structures and capabilities of the collectivities in Martinique are the same as those in the metropole, their mechanisms of functioning respond often to a logic which takes into account both socio-economic and cultural factors. More than ever, the economic and social factors in Martinique are intimately linked with administrative action.[10]

The direction of economic life by the administrative authorities occurs through the intervention of specific institutions such as FIDOM (Overseas Investment and Development Fund) funded by state credit, and SATEC (Technical Aid and Co-operation Society) which, through its opinion and advice, has influenced the management of economic activity.[11] At a strictly local level, those elected use a substantial part of the budget for economic and social aid. In order to compensate for unemployment figures which are comparatively more important than in the metropole, the working expenses of the municipalities go principally to social aid and to personnel expenses, which total 51.3 per cent of the budget.[12] This existing structure creates an over-abundance of often under-qualified personnel. However it is unclear whether this spending is directed only by humanitarian concerns. Although such recruitment makes heavy demands on the budget, it establishes a sort of personal dependence of the individual recruited on the mayor and thus supports a complex of clientilistic (patron-client) working relations in the municipality.[13]

After reassuring him/herself that the candidate for recruitment is definitely from his/her commune, the mayor will employ the individual according to the limitations of the budget. In reality, competence and merit are not always the determining criteria for recruitment, the importance always being the tacit obligation of the recruited to openly support the mayor, particularly through electoral support in favour of his/her benefactor. This relationship is characterized by the fact that it is particularist, that is, it associates two partners in a quasi-exclusive exchange. It is also voluntary to the extent that no formal rule obliges the recruited to vote for the person in power.

In reality a solidarity exists between the two partners, the elector-client is the beneficiary of employment, who returns the favour with his/her vote and that of the family, in support of the elected-patron. This relationship of vertical solidarity is established between two unequal actors. Although there is an exchange of favours, the mayor is above-all the 'boss' and at the head of a source of supporters fed by diverse public resources. This type of quasi-generalized relationship pervades the communal framework. The situation becomes more complex the moment that the initial partners and resources exchanged diversify. Far from restricting itself to the difficult socio-economic context of rural society, the 'clientelist' relation also penetrates the bureaucracy and the rapport between civil servants and those elected.[14] In this latter context the resources exchanged vary with the objectives of the partners and the time period in question.

Until the decentralization reforms in 1982, the French politico-administrative model allowed the elected and the civil servants to be alternatively patrons and clients. Centralization gave the civil servants (prefect, general treasurer, peripheral directors of external services) a decisive role in terms of control of local affairs. Lacking technical competence, the locally elected officials were often forced to enlist the expertise of state representatives. When not actually substituting the choices made by the local officials, the recommendations of these experts directed these choices. Concerned with their public image and the renewing of their mandate, the elected considered their dependence on the expertise of the civil servants as a resource. In return, the representatives of the centre, preoccupied by their careers, did not hesitate in certain cases to overstep the limits of their competence, when the attitudes and judgements of the elected contributed to their own promotion. In this complex exchange, the elected were not always clients. Certain among them benefited for political or personal reasons through their contact with supporters within the civil service, while others encouraged both a national and local mandate. All in all they succeeded in setting up a strong network with which they could pressurize the civil servants in the collectivity. These dispensers of public resources found themselves in a subservient position to the elected representatives.

The juridical rigour of centralization nurtured the established informal working of the French politico-administrative model in Martinique. The elected officials therefore managed to pass legislation, satisfy their 'clientele' and renew their mandate. The state, thanks to the informal actions of its representatives satisfied itself with the maintenance of order and the acceptance of its presence, a presence which was considered a necessity by the elected, including those who condemned it in their discussions.[15] As the tenants of organizational sociology have shown, such a system of transgressing the rules proves itself functional to the extent that the principal actors concerned in withdrawing mutual advantages help maintain the permanence of the politico-administrative model.[16]

However, although the recent laws of decentralization have not completely modified the system, a double movement is being created. On the one hand, the efficiency of certain informal contacts between the civil servants and the elected have been explicitly recognized by the legislator. Henceforth, through accepted practices reinforced by dialogue, relationships, informal up to now, have moved from a stage of quasi-normal to that of rights granted to the peoples' representatives by legislation. Parallel to the recognition of the efficiency of certain informal working mechanisms, they also support the elected in their struggle to assume fully their new powers created by decentralization. This is manifested by the employment of highly-qualified personnel, which not only limits the technical control of the state, but allows the elected officials to elaborate and realize more easily their political objectives.

Most of the analyses that follow can be applied to other overseas departments and to metropolitan collectivities, in particular to the relative development of the relationship between civil servants and the elected. The complicity between representatives of the state and the representatives of the people at a personal level is not only found in the periphery. However, other aspects of local political and social relations considered only concern Martinique. In effect the contemporary history, and maybe the future, of this country is strongly influenced by the thought and action of one man: Aimé Césaire. More than the individual, it is the political system that he has consciously or unconsciously put in place that must be analysed, taking into account his input on the working and objectives of local society, and the relations between the French centre and the overseas departments.

## The importance of the Césairean political system on local society

Deputy of Martinique in the French National Assembly and mayor of the capital of Fort-de-France since 1945, Aimé Césaire was regularly re-elected to his post until his retirement from the French National Assembly in 1993. Writer and founder with the ex-Senegalese president Léopald Sedar Senghor, and the Guianese Léon Gontran Damas of the political cultural model of Négritude, he influenced and still influences the black world and national minorities. Maybe it is not an exaggeration to say – considering the prestige which Césaire enjoys outside Martinique – that the system which he laid out and which has its roots in his native country, has determined to a large extent the institutional forms of the rapport between the French centre and the whole of its overseas departments beginning in 1946, and since 1981.

In order to study what we have called the Césairean system, we have been inspired by the 'systems analysis' such as that conceived by David Easton,[17] following work carried out by Norbert Wiener.[18] Like von Bertalanffy,[19] Easton stresses the study of exchanges between the system and its environment, while ignoring what happens in the interior of this system, considering it in the tradition of Wiener as a black box. Easton's originality is that he is interested in the political system and more precisely in the influences of the environment on the system; in the reaction of the latter and the means deployed by it to maintain its equilibrium. Although inspired by Easton, this study elaborates further on two points.

The object of this analysis, built along the lines of the systems approach, is reduced to the exchange between, on the one hand, a way of thinking and acting set up in the system, and on the other hand to a divided environment. Besides this, contrary to Easton, consideration is taken of what occurs in the heart of the black box. It appears to us that the nature of the reaction can vary with the contents between the black box and the outside; the importance of the influence of the environment on the system, the nature and strength of the reaction of which can depend on what happens within the black box. The approach illustrates a system including authority structures, roles and a set of values linked to a double but connected environment: the local society and the French state. Altogether this forms an integrated model, the permanence of which is assured by a continual movement of exchanges between the black box and the exterior, through 'inputs' and 'outputs', following the classical schema of system analysis. The centre of this model is made up of structures and of political roles such as the post of mayor of the capital city of the *département*, of deputies and senators of Martinique. These political positions are accompanied by the control of numerous institutions for the allocation of resources.

We have also included a group of non-exhaustive values classed in two categories, namely intangible and flexible values. The former are based on numerous ideas among which is the recognition of the grandeur of French culture. The most striking illustration of this idea is the pleasure with which Césaire, as a writer, enjoys to manipulate and to 'bend' the French language, contributing also to its enrichment. This admiration for 'French' culture does not always exclude the affirmation of a Martinican specificity and identity; an identity based in particular on the multiplicity of component parts of the Martinican culture and the importance of the black presence. The specificity is made apparent by the youth of 'his people', by the originality of the historical trajectory of his country, and the social and economic issues which this country must face.

On a political level, the presence of a republican France with its universalistic values, implies for Césaire social equality between the metropolitan citizen and the French citizen of Martinique. One must thus consider that the egalitarian demand is a recurrent aspect of Césairean discourse, the objective being to assure the security of the people by the benefits of social laws applied in France. Such a demand brings as a consequence a secession in as much as the Martinicans will not have the means to assume independence. Will they be able to one day? Nothing is less sure in the approach of the deputy-mayor. Since 1958, after his resignation from the French

Communist Party in 1956, he has rejected all political formulas which would distance the island from France. Refusing independence and an 'autonomy of misery', he argues for regional status, regretting that 'we do not find this word in the French constitution'. According to Césaire, regionalization in 1958 would have allowed for the combination into one concept the recognition of Martinican specificity and its belonging to France. In Martinique, recent debates on the institutional evolution of Martinique do not touch on this issue expressed as an interest in belonging to France, and a refusal of the 'misery of sovereignty'. These different ideas are here considered intangible because they are based on past and actual political acts of Aimé Césaire, despite certain variations according to the circumstances.

If Césaire appears momentarily to abandon these principles, it is in order to state better the particularities of Martinique without going as far as to demand independence. In reality this demand is part of the category of values which have been called 'flexible'. Stronger or weaker according to the government and the overseas minister in power, this political demand always takes the form of a peaceful request against measures taken, or the inadequacy of central politics in terms of the periphery. This is behaviour according to circumstance, which is manifested by the defensive action of questioning the French presence. The offensive dimension of the disagreement is social and security-oriented. It is not an identity-oriented problem except by reference to the affirmation of a Martinican specificity. But it does tend to diminish and may be suspended when the egalitarian resources distributed by the state rise. From this we should consider the demand as circumstantial and variable.

The same can be said of the attachment to France. In the works of Aimé Césaire and his followers, this choice is expressed in different ways. It oscillates between 'permanent and definite belonging', the reinforcement of local power and the possibility of independence. When the latter option is envisaged, the response of Césaire as an individual differs from that of the politician. The individual believes that 'Martinique will be independent. The political man thinks that the circumstances should be taken into account, that a title is of no value unless it is adapted to the prevailing conditions'. He 'does not really believe that the Martinican people will take up the call for independence'. Although Césaire's personal thoughts illustrate a certain flexibility, the politician suggests the idea of an attachment to France in the name of being realistic.

Another flexible aspect of the Césairean system of values is the charisma of the political leader. This characteristic, maintained voluntarily or not, is tied also to circumstances, but above all to the role of the deputy-mayor. It is less the man of letters unknown for a long time in his community, than the dispenser of material resources which gives Césaire prestige, adulation and allegiance from numerous electors, as well as a large influence among the local political class. The qualities of the writer did no more than add to the political capital held by the deputy-mayor. This political charisma risks, however, being eroded with time, as the new generations do not have the same rapport with this leader, who is less and less present on the political scene. More important is the increased rationalization of the politico-administrative management, consecutive with decentralization, implying more responsibilities for the elected, which tends to modify the forms and capacities of allocation of material resources. It will become more and more difficult, for example, to employ individuals in large numbers on a basis other than merit and real needs of the service.

This social dimension which has contributed and still contributes to the success of the Césairean system, corresponds to that conveniently called in the systems approach 'outputs'. The 'inputs' include both the demands emerging from local society and the supports which are manifested in particular by affection, recognition and adulation. In truth the reality is more complex. The 'inputs' directed at the system, including demands and supports, come from the two levels of the environment which make up the local society and the French state. If employment and material advantages are the principal demands of the inhabitants of Martinican society and Fort-de-France, of which Césaire is mayor, one must add to these a certain number of diverse symbolic demands, such as the defence of a cultural identity. For consideration, these demands must traverse certain institutions including partisan organizations, municipalities, and the reception of citizen problems by parliamentarians, all of which function principally to avoid an overload of the system.

There are corresponding responses to these solicitations in terms of employment, and individual advantages gained from public politics. In cultural matters, for example, the response takes the form of putting at the disposition of the population a municipal cultural service (SERMAC), which manages numerous cultural centres in the area, providing open free workshops for all Martinicans; the first objective being 'the fight against alienation', which accompanies or takes the place of a desire to make culture available to all. It is equally necessary to mention the cultural festival set up by Aimé Césaire for which the expenses have for a long time been supported by the municipality of Fort-de-France. A study of the social functions of this cultural service should be undertaken. In effect it has allowed for the socialization of numerous young persons out of work, delinquents and quasi-delinquents. From this point of view, the social response of a cultural structure to a latent demand of integration merits recognition. The responses of the system to the environment (feedback) allows the municipal authorities and the parliamentarians to measure the popularity of the values defended, to receive the support of the local society, the most important being the electoral allegiance of numerous citizens and in consequence, the renewing of the mayor's and parliamentarians' mandates.

The influence of the system is not limited to its action on the general population. In the majority of the two principal local assemblies (the general and regional councils) the supporters of the system influence the management of numerous communes of the island by technical aid and advice on cultural matters. These happenings have allowed Fort-de-France to place at the disposal of numerous municipalities its material, for example the lending of large and often expensive equipment. They have also contributed to the increase in the number of offices or municipal services of culture and cultural festivals, inspired by that of the main town.

Resituated in a different and larger environment, that of the French state, the 'inputs' and the 'outputs' change. With the central authorities the exchange is first a partial one. The demands on the metropole concern principally maintenance of French sovereignty in Martinique and the spreading of French influence in the Caribbean. In order to achieve this the metropolitan authorities offer finance, structures, and personnel. But the success and efficiency of state public policy in the local arena presupposes the agreement, participation and initiative of the local representatives. Finally the treatment of central demands by the Césairean system is less conflicting than what is shown by the political discussion and practices. These demands have that much more chance to succeed in their objectives when the authorities and the values of the system are not really hostile to one another. The deputy-mayor, in support of a re-working of the relationship between the centre and Martinique, does not oppose French sovereignty. The analysis of the response of the system to this sort of solicitation must always take into account the historical situation.

Speaking for the middle and lower classes, Césaire and his Parti Progressiste Martiniquais channelled for a long time political enquiry and limited the waves of violence which could have negatively affected the authority of the French state. This differed from Guadeloupe where political disagreements have occasionally taken the form of

bomb scares against state symbols. It was during this period, therefore, through the stabilizing efforts of populist leadership that the
Césairean system responded better to the needs of central authorities. From 1981, the date of François Mitterand's election to the presidency, to 1990 the moratorium proclaimed by Césaire on the
question of the statute of the island, was actually a response in antici-
pation of the promises of support from first the candidate, then the
French president. Suspending all debate on the political evolution of
Martinique in the name of the necessity for economic development,[20]
Aimé Césaire led the entire political left into the discussions and
practices of managers, focusing on the necessity to reinforce the productive system, and the distribution of aid to the different economic
sectors, in particular agriculture and tourism. In setting up an apparent consensus on the secondary character of the institutional debate,
the supporters of the moratorium responded also to a wish of the
French centre to calm the political climate in the overseas departments.

It is during this period that the Césairean system and local society have received the most support from the state: financial aid has
multiplied. Césaire's contributions to French culture were celebrated
with the performance of one of his works at the Comédie Française.
At many points, members of Césaire's party were appointed to
French government positions.[21] From 1981 to 1990, it appears that
dependence on terms of the French state was fully utilized as a
resource by all political actors of the left and the right. Contested
before 1981 because it was non-egalitarian and centralist, dependence within a framework of decentralization reinforcing local power
satisfies one of the demands of the Martinican left, that is the recognition of difference, while maintaining the egalitarian advantages of
departmentalization.

This analysis of the Césairean system does not exclude the possibility of malfunctioning and conflict, which could stem from internal weaknesses, and/or come from outside. The filtering of demands
can prove to be inefficient. For example the partisan organizations
and the Césairean militants sharing the immediate benefits of power,
do not always have the necessary fighting spirit on the field to impose
themselves as intermediaries between the society and the authorities.
The open or latent conflict between people and political actors can
be explained both by a disaffection of the electorate with their political representatives, and a lack of adaptability of the responses of the
system to the issues of the moment.

The hypothesis of a breakdown or fault in communication can
be proposed in the light of international changes, or more precisely,

on the effects of the opening of the European Community which pre-occupies all Martinicans. Conflict can creep in between local authorities and the French state, and this is how one can explain feeble support from which the system benefits; this does not always coincide with the demands of the metropolitan centre. The system can either benefit from or enter into conflict with the changing environment. In the latter case, if the system does not adapt it may cave in.

In conclusion, numerous observations are apparent from this study on Martinique. The French politico-administrative model seems to be agreeable to all political actors, including the independentists who see in it a means of controlling some power. Apart from this, without attributing the cause to decentralization, two phenomena will probably mark the political life of Martinique. The first is the spectacular entry of the independence movement into the heart of municipal and regional councils. From 1986 to 1992 (the date of the most recent regional elections), the number of supporting votes for the independence movement tripled, passing from 7.9 per cent to 23.4 per cent. Absent until now from the regional council, they have gained nine seats out of forty-one in the Assembly. Another event was the end of the moratorium in 1990 and the subsequent resurgence of the question of political status. The different leftist movements, with the exception of the Federal Socialists of Martinique, have laid out a project on the future status of Martinique, which evokes the necessity to go further than decentralization, which in their words, has reached its limits.[22] These two events coincided with an erosion of the Césairean system which is submitting to the rebuffs of environmental pressure.

This change in the strategy of leftist political groups seems to have been stimulated by the success of the independentists, a success which itself is explained to a certain extent by the fear engendered by the prospects of the European market of 1993. In short, the French politico-administrative model and the Césairean system must face up to the limitations of the European set-up. It seems that, little by little, a third level of environment is taking shape, of which its pressures, comparable to successive waves, influences with more or less force the behaviour of all the authorities and the local society.

## Notes

1   From the extensive literature on this subject, reference can be made to the work of authors who have applied these theories to the Caribbean; see for example: André Frank Gunder, *L'accumulation dépendante*, Edition Anthropos, 1978, p. 67.

Philippe A. Blérald, 'Etat idéologie et développement à la Guadeloupe et à la Martinique', doctoral thesis in Political Science, University of Paris I, 1981.

2  Fred Reno, 'L'exportation de modèles d'administration opposés: le cas de la Barbade et de la Martinique', doctoral thesis in Political Science, University of Paris I, 1987, pp. 18–21.

3  It appears that there are two compatible conceptions of the state in the works of Marx; see Karl Marx, *Préface à la contribution de l'économie politique*, Editions Sociales, 1957, p. 4.

4  Bertrand Badic and Pierre Birnbaum, *Sociologie de l'Etat.*, Grasset, 1979.

5  The majority of the indigenous population had been exterminated. In certain cases, for example Barbados, the territory was uninhabited.

6  See the comments of J.F. Bayart in the 'forward' of *La Revue Française de Science Politique*, December 1989, 39(8), p. 789, which deals with the origins of politics.

7  François Miclo, *Régime législatif et réglementaire des Départements d'Outre-Mer*, Edition Economica, 1982.

8  Sylvie Jacquemart, *La Question départementale outre-mer*, Presses universitaires de France, 1983.

9  Created by law on 11 January 1892, this tax represented in 1982, 39.78 per cent of the working expenses of all the communes. Extracted from certain imported goods, it works contrary to European legislation according to which it should be extracted from locally produced goods.

10  See M. Alliot and G. Tinisit, 'L'administration des Départements d'Outre-Mer, une administration du développement', *Revue d'Administration Publique*, No. 31, 1984.

11  During the 1960s this institution modified the traditional relationships in the countryside, in particular by the codification of the rapport between large and small landowners. See Reno, *op. cit.*, pp. 263–95.

12  Justin Daniel, 'Pouvoir central, pouvoir local: essai de sociologie de l'administration à la Martinique', *Revue d'Administration Publique*, No. 31, 1984, pp. 71–89.

13  On this question, see Justin Daniel, *Administration locale et clientélisme: le cas de la Martinique*, doctoral thesis in Political Science, Paris, 1983.

14  J.F. Médard, 'Political clientelism in France. The centre-periphery nexus reexamined', in *Political Clientelism, Patronage and Development*, (ed.) S.N. Eisenstadt and R. Lemarchand, Sage Publication, London, 1985, pp. 125–71.

15  Fred Reno, 'Types d'états et contestation politique', *Cahiers de l'Administration Outre-Mer*, No. 2 (1989), pp. 15–42.

16  Pierre Gremion, *Le Pouvoir périphérique*, Editions du Seuil, 1976.

17  David Easton, *A Framework for Political Analysis*, Prentice Hall, 1965.

18  N. Weiner, *Cybernetics*, Hermann, 1948.

19  L. von Bertalanffy, *Théorie générale des systèmes*, Dunod, 1973.

20  The moratorium was declared on 23 May 1981.

21  The deputy mayor Césaire and the deputy Claude Lise, both members of the PPM, were selected in 1981 and 1988 to be members of the French government.

22  It appears that there is a convergence between these parties and the government, the latter of which, according to the Minister of the DOM-TOM, envisages changing and adapting the status to each collectivity.

# CHAPTER 3 | Guadeloupean consensus

*Jean-Paul Eluther*

Unlike many territories of the French colonial empire, Guadeloupe opted, in 1946, for complete integration into the French Republic in order to ensure its economic and social development and the advancement of its population. This attitude seems in principle paradoxical, given the crimes committed during the slave epoch and the tremendous attraction exerted by the ideology of decolonization during a great part of the twentieth century which saw, in the acquisition of independence, a necessary condition for the development of colonial territories.

It is all the more paradoxical in that certain French West Indian élites, which had participated directly in the adventure of Négritude, the ideological basis of decolonization in Africa, actively participated in this option by presenting to the French Parliament in 1946 the proposal recommending the legal and political assimilation of the French West Indies. But this attitude is not as paradoxical as it first appears. The drive towards integration into the French Republic, in order to resolve the problems of inequality provoked by colonization, is linked to the fundamental dynamics of Guadeloupean society, which cannot be understood without a grasp of how that society was formed. Moreover, the decision of 1946, after a brief and sometimes violent period of contestation, has favoured the appearance of a consensus around the idea of a necessary integration into France. This faces Guadeloupe with new problems bound up with the fact that it forms a minority within the French national ensemble and, shortly, with the European ensemble if the dynamic of unification continues.

The choice of integration into France was not fortuitous. It formed itself little by little even as the society – created piecemeal by the French occupier – evolved. Guadeloupe is a creation of France: no Guadeloupean community pre-exists conquest, colonization and occupation by France. Populations of diverse origins were brought there and learned how to coexist on the basis of criteria furnished by French society and culture. These criteria, unlike those of other forms of colonization, were always strongly oriented towards assimilation and the systematic reduction of differences.

Thus, in a manner that was distinctively and typically French, a contagion of cultures or infusion of mores was realized. All the major French institutions combined their efforts to suppress the cultural differences of Guadeloupe and to form its population according to the national mould. The education system, administration and religion were particularly effective in this global process of socialization. The success of assimilation was all the more comprehensive in that slavery, and the atomization of society that it had institutionalized by mixing Africans of different ethnic origins, had suppressed most of the differences of those who would subsequently become Guadeloupeans.

Accordingly, there is no evidence of the traditional double process of colonization: on the one hand, the destruction by the colonizers of an inferior material civilization and, on the other, its replacement by wholly new and superior structures. More precisely, the double movement occurred but was accompanied, first of all, by the genocidal killing of the original civilization of the first inhabitants by the colonizers and, subsequently, by its replacement by a new society and new peoples.

The result of this was that the system of colonial justification – that is, the set of rationalizations whereby the colonizer explains his position in the colonized territory, his superior situation and his conduct towards the dominated peoples – had perceptibly more success in Guadeloupe (and in Martinique) than in other colonized territories which had available to them deep and age-old historical and cultural roots.

The psychological attitudes, the behaviour patterns traditionally encountered in colonial societies (for instance, the ambivalence of the colonized who takes over the image that the colonizer has forged of him, the colonized's tendency to wish to resemble the colonizer who becomes a point of reference for him) – all this imposed itself more rapidly in Guadeloupe.

This option for France was reinforced by three important factors:

1 In the first place, the adherence on the part of the Guadeloupeans to the idea of a universalist, generous and egalitarian France born of the Revolution of 1789 and whose principles are incarnated in the Declaration of the Rights of Man and of the Citizen.

In point of fact, Guadeloupeans found in the ideologies produced by republican France a response to the depersonalization and psychological fragmentation provoked by colonization. The decolonization to which they had long aspired, rather than being conceived of as a break with the colonizer's order, was seen rather as a demand for total, unqualified French citizenship, the precondition of a social, cultural and economic revolution that would suppress the socioeconomic structures inherited from colonization.

The promoters of the law of departmentalization of 1946 were insistent on this second point. This form of decolonization was conceived above all on the basis of socialist ideologies (Marxism and pluralistic socialism). It is for this reason that egalitarian socialist ideas had, and still have, a profound resonance in Guadeloupe. In short, and rather paradoxically, France produced both a model of colonization and a model of decolonization that were distinct from those models that condition and foster the accession of colonized peoples to independence.

2  The separation of debates concerning French citizenship from the social conflicts which have dominated the world (including Guadeloupe) throughout the twentieth century, and that in spite of the searching criticisms made of departmentalization by certain élites and certain parties of the left (communists and the nationalist ultra-left).

Marxism, which furnished the ideological base for all these forms of contestation, linked colonization to the exploitation of the working classes. In fact, colonies were considered as appendages of the developed capitalist societies of the centre to whom they served as outlets in order to arrest the downward curve of profitability which, according to Marx, was the fate of the capitalist system.

In this perspective, the colonial working classes were subject to a double exploitation: first, in the context of the world capitalist system through the mediation of the mechanisms of imperialism which blocked the development of peripheral capitalist economies; and secondly, on the internal plane, by the internal owner class which represented world capitalism. It was thus vital to break with the logic of colonialism by using the working and peasant classes in order to liberate the whole society and thus permit the development and advancement of the whole population.

In the colonies, as in France and the developed countries, one encountered the same discourse concerning the necessary transcendence of capitalist society by a revolution initiated by the working classes. This conception, which had the advantage of being coherent and straightforward, was extremely seductive. In certain colonized colonies, it made possible a victorious mobilization of the working and peasant classes and an accession to independence.

In Guadeloupe, despite the efforts made by certain political and trade union groups, workers and peasants rarely adhered to this discourse, even when they voted for autonomist or independentist parties. Indeed, contestation of the departmentalist order rarely brought into opposition the classes that made up Guadeloupean society. In each social group and social class were encountered both partisans and opponents of departmentalization. It was precisely this sociological characteristic of the anticolonialist movement which explains why contestation of the departmentalist order remains such a heterogeneous phenomenon made up of 'defectors' from each and every class with, however, a preponderance amongst certain well-off social classes closely linked, by education and situation, to France.

The consequence of this was that the anticolonialist movement was never able to acquire the dynamics, that capacity for destruction and enthusiasm, which are alone capable of provoking breaks in the structure of society that may lead to its collapse. Opposition to the departmentalist order thus remained a diffuse movement, a set of demands made by intellectuals remote from social realities. It was transformed into a kind of salon entertainment. This is illustrated, in particular, by the embarrassment of those political parties with a certain influence when it became necessary to explain their calling into question of departmentalization. Thus the Communist Party and its satellites which, as early as 1958, had adopted as its programme a partial break with departmentalization (autonomy within a continuing relationship with France) were rarely able to deploy this slogan in day-to-day political conflicts. More recently, the Union Populaire pour la Libération de la Guadeloupe (UPLG) was obliged to put its demand for immediate independence in the broom-cupboard of superannuated ideas.

> 3 Finally, departmentalization permitted the Guadeloupean community to make quantitative and qualitative progress of a kind that its members could scarcely have dared believe in when the law of 1946 was passed.

This attitude is hardly surprising when one takes into account the penury the country had known from time immemorial. All the indicators go to prove the same thing. The standard of living in Guadeloupe has improved more or less in line with the average for France as a whole. Educational levels, social security, the availability of social services, remuneration for employment or unemployment which make up this standard of living – all have increased. Guadeloupe today has all the features of a developed society with consumer patterns identical to those of metropolitan France. In this perspective, it can be said that the revolution expected by the proponents of departmentalization in 1946 has been fully realized.

Indeed, such results are unsurprising. Once the more developed metropole took the decision to share its resources with Guadeloupe, the cause was won: Guadeloupe's standard of living could only improve. The mechanisms of national solidarity – the right to state subsidies, the right to the same standard of living as the rest of the nation – performed the role which, in another context, would have been performed by internal mechanisms of economic growth. Indeed, national backing probably allowed Guadeloupe to go further and faster where economic development was concerned. Had it been necessary to wait for development to be initiated by internal factors, Guadeloupe would not yet have reached the level of development it enjoys today, as a result of certain constraints which hamper economic growth, such as the absence of primary materials, the restrictedness of the internal market and its own insularity.

It is surprising, therefore, that in these conditions and considering the progress made, certain commentators insist that departmentalization has been a social and economic failure. Certainly not everything has been perfect in the process initiated by departmentalization in 1946. The rise in living standards, the institution of social security and the development of education have been accompanied by often spectacular negative features. Economic growth has been modest and, in any case, disproportionate to levels of consumption, giving rise to a marked tendency to import. Unemployment is endemic, affecting 20 per cent of the active population and falling especially heavily on women and young people under 25. Social security has fostered a kind of dependence on the state and a reluctance to work, given that unemployment benefits are often superior to wages.

People have spoken, with justification, of 'skewed development', but have drawn misleading conclusions from a phenomenon which, after all, is normal when a less developed social formation is integrated into one that is more developed. The same phenomenon can be observed, *mutatis mutandis*, in Germany today. The integration of former East Germany into former West Germany is being achieved at the price of increased unemployment, widespread recourse to social security and a collapse in production. The more developed economy draws the less developed one upwards, brutally and very rapidly, preventing the latter from adapting gradually to the new conditions brought about by integration.

A striking instance is afforded by consumption levels. The increase in wages and other forms of income creates demands which can only be satisfied rapidly by importing goods. Families can hardly be expected to wait until local production is capable of fulfilling their demands as consumers.

One can readily understand, given these conditions, why those who have challenged and criticized departmentalization have had little success. On the one hand, the bases of their argument were fragile and, on the other, public opinion is more realistic than is believed or affirmed and has a more sophisticated understanding of this complex phenomenon.

The only obstacle to the development of Guadeloupe could come from a serious down-turn in the economic growth of metropolitan France, and this did not happen even at the time of the world crisis of 1973. Improved living standards are closely linked to the dynamic of the French economy. Local opinion has fully understood this for 40 years and more; and it continues to do so, despite the criticisms which, in other respects, it addresses to a system which is not always as positive as it would wish and whose performance is often felt to be lacking.

## The new consensus

Guadeloupe, then, has reached a new consensus which is not without parallel with that of 1946 when all local political tendencies had supported departmentalization. Today, no political movement of substance stands for leaving the French national ensemble. The most radical movements, those which formerly aspired to immediate or ultimate independence on the grounds that departmentalization was simply a modernized form of colonialism, have been compelled seriously to modify their traditional point of view. On the other hand, those who formerly stood for departmentalization pure and simple – a departmentalization that would have suppressed all local institutional specificities – have likewise changed their tune. Only a handful of political movements – Trotskyist formations on the far left – continue to stand, come rain or come shine, for a form of decolonization conceived of as a total break with France.

People's fears concerning the acceleration of European unification are grist to these extremists' mill, but do not, however, call in question the foundations of the new consensus. This consensus is indeed stronger than people think, since it is based on a kind of social and economic necessity which became fully evident once the euphoria of decolonization came to an end. Decolonization has not, contrary to what was thought in the 1960s, turned out to be the catalyst which would favour the economic, social and human development of the now nominally independent ex-colonies. On the contrary, with the exception of some Asian countries which, after decolonization, succeeded in creating high-performance economies, a relatively solid state and some measure of social progress, the effects of decolonization on former colonies, especially in Africa and the Caribbean, have fallen short of expectations. Most commonly there has occurred a regression of the economic, social and cultural levels, and a decline in public and political freedom. Decolonization for many countries has become a tighter, harsher straightjacket than ever colonization was. It is hardly surprising, in these circumstances, that some are seeking recolonization.

This negative balance-sheet of decolonization, responsibility for which is not limited simply to world patterns of domination, came as a surprise to Guadeloupe and deeply marked their unconscious, and it is this which explains why the best way for a political party to marginalize itself once and for all is to clamour for independence. But the new consensus has not totally suppressed all differences of opinion concerning the problem of the status of Guadeloupe as part of the French Republic. There are still great differences between those who would like to create a new formation within the context of the Republic, those who seek a deepening of decentralization, and those who favour the creation of a state associated with France. None the less, these genuine divergences have not created deep and insurmountable divisions and they do not prevent the consensus from working, all in all, smoothly.

Furthermore, consensus has not completely suppressed differences of opinion between our community and France. On the one hand, the people of Guadeloupe have not ceased to assert themselves over the last decades. Once an inferior, fearful community, afraid of expressing its cultural originality, it has become a dynamic community, more sure of itself and more secure in its cultural originality which it sometimes clumsily asserts. The changes that Guadeloupe has undergone, the shift from a situation of penury to one of relative abundance with all that that implies for ways of living and acting, have probably accelerated a movement which has its origins in the very constitution of the society.

The Guadeloupean community is increasingly attached to its originality. Négritude in its different forms has exercised a considerable influence in this discovery and affirmation of an identity, and has been followed by the East Indian community which, over the last ten years, has affirmed with force and persistence its presence in the community and culture of Guadeloupe. Moreover, the white community, for a long time hesitant or absent, seems keen to affirm its presence whilst abandoning, at last, its former pretensions to hegemony. Finally, at the same time that these necessary affirmations of particular identities have taken place, a process of fusion has begun which will give the Guadeloupean community its permanent shape for the coming decades.

# CHAPTER 4

## Society, culture and politics in French Guiana

*Bridget Jones and Elie Stephenson*

## Introduction

When the French Antilles and French Guiana are combined under the label 'French Departments of America', very disparate partners are brought together. If the profound differences between Guadeloupe and Martinique are apparent as soon as one looks closer, how much more different is French Guiana from the island departments. A geographical position on the South American continent, a history shaped as much by the Gold Rush and deportations to the penal colony as by the plantation system, very slow population growth but of an extraordinarily diverse kind: these are some of the major factors which determine the specific character of French Guiana. Whereas the concrete location of the French West Indies demands a re-appraisal of their situation at the heart of an archipelago, French Guiana belongs in reality to other groupings:[1] firstly the Guianas, ranged like a set of samples of European colonisation en route for El Dorado, and then to the South American continent. On topics like the protection of the natural resources of Amazonia, land rights for Amerindian peoples, Brazilian expansion, French Guiana has quite other concerns from the islands, while nevertheless sharing with them the same contradictions: an overseas department combined with a region, soon to be theoretically part of 'Europe', torn between economic dependence and the challenge of taking on responsibility for its own future.

One glance is enough to take in the endless green horizons of the most extensive French department, and geographical features which are on a continental scale.[2] In contrast to the dense and circumscribed Lesser Antilles, French Guiana covers a surface of some 90,000 square kilometres, about one-sixth the size of France, and has long permeable frontiers with Brazil and Surinam. It is still 90 per cent covered in tropical forest and segmented by mighty rivers, with abundant vegetation resulting from an equatorial climate: heavy rainfall averaging at least 2m annually, heavier on the eastern side than towards the west, and a temperature which shows little variation around an average of 26° C. A French Guianese lives with the forest at his back; once the refuge of the Boni Maroons, it creates a protective habitat for the Amerindian, a paradise for the Creole hunter, but its green curtain is only kept at bay by the human will.[3] Though a precious resource in an over-crowded planet, the ecology of this forest more readily supports an abundant population of insects, reptiles, birds and small animals than larger mammals like man.[4] It is an arduous task to cut and maintain land routes into the interior, and away from the main road axis linking Cayenne to Saint-Laurent-du-Maroni, the transport network still relies heavily on small planes and even canoes.

There are substantial mineral deposits in the old rocks of the Shield which acts as a watershed between the Amazon Basin and the north-flowing rivers of the Guianas, but they have not been systematically extracted or even fully surveyed. Above all there is, of course, gold, the driving force for early exploration and peopling the interior after 1855,[5] but the bauxite deposits of Mount Kaw, and kaolin have also raised hopes of viable resources. Apart from solar power, the only local source of energy is hydro-electricity, at long last to be productively harnessed in the Petit-Saut dam project under way on the Sinnamary river.

Out of the three Guianas, French Guiana has the narrowest strip of coastal land suitable for farming, and agricultural development on the basis of polders has never been on the scale found in Surinam or (ex-British) Guyana. The traditional technique of the 'abattis' (cultivation for a few seasons in a forest clearing created by tree-felling and burning off scrub) is suitable for a low density of population, and only recently have sustained efforts developed projects of some size in cattle-raising, rice cultivation and vegetable gardens. The coasts and creeks are rich in fish (there is a significant export volume of shrimps) and conditions are very favourable for fish-farming. It should be noted that the most successful projects have benefited from considerable official support, very often in the context of a plan to settle newcomers and boost the active population, as in the case of the H'mong refugees.

That was merely one example among many projects to 'populate French Guiana': a constant concern of the colonial administration but seldom well received by those on the spot most intimately involved. In outlining the main groups which compose the population, we can see their wide diversity of origins, as well

as a quite spectacular increase in numbers over the last twenty
years.

## *Population*

### Distribution and ethnic characteristics

The 1982 census calculated the number of people living in French
Guiana as 73,012. On 1 January 1990 INSEE estimated that the population amounted to 97,300 souls. But the experts maintained that
the actual population was higher, somewhere between 100,000 and
120,000 people. Whatever the true figure, the average density does
not exceed 1.2 inhabitants to the square kilometre. Moreover this
meagre population is very unevenly distributed, with more than
85 per cent of those living in French Guiana concentrated on the
coastal strip. The 'island' of Cayenne alone (Cayenne, Rémire,
Montjoly and Matoury) musters 55 per cent of the total population
and Kourou 15 per cent.

The population consists of Creoles, Maroons ('Bush Negroes'),
Indians, Europeans, Asiatics, Syrians and Lebanese, and various foreign nationals (Haitians, Brazilians). Given the small total population this variety is a feature of unusual socio-economic interest.

The Creoles are black or of mixed race and constitute the
largest group numerically; about 72 per cent of the total population.
(In French Guiana, a 'Creole' is one whose lifestyle is based on
European norms. Hence the descendants of the 'unseasoned'
African Maroons: Boni, Djuka, etc. who have retained their tradi-
tional lifestyles, are not counted as Creoles.)[6]

The Maroons are essentially rebel African slaves who came
across from Surinam in the eighteenth century. They are distributed
among four tribal groups: Djuka, Paramaka, Boni and Saramaka.
They occupy the valley of the Maroni between St-Laurent and
Maripasoula. They constitute 6 per cent of the population.

The Indians (Amerindians) 'descend from the ancient indigenous tribes originating in the Tupi-Guarani, Arawak and Carib linguistic groups: in French Guiana they numbered about 30,000 in the
seventeenth century when colonization began. The diseases brought
by the Europeans almost wiped them out, and for a time it was
feared that these peoples would disappear completely'.[7]

The white population resident in French Guiana is essentially
composed of Europeans and North Americans. The majority of
the Europeans are French: in general employees of the state on civil

service contracts of two to four years. Before 1976 there was a relatively small population of European origin with only a limited impact on the local economy. However since the celebrated 'Plan Vert', launched in August 1975 by the then Secretary of State for the DOM-TOM, Olivier Stirn, the number of French people settled in the country has shown a considerable increase. In 1986 INSEE estimated that 8.5 per cent of the population was of European origin. The population hailing from Asia contains groups of Chinese, Indonesians, Javanese and H'mong (refugees from Indochina). The older generation of Chinese in French Guiana migrated from Shanghai and Canton, and almost all belong to the Ho clan. But a good number of the younger settlers today have come from Surinam. The Chinese and the H'mong constitute closed groups, showing considerable social and economic solidarity: 1700 were counted in 1986, that is to say about 2.2 per cent of the population.[8]

The other minority groups are essentially the Brazilians, Surinamese, St Lucians, Haitians and Guyanese. Most of the Brazilians supply agricultural or construction project labour at bargain rates, unintentionnally competing with local-born labour, whose rates are based on the French labour market. Most of the St Lucians, a mainly agricultural population, have been settled for some time, and have practically merged into the local Creoles. As for the Haitians, much more recent migrants, they are mainly hired for agricultural work or various other manual tasks which local labour is reluctant to accept. All these groups, with the exception of the Europeans, speak Creole, which functions as the language of communication between the different communities.

## Demography: rate of population growth

Between 1954 and 1982 the population increased by 62 per cent. The annual average increase is accelerating: from 3.4 per cent in 1967–74 to 5.8 per cent per annum between 1982–90, or 57 per cent over this 8-year period, taking 114,600 as the 1990 total. Thus in 15 years the population has more than doubled.

## Profile by age-bracket

In 1961, 43 per cent of the population of French Guiana was under 20, while in 1974 this group accounted for 48.4 per cent of the total, 44.6 per cent were between 20 and 59, 7 per cent were sixty and over.

The 1982 census shows a significant change, with 49 per cent of the population aged between 20 and 60, 44 per cent under 20 and 7 per cent over 60 as before. This gives a measure of the extent of immigration (especially of young adults) into French Guiana between 1974 and 1982. The population continues to be predominantly very young, with 33 per cent below the age of 15 in 1989–90.

## Labour force

In 1989 the Departmental Labour Board (DDT) gave a figure of 31,183 for the active population, with 17,208 wage-earners. They are mainly distributed between Cayenne (65 per cent of the active population) and Kourou (12 per cent). The distribution in terms of activity shows an explosive growth in the tertiary sector which now occupies 70 per cent of the active population (67 per cent of salaried employees), reducing the other two sectors, agriculture and industry/craft to the meagre share remaining. By contrast, in 1974, for example, the secondary sector still employed 21.3 per cent of the active population, and the primary sector close on 18 per cent. The direction of growth has confirmed and much reinforced the dominance of the service sector in the economy. The development of service industries has promoted especially the employment of women, who now comprise 37 per cent of the active population.

### Unemployment

Measuring unemployment in a country like French Guiana poses particular problems (inadequate means, local social structures and practices, etc.) to the extent that information is scarce, unreliable and sometimes even contradictory.

According to the INSEE statistics for 1982, unemployment stood at about 18 per cent, with more women unemployed than men. The IEDOM Bulletin for 1989 maintained that unemployment was keeping pace with the growth of the active population, and that the number of unsatisfied requests for jobs doubled between 1982 and 1986 (to 3,806). Yet the same publication only assesses the rate of unemployment for 1989 as 12.2 per cent!

This confirms our feeling of scepticism over the official figures for unemployment. They can only reflect the official labour market as defined and quantified by the DDT, leaving out of account the number of people under-employed, those who live by short-term jobs of various kinds, are employed sporadically on the land or in workshops, young people leaving high school or technical college but not finding work and living 'as usual' supported by the family structure. On the other hand, the collapse of many Latin American and Caribbean economies just at the time when what are called the 'Grands Programmes'[9] came on stream in French Guiana provided a powerful drawing factor, bringing many workers who often arrived illegally. Most of these people would not be registered with the social security, many would never 'check in' for the labour inspectorate. All this, of course, makes the accurate evaluation of unemployment virtually impossible. Where does it begin in French Guiana? Where does it end? At what point does an individual consider her or himself unemployed? At what point should he or she be counted as such?

In any case, we view the figure of 12.2 per cent as distinctly unrealistic, and would put forward a figure of our own more of the order of 20 per cent.[10]

## Productive activities

### Agriculture

Agricultural holdings in French Guiana divide into three main categories:

1 Traditional agriculture based essentially on the 'abattis' technique (a shifting pattern of 'slash-and-burn' forest clearings) sometimes accompanied by raising livestock and poultry, usually free-range.
2 Non-traditional farming ('semi-modern' for want of a better term) cultivating and stock-raising in a fixed location.
3 Mixed farming, where the 'abattis' is supplemented by non-traditional techniques such as fruit-growing, cattle raising and hydroponic methods of market gardening.

The average area per holding varies between 3 and 5 ha. In 1982, a total of 10,436 ha were under cultivation, as opposed to 5,832 ha in 1978. However, over the same period, the number of individual holdings dropped quite noticeably (from 2,950 in 1976 to 2,250 in 1982), but has now increased again, rising to 4,500 in 1989. The land area in productive agricultural use has gone from 12,081 ha in 1984 to 20,600 in 1989, largely as a result of the development of rice-growing.

Farm labour is still mainly supplied by the family.

## Agricultural production

The statistical figures concerning agricultural production are most often estimated gross approximations; moreover products are not always classified under the same headings from one set of figures to another. To give one example, in the category bananas might be collected either as the combined total for cooking bananas (plantains) and dessert bananas, or only the production figures for plantains. However, the information we have is enough to judge the level and general state of agricultural production in French Guiana.

From 1959 to 1977 the overall total production of food crops registered a fall of 47 per cent (down from 42,005 tons in 1959 to 22,170 tons in 1977). This situation can be explained by a substantial decline in the production of sugar-cane and cassava. The improvements recorded subsequently are not entirely convincing in so far as production can vary quite considerably from one year to another.

Fruit growing is concentrated in the area around Cayenne (Matoury, Rémire, Montjoly) and Saint-Laurent-du-Maroni (including Mana). After a crisis period in the 1960s, orchards of fruit trees are increasing (109,200 trees planted in 1977 compared to 83,985 in 1971), while the area planted has gone up from 638 ha in 1978 to about 990 ha in 1982. However French Guiana is not self-sufficient in fruit, as only 50 per cent of the local demand for fruit is met, the remainder being imported.

Production does not cover a very wide range: citrus, dessert bananas, granadillas and pineapples (a recent addition). Production amounted to 1,020 tons in 1984, rising to 2,180 tons in 1989.

## Livestock

Stock farming in French Guiana is not very developed and encounters all kinds of difficulties and obstacles. Although for a time during the colonial period the territory raised enough livestock to satisfy local demand and even export to the Antilles, in recent decades this has not been the case. Local production now falls far short of the demand. Thus only 26 per cent of the beef consumed in 1989 was locally produced: pork production only met between 19 and 20 per cent of demand, and in the case of poultry, where consumption is heavy, local producers could only cater for 15 per cent of the demand for chicken and 45 per cent for eggs.

# Forestry

The complex and varied nature of the forest in French Guiana, which contains a great diversity of different types of trees (on average 30 to 60 species per ha) makes it difficult to extract any one particular type of timber. The trees are fairly small in diameter, and the wood often hard, so that felling and sawing pose difficulties. The lack of accurate knowledge, not so much of the precise composition of the forest as of the economic potential of the marketable timber, combined with the factors already mentioned, make it difficult to draw up plans for viable development in forestry. The absence of a road network, the difficulties of transport and navigation by river due to the rapids and waterfalls, effectively prevent the economic use of extensive areas in the interior of virtually virgin forest.

These are the major handicaps impeding development in forestry, but there is also the question of markets. The limited scope of the local market makes it essential to secure export outlets. However the high cost of labour and of freight for lumber loaded in local ports for destinations in the United States or Western Europe also acts as a brake on forestry development.

Virtually all the forests are owned by the state, which is to all intents and purposes sole owner of the 8 million ha of French Guiana under forest. There are at present 23 lumbering and saw-mill businesses in operation. About 100 firms working with wood – carpenters, cabinet-makers, etc. – are active.

From 1960 to 1968 forestry passed through a phase of major expansion (the production of logs more than doubling between 1964 and 1968, from 33,200 to 76,000). Then came collapse, and not until the beginning of the 1980s did production and export return to these levels. But the whole sector remains very vulnerable, not least because on the West Indian market French Guiana now comes up against competition from Brazilian timber available at very competitive prices.

# Fishing

There is fishing in French Guiana both on a small local scale and as a modern industry. Local fishermen operate near the coasts, in small open boats, Creole or Indian style, using nets, lines, and 'Chinese gates' (nets suspended on a bamboo framework). For the open sea, there is a fleet of medium-sized vessels, between 15 and 25 m, and trawlers.

The catches vary (mudfish, scaly fish, red fish from the deeper water, tuna caught in traps, shrimps) with the aim of catering for the requirements of the local market. The red fish, which is not much appreciated in French Guiana, is mainly exported to the islands.

Fishing on a relatively small scale supplies the requirements of the local markets, and more than satisfies the existing demand. Shrimp fishing for the variety called 'sea-bob' is also practised on traditional lines, using the 'Chinese gates'. It has developed on the rivers, especially in the estuary of the Cayenne river.

The fishermen have gradually become more organized: an Association for the Organization of Fishing in French Guiana (AOPAG) was set up in 1982, which created a co-operative (COPEDAG) in order to improve methods of storing and cleaning their catches, as well as marketing them.

Fishing on a larger commercial scale began in French Guiana about 1961–62, and mainly concerns the variety of shrimp found at depths of 60 to 70 metres in the open sea. Since 1982 the government has taken steps to implement a policy of national ownership for this fleet, so that there are no more ships operating in the waters of French Guiana under the Japanese flag. There are 16 American trawlers and 56 French-registered vessels. It is an important activity from every point of view. Although there has been some overall variation in production, it has almost invariably kept to a substantial level. Between 1979 and 1982 output went up from 2,255 to 3,221 tons, and after dropping again to 3,061 tons in 1985, it rose to 4,129 tons in 1990, with the same fluctuations observable in the level of exports. Nevertheless fishing represents one of the very few dynamic sectors in the economy of French Guiana as a region.

## Industries and crafts

Let us begin by making the point that we are talking about industrial activity in French Guiana only for lack of a more accurate term. In actual fact an industrial sector cannot really be said to exist. Hence we are collecting under this title various activities involving the transformation of materials on a larger or smaller scale, stemming from agriculture, lumbering, construction work, etc. and also craft work, as the distinction between the two types of activity is not always very clear.

Most of these concerns operate on a small scale. In 1989 93 per cent of them employed fewer than six people, and only 20 per cent have more than 20 employees. In the building industry in particular, small-scale private firms are very numerous (65 per cent of the total in 1989). Activity on a genuinely industrial scale is thus rather rare (10 per cent of the total number of businesses in 1989), and would seem at present to employ only about 10 per cent of wage-earners. By contrast, there is a marked expansion in cottage industries and craft. In 1989 2,580 skilled workers were counted (compared to only 1,579 five years before). Wood-working and furniture-making take the lead (24 per cent of manufacturing firms), followed by food products derived from farming (17 per cent).

## Extractive industries

Mining activity means essentially gold production, which, after a spectacular decline in 1963–64, progressively returned to a healthier position. Production, which was only just over 73 kg in 1970 more than doubled in seven years to 150 kg and reached 544 kg in 1989. There are only two companies working on an industrial scale, and about 20 small firms. The rest is extracted by independent individual miners, but these nevertheless account for 41 per cent of total production.

## External trade

The traditional exports from French Guiana: timber and other forest products, gold, rum, and, since 1963, shrimps, amount to little and are very irregular, reflecting the economic situation of the department. Imports, on the other hand, have always been substantial, hence necessarily perpetuating a negative trade balance.

### *Imports*

Ever since French Guiana became an overseas department, annual imports (with a few rare exceptions) have risen continually in value and quantity. If we compare the value of the global imports of consumer goods (foodstuffs, cloth and clothing, private cars, etc.) with that of goods relating to production and development (building materials, fertilizer, service vehicles, etc.), it becomes evident that, between 1968 and 1976, imports for consumption practically doubled while imports for production lagged far behind. After 1977–78 the picture is modified and goods for production have grown at a slightly faster rate than consumer goods (40 per cent as opposed to 37.8 per cent).

## Exports

Whereas in 1960 gold (69 per cent) and timber (20.2 per cent) consti-
tuted almost 90 per cent of exports from French Guiana, today
shrimps count for 56 per cent of the total value, timber counts for no
more than 11 per cent, with gold, and also rice, both standing at 8 per
cent of exports by value.

## Trade balance

French Guiana is very far from covering its imports: the deficit in the
trade balance is a permanent characteristic of the department's economy which nothing seems to change. Although on two occasions
between 1945 and 1952 there was a positive balance, since then the
adverse balance has done nothing but increase. Exports, which covered 14 per cent of imports in 1988, only accounted for 10 per cent in
1990.

The principal trading partners are metropolitan France, the
Antilles, the EC, the United States, Japan, and for petroleum products, Trinidad and Tobago. Among them France of course takes the
lion's share, accounting for almost 65 per cent of commercial transac-
tions.

## Comments on the economic situation

Ever since French Guiana entered the space age, and specifically
with the development of the European Space Agency programme of
Ariane launchings, there has been more and more talk of 'strong
growth' in the economy. However it is vital to bear in mind that this
development is essentially demand-led, and in particular based on
demand for consumer goods. This in turn is largely fed by transfer of
public funds. As is implied by the weakness of the industrial fabric
and confirmed by the distribution of the labour force, the motive
force of the economy is paradoxically the tertiary sector, services.
This service sector has not developed as a consequence of industrial
activity or following growth in the secondary sector but seems to
precede them – for they are still-born – quite simply because the
economy is fed artifically by injections of money from the metropole.

The other main planks in this 'development' are the large construction sites, the PHEDRE programme[11] and the activities of the
Centre Spatial Guyanais at Kourou. However, the construction sites
have a limited lifespan, hence their impact on the economic level has
also to be seen as of limited duration. The PHEDRE programme

essentially consists of a total budget provision of 1.2 billion francs, in other words is not much more than another form of transfer of public funds. As for the activities linked to the space programme, their effects, both direct and indirect, tend to be limited in scope, making an impact in well-defined sectors which do not necessarily play a dynamic role in promoting economic growth. It is possible to maintain that concentration on the space base even risks having an adverse effect on social and economic development for French Guiana as a whole.

Moreover, none of the elements on which this much vaunted economic growth is based come under the control of the French Guianese people, rather they intensify dependency on France and on Europe in general – as can be seen by the structure of external trade – even before the dependency on external sources for energy and food supplies is taken into consideration.

It all adds up, in fact, to underwriting a state of social and economic non-development. How is it possible to talk about growth (still less of development) when a country is unable to meet in any rational way its basic needs? When strictly speaking there is no agriculture or livestock production, no industry? When the place depends almost entirely on outside sources for its food, clothing and building? Can one seriously speak about growth, or development?

The year of the grand European market, 1993, arouses expectations in French Guiana as elsewhere of an extraordinary event. But there will certainly not be a miracle. With the entry into Europe, and the opening-up to Europe, there is a real risk of making the economy still more dependent and vulnerable. But above all there is the risk that French Guiana will escape completely from the grasp of its own inhabitants.

## Political aspects

For a closer look at the nature of the political evolution which has led to this situation, it is mainly relevant to look at the period since 1946. However, it may be worth recalling that democratic institutions have had a shorter and more chequered history in French Guiana than in the Antilles. From shortly after emancipation until 1875 there was no local representation,[12] and the extensive powers of the Penal Administration for many years reduced the scope of the civil authorities. The persistence of this authoritarian reflex might be detected in the action of the prefect, closing access by decree to some of the areas of the interior peopled by the Indians.

## From departmentalization to demands for independence

In 1932, Gaston Monnerville was elected deputy and it was due to his influence in particular that French Guiana became an overseas department just after the Second World War. In 1946 (the year when departmentalization took effect), René Jadfard, a socialist hostile to the notion of departmental status, defeated Monnerville and became deputy for French Guiana. In November 1947 Jadfard was killed in a plane accident at Sinnamary.

Léon Damas, viewed as his natural successor, inherited the seat. A convinced opponent of departmental status for French Guiana, he had already composed a critique of France's Assimilation policy in his book *Retour de Guyane*.[13] In 1951 Damas was opposed by a pro-departmental candidate, Edouard Gaumont, and was not re-elected. But the most significant political figure of this period is undoubtedly Constant Chlore, Mayor of Cayenne in 1945, and the first to lay the foundations of a trade union movement. He had founded a communist party, the Parti Communiste Guyanais (the only one which has ever existed in French Guiana), and he was the first political organizer to work with the mass of the population. He abandoned the political arena as a result of personal problems and died in Cayenne in 1967.

Radical criticism of departmental status developed with increasing force after 1958 with the founding of the Union du Peuple Guyanais (UPG) and the Parti Socialiste Guyanais (PSG). The UPG was founded in 1958 by a group of young Guianese on their return from studying in France, and demanded quite simply self-government. It was a clear-cut and straightforward rejection of French supervision and the departmental system. For reasons which we will not go into here, the UPG never succeeded in mobilising the support of the 'masses', still less that of government employees. Although purely at the level of polling votes there is no denying its failure, on the ideological plane, this party contributed a vital new ferment in promoting the idea of self-government.

The PSG had been founded in 1956 by Justin Catayée (who had previously been responsible for starting a local section of the SFIO, but left that grouping as a result of internal differences of opinion). From the outset, Catayée's action was aimed at gaining power, but within what framework? That was not yet defined, but it was a question of securing a type of statute resembling decentralization: an increase in local decision-making while retaining the overall structures of a department. The status envisaged and its content would become clearer in 1960: a package specifically for French Guiana, embodying demands for financial devolution, an elected regional Assembly, a local executive, etc.

In no time at all the PSG and the UPG were at daggers drawn: at that time the PSG was firmly against self-government and saw the UPG as dangerous 'Reds'. In fact it is quite probable that Catayée's conception of a special status became more clearly defined in the course of this polemic.

Catayée was elected as deputy in the November of 1958. On 14 June 1962 all the parties of the left (PSG, RPG, UPG, SFIO) and the trade unions organized a demonstration to protest against the stationing of the Foreign Legion in French Guiana. The mass protest was harshly put down by the security forces. Catayée, who was in Paris at the time, caught a plane to return to Cayenne on 22 June. He failed to reach his destination as the plane crashed in Guadeloupe.

Heder, his second-in-command, was all set to complete his term of office, but in July the National Assembly was dissolved and new elections held. Heder, supported by all the parties of the left who combined in the 'Front Démocratique Guyanais', was elected with an overwhelming majority. In 1967 he was beaten by the departmentalist candidate, Hector Rivierez, but was nevertheless elected Mayor of Cayenne. The Democratic Front, meanwhile, had quietly ceased to exist. The UPG and the local section of the SFIO were also no longer playing any significant political role, which left the PSG as the only upholder of the left to confront the parties which supported departmentalization (UNR, later UDR, and RPR). However, 1970 saw the birth of a number of political splinter groups, demanding self-government or independence, Marxist or nationalist in orientation, making radical demands but lacking any real popular support. Meanwhile the PSG concentrated its thinking around the idea of greater autonomy.

Over the next ten years French Guiana seethed with political ferment, typified by the all-out activism of young 'Revolutionaries', some of them heirs of the UPG, while others were formed directly by the events of May 1968. Groups, movements, parties flourished: MNG (Mouvement National Guyanais) which arose from the transformation of a Marxist study-group formed four or five years previously; the FNLG (Front National de Libération de la Guyane) whose leader, Raymond Charlotte, spent two periods in French gaols; MOGUYDÉ (Mouvement Guyanais de Décolonisation) which for a spell had a great deal of influence among young people in high-schools and colleges. In contrast to the MNG based on Marxist-Leninism, and the FNLG which claimed to be Maoist, MOGUYDÉ had no clearcut ideological position: anti-colonialism and nationalism seemed to define its platform. The individual action of the late Felix Bade should also be noted, as expressed via the bulletin of the Union of Bakery Workers, and later in his newspaper *La Jeune Garde*. He was an uncompromising nationalist, who formed alliances according to circumstances with anyone who could help him combat his avowed enemies: 'the bourgeois clique of French Guiana'. Somewhat later, in 1977–78, a party for 'Guyanese Unity' was set up with the aim to bring together all these small groups (who competed with each other, even at times opposed each other) into one unified movement, which would water down its Marxism but remain strongly anti-colonial.

Despite their differences, which were often quite trivial, these groups had several common concerns: they were all against departmental status and for independence. They all preached a radical nationalism in the name of the people, and even if they were not Marxists, they all rejected capitalism as the way forward. They were also unanimous in condemning the ill-defined political goals and opportunist vote-catching of the PSG. In the final analysis, they failed because of their sterile internal disputes, their lack of knowledge of the local political terrain, poor choice of tactics and a faith in ideas which cut them off from reality, underpinning a belief that it was enough to have your heart in the right place ... always a detrimental attitude. Suffering from various forms of repressive action and/or constraints, towards the end of the 1970s these movements – and their leaders – began to experience serious difficulties. However, it was the accession of the socialist government to power in France which struck the fatal blow. The reversal of the political situation in France provoked in French Guiana a reflex of caution and 'cupboard love', bringing about a wholesale shift of political and electoral loyalties, which operated much to the benefit of the PSG, and of sundry tacticians and young Turks.

The local far left believed that the socialist victory in France would radically change the balance of political forces: hence many of them rejoined the PSG. The 'Unité Guyanaise' group in particular broke up when several prominent members turned to the PSG, while its militants grew scarce. A new mirage was going to everyone's head ... it was all going to turn out right with a strong and popular left-wing party in French Guiana and a socialist government in power in France. In the event, the political decentralization that the socialists and the PSG set such store by made no fundamental change in the relationship between the overseas department (as colony) and the metropole. On the other hand, the face of the struggle within French Guiana underwent a transformation.

Gone are the days of ideologies and aspirations towards national dignity and pride, now is a time when opportunism can flourish and new alliances are brokered to profit from all manner of schemes. Even the far right is finding support, especially in Kourou, an urban area experiencing the strains of rapid multi-racial expansion,[14] and at Saint-Laurent, another meeting-point, the PSG does not receive the same hearing as in Cayenne. The PNPG (Parti National Populaire Guyanais) with Claude Robo as general secretary, has more or less regrouped the surviving *indépendantistes* from the 1970s, while elsewhere the workers' union, the UTG, holds the last reserves of anti-colonial popular feeling in a perspective that is both socialist and pro-independence.

## Dimensions of culture in French Guiana

The complex process which has presided over the birth of French Guianese society, and especially its plurality of population, have led many people to call in question the existence of a specific national culture. This reasoning runs as follows: French Guiana is peopled by very diverse ethnic groups, each with their own culture, therefore one cannot speak of a culture in the singular, it must be plural.

In reality this attitude is based on a widespread confusion between creole culture and French Guianese culture. Although the creole group comprises by far the largest in the population, and historically speaking engendered this society, strictly speaking the culture of the Creoles does not coincide with that of the whole population. The culture of French Guiana is a 'supra-ethnic' product of the historical situations, economic conditions and human migrations we have been discussing. All the groups currently resident in the country, as soon as they occupy a space there, are affected by the overall situation: they experience it, submit to it, integrate it, each in its own way. Whatever cultural features existed when the group arrived will be transformed to some extent and at varying rates in contact with the new milieu and in relation to their participation in the life of the community. No ethnic group preserves its culture without undergoing change. It is interaction and participation which create a base for the culture of the country.

This culture is the point of convergence of everything that is shared, whether or not at a conscious level, by all the groups: techniques, attitudes, ways of thinking, can supply concrete instances. Take the case of the art of cooking for example: creole cooking has been modified in some ways by contributions from Asia, but equally

Chinese cuisine has in turn been influenced, and some of its original features have evolved differently in French Guiana. Another example is carnival, where the way carnival manifests itself in French Guiana has had an impact on other ethnic groups living there, particularly the Antillais, who over the years appear to be modifying their own conception of carnival and responding to its more ritual aspects. In literature it is particularly the theatre which offers a privileged site for cultural interaction.[15]

Thus the culture is a product of the multiple and reciprocal influences which the various ethnic groups exert on one another, and although the Creole group has a central role and is the main medium for developing and transmitting the culture of French Guiana, creole culture should not be identified with the larger whole. Equally it is reductive to speak in the plural of the cultures of French Guiana, as in that case the individual is given priority over the general, differences are stressed instead of convergence,[16] promoting a hierarchical view of culture if not an exclusivity all too liable to be extended into social and political domains.

## The problem of identity

The difficulty experienced by some people in admitting the existence of a French Guianese culture is in fact a byproduct of the problem of identity. As much cultural identity as political, that is to say national. In practice there is constant interference between the two spheres, and that is where the status of overseas department complicates the situation further. There is not yet a national consciousness. Not only due to being a DOM but especially because of the diversity of ethnic groups. The 'nation' for the inhabitants of French Guiana is France. The 'state' is also France.[17] Only the Indians and the Boni to some degree distance themselves from this vision, without making much difference to the fundamental problem, the absence of identity. For groups and individuals to identify with a nation there has to be a history, with specific social and political actions. The nation is a more or less willed creation created with a sense of a shared future, in which the groups and individuals involved in the shaping recognize some part of themselves. National identity thus necessarily appears as the result of various struggles, creating through time some solidarity between the ethnic groups involved. French Guiana remains torn apart. Despite quite strong racial divisions, Surinam and Guyana have their own identity. All the different groups recognize it, even claim it. This is not the case for French Guiana.

This absence of identity makes necessary the constant reference to a supervising power, and to value systems external to French Guiana, which thus become a check impeding the expression and the expansion of its own culture. This is why every assertion of identity, of a personality or merely of a cultural specificity for French Guiana leads back to the political problem. So we maintain that any discussion of the culture of French Guiana comes back to the burning question of national identity, this is the only meaningful level at which cultural problems can be resolved.

## Notes

1 Note essay by F. Schwarzbeck in *Dual Legacies in the Contemporary Caribbean*, (ed.) Paul Sutton (London: Cass, 1986).

2 Consult that very useful book, the *Atlas de la Guyane* (CNRS-ORSTOM, 1979).

3 A graphic example shown at Guisambourg (G.Prost, *Histoire-Géographie Guyane*, Armand Colin, 1988, p. 70).

4 J.-C. Giacottino, *Les Guyanes*, PUF Que sais-je?, 1984, p. 22.

5 J. Petot, *L'or de Guyane*, Editions Caribéennes, 1986.

6 See the research of M.-J. Jolivet, especially 'Une approche sociologique de la Guyane française: crise et niveau d'unité de la "société créole" ' (*Cahiers de l'ORSTOM*, 1971); *Etude de la société rurale guyanaise: le cas de Mana* (ORSTOM, juillet 1971); *La Question créole: Essai de sociologie sur la Guyane française* (ORSTOM, 1982).

7 J.-M. Hurault, *Français et Indiens en Guyane* (Guyane Presse Diffusion, 1989). See also 'La population indienne de la Guyane française' in *Population*, No. 4 (juillet-août 1965); *La vie matérielle des noirs réfugiés Boni et des Indiens Wayana* (Paris: ORSTOM, 1965); 'Les Indiens Wayana de la Guyane française: structures sociales et coutumes familiales' (Paris: ORSTOM, 1968).

For a recent survey see: Pierre et Françoise Grenand, *Les Amérindiens: des peuples pour la Guyane de demain* (Cayenne: ORSTOM, 1990). This work is designed to guide and inform local opinion and contains a selected bibliography.

8 M.Fauquenoy 'La colonie indonésienne de Sinnamary' (Cayenne: ORSTOM, février 1968); 'Les problèmes sociologiques du littoral', (Cahiers ORSTOM, juin 1967). By the same author 'Dimensions de la guyanité: langue et identité en Guyane', *Contemporary French Civilization*, XIV/2 (Summer/Fall 1990).

9 Involving some very substantial programmes financed by the ESA for the upgrading of the space centre, in particular the construction of a third launching pad for Ariane 5, which would be a new type of launcher using, for the first time, some locally produced components. Other projects under way include improvements to port facilities at Kourou-Pariacabo, and the heavy construction work for the hydro-electric dam on the Sinnamary river at Petit-Saut. The plans for the space shuttle Hermes contain examples of the official discourse on economic integration, expressing the wish to move on from the stage of building up the infrastructure and expanding the demand for services to that of functioning local production.

10 Borne out by the findings of a survey (23.4 per cent along the coastal strip. See *Guyane: Tableaux Economiques Régionaux* (INSEE 1990) p. 40.

11  The 1989 PHEDRE (Hermes Partnership for Regional Development) plan provides for a housing construction programme and development of facilities like schools in the area of the CSG (Kourou-Sinnamary), improvements to roads, ports and airports, and a 'solidarity' programme intended to assist other parts of Guyane.

12  Cf. S. Mam-Lam-Fouck, *Histoire de la société guyanaise*, Editions Caribéennes / CEGER, 1987, p. 216, 'Le dévoiement de la démocratie'.

13  José Corti, 1938. This work was withdrawn and largely unread in French Guiana. Only a few copies survive.

14  *Le Monde*, 19 juin 1991.

15  Consult the edition of *O Mayouri* (Théâtre guyanais) by Elie Stephenson with commentaries and bibliography by M.Fauquenoy (L'Harmattan, 1988).

16  The literary magazine *La Torche* offers an interesting example: founded in 1978 in hommage to Léon Damas with a militant Négritude platform, it subsequently opened its pages to a much wider range of cultural experience.

17  Some striking examples in the writings of some of the leading figures of the PSG, for example E. Castor, *1981–1985 La gauche au pouvoir* (L'Harmattan, 1986).

## Statistical sources

IEDOM Bulletin for 1986–87–88, for 1989 and 1990.
INSEE Annuaire statistique de la Guyane 1970–77.
INSEE Recensement général de la population 1974 et 1990.

# CHAPTER 5

# Dialectics of descent and phenotypes in racial classification in Martinique

*Michel Giraud*

Given the multiplicity of 'racial' typologies throughout the world it has often been said that the human mind has a universal tendency to categorize things. But this tendency, in so far as it exists, is simply an inherent capacity. Typologies, and the stereotypes they contain – which are supposedly the result of this capacity to categorize – are in fact the product of particular social histories. Thus, if we push the logic of this to its limit, we might say that each society has its own system of racial classification, which is an expression more of the dominant social representation of existing phenotypical variation than an objective reflection on the latter. Roger Bastide puts his finger on it when he says:

> Each nation has its own ideology of race and censuses reveal that ideology more than any demographic reality. In the USA every individual who has a drop of black blood in his veins is looked upon as 'black'; in Brazil, every individual with a drop of white blood in his veins, particularly if he has a certain social standing will be considered 'white'.[1]

This means that an analysis of popular racial taxonomies needs to have recourse to anthropology, which is here defined as the study of the variability of social and cultural forms. Within the framework of this analysis the term 'race' is not to be taken to have its usual 'scientific' definition – a much debated definition anyway, and one which can only indicate a constant – but the meaning that sociologists give to it when they speak of 'social race', namely 'the way in which the members of a society categorize each other according to their physical characteristics',[2] and which differs from one society to another.

The diversity of popular racial classifications arises from the fact that they are based on different combinations of a small number of general principles.[3] This is why, whenever a society is under examination it is to the evidence of such combinations that we must look primarily, as we will be doing here in the case of Martinique.

## The traditional model of racial typology in Martinique

Schematically speaking, this can be reduced to two fundamental rules,[4] and its social legitimation resides in a body of particularly significant stereotypes.

### The descent rule

It is an individual's filiation, as defined by popular genealogical tradition, which determines into which racial category they are put. Thus 'someone whose antecedents are in principle exclusively white is white; someone who is of mixed blood is a mulatto, and someone whose antecedents are essentially black is considered to be a black.'[5]

The phenotypical modalities (particularly those relating to skin colour, hair texture, or lip and nose shape) – in so far as they are attributed differentially to each of the typological categories under consideration – serve as clues from which the genealogy of individuals can be deduced, particularly when their parentage is unknown to those doing the categorizing. But, and it is important to stress this, phenotypical characteristics are not necessarily the criteria of definition of racial classification in Martinique. This is why two individuals with similar physical characteristics can, because of their different origins, be placed in separate categories; similarly two siblings of quite different physical appearance will more often than not be placed in the same racial category. In Martinique, racial prejudice, even if it is often called colour prejudice, is initially more a prejudice based on origin than on appearance.[6] Nevertheless it is true that over time, once the depth of genealogical knowledge has gone beyond the point where oral tradition can operate, the descent rule has had a tendency to disappear gradually to be replaced by classification by phenotype.

### The inequality rule

Martinican racial typology not only presupposes that the criteria determining who belongs to the categories of which it is composed should be defined, but also that these categories should be ordered hierarchically, in other words the typology is based on 'colour' prejudice. This hierarchy traditionally reaffirms the superiority of white over the black in such a way that the closer a category is to whiteness, the more it is esteemed. This supremacy of whiteness (the *sine qua non* of which is the inferiority of blackness) in Martinican racial classification springs from the history of European colonization and reflects the social structure which colonization imposed. Indeed, the conditions in which Martinican society was formed, the very facts of the island's colonization by French merchant capitalism and the introduction of slavery which followed, mean that this society is socially stratified according to racial differences. Thus, the demands of colonialization – and in particular the population factors this implies – created a situation where slave owners and white colonists of European origin on the one hand, and black slaves of African origin on the other hand, met face to face. The addition to this initial bipolarity of a third group, the offspring of interbreeding between masters and slaves, namely the mulattos (often freemen but situated socially in an intermediate position as small farmers, artisans or shopkeepers), added to and further complicated the situation with regard to social class hierarchies and also the hierarchical structures based on race, of Martinican plantation society.

## Racial stereotypes

The position of inferiority or superiority that each category occupies in popular racial classification is legitimized socially by value judgements or stereotypes,[7] which attribute in gross terms both moral and physical characteristics to the members of each category regardless of individual differences. Thus, in Martinique when it comes to physical characteristics, the criterion of beauty is, generally speaking, defined in relation to the white phenotype which in this case is taken as the model, and which is, as the anthropologist Hermanus Hoetink put it, the 'somatic norm'.[8] Beautiful hair is 'flat', 'smooth', 'straight', as is evidenced by the widespread practice by women, and also by certain black men, of having their hair 'straightened' or 'improved'. It is equally to be noted that more recently there has been resistance to this practice, with the increasing popularity of 'Afro' style hair. The beauty of facial features is associated with 'fineness'; the nose must be 'straight', 'pinched'; the mouth 'small'. Black features are often considered to be 'thick', 'heavy', 'crude', even. The lighter the skin colour, the more it is valued. Such skin is described in glowing terms: 'iris milk' for the whites, rosewood for certain mulatto women, etc.; whereas a very dark skinned negro might be described disparagingly as a '*nègre gros sirop*' from the dark colour of molasses syrup; or 'blue' if he is very dark.

The stereotypes related to the moral and intellectual capacities of the different racial groups also underline the inferiority of the blacks. Intelligence is, for example, an essentially white (although sometimes mulatto) quality. According to the participants in a socio-metric study we carried out in certain schools in Martinique,[9] intelligence is widespread among Europeans, rare among blacks. The same subjects describe the negro as being 'aggressive', 'a brawler', and by way of explanation point out that the negro has retained something of his savage ancestry. Frequently the negro is described as 'crude' or 'ill-mannered'.[10]

In short, in the language of traditional colour ideology in Martinique, white is from every point of view synonymous with everything that is good,[11] and black with everything that is bad. The dominant feature of this ideology is revealed in the way that the stereotypes it proposes are essentially identical in the different groups; indeed, there is no substantial difference in the way each group perceives itself (autostereotypes) and the way it is perceived by the other groups (heterostereotypes).[12] The discriminatory values and ideals of the dominant racial ideology in Martinique are widely internalized by the majority of Martinicans, including those who are its principal victims. Thus the deep awareness of their identity revealed by whites, and to a lesser extent by mulattos, and the pride they derived from belonging to those groups, contrasts with the 'self-rejection' often shown by blacks. Thus, too dark a skin can some-times cause suffering, shame or resentment on the part of the individuals concerned; consequently it sometimes happens that the individuals attempt, as much as is humanly possible, and even beyond, to fantasize to the point of rejecting their hair colour. The negrophobia manifested by numerous coloured men, some of them blacks, is only in fact paradoxical, as Fanon has pointed out, for those who pretend to ignore that these men are the victims of a cul-turally imposed situation which tends to convince them that whites represent the ideal; and that therefore they have only to identify with them to move up in the social hierarchy. From early childhood, young Martinicans are invited by the strip cartoons they read, the films they watch and the stereotypes which prevail in their social environment to accept this identification.

# The misfortunes of the descent rule

None the less, since historical forces, particularly after the abolition of slavery in 1848, facilitated the upward social movement of certain coloured people – in the first instance the *'anciens libres'*[13] and their descendants – the traditional super-imposition of classes and races in Martinique was, as a result, somewhat distorted. Not that the racialization of social relations – a prominent trend in Martinique – was halted; phenotypical and hereditary diversity continued to form a basis for social differentiation. Since then, in Martinique, race has remained a sign[14] by which the social status of individuals is indicated.

On the island of Martinique both economic and political power, and the lack of it, have retained their colours in everyday language; white is synonymous with power and wealth, black with poverty. Hence the expression *'Béké'*, which strictly speaking is a white man, can also sometimes mean a boss, or a rich man, regardless of the colour of the individual concerned. A coloured person can also (in certain circumstances) be called white provided he has a recognized social position. As for the term 'negro' (*nègre*), it is associated not only with the physical characteristics of an individual but also with their social circumstances; a negro symbolizes all that is misfortune in the world. When visited by a negro people might say 'What bad luck is he bringing with him?' Martinican writers, as privileged observers of life on the island, have always been highly aware of this racialization of the social scene; shown, for example, by Joseph Zobel: 'In Martinique we were poor, you could tell by our colour, as black as poverty';[15] and Aimé Césaire: 'The white man symbolizes capital, just as the negro symbolizes labour.'[16]

The logic whereby race is an indicator of social position strongly implies that any upward social movement on the part of an individual is accompanied by their 'racial promotion', by a 'whitening'; what Michel Leiris has called the game of adjustment between social status and racial group,[17] as illustrated for example, in the creole saying 'Any rich black man is a mulatto'.[18] In Martinique, as in many other places, money, education, or social success have a whitening effect. From that moment on, racial categories can no longer be said to be defined exclusively by filiation; the descent rule must now be intertwined with what Pierre Crépeau calls the 'assimilation law. People are classified racially by assimilation to a racial type corresponding to their social status.'[19]

The assimilation law adds a new dimension to the process of racial classification, contributes to a transformation within the typology which that self-same process had long confirmed, and creates contradictory views of that typology within the various groups. Indeed this law, which assumes that upward social mobility must be realized by assimilation to the categories which are closest to the white man, lead coloured people who move upwards in the social hierarchy, as several field studies show,[20] to multiply the intermediary categories of racial classification (and, as a consequence, to extend as much as possible the variety of phenotypes), in order to confirm their upward mobility. They do this by creating the greatest possible number of gradations between the 'white world', associated as it is with the dominant classes, and the 'negro world', associated with the proletarian and peasant classes. This enables them at one and the same time to reduce the gap which still separates them from the first 'world',[21] and to distance themselves from the second.[22] Conversely, at the two ends of the socio-racial hierarchy, the members of the white bourgeoisie and those of the black working class attempt to counter this strategy of the coloured middle classes, which threatens their interests. This they do by simplifying the classification of the races, and particularly by reducing it as much as possible to a simple white/black dichotomy which reflects the fundamental polarization of the Martinican social system: that between the big land-owners and industrialists, and the poor workers and peasants.

On the one hand, while colour ideology maintains its hold on Martinican society, at the same time, as we have already indicated, the traditional correspondence of race and class has been somewhat distorted. This same distortion has tended to confer upon colour differences a greater categorizing function. For 'with classes becoming less homogeneous in their ethnic composition, phenotypical characteristics acquire a value in their own right'.[23] Placing someone in a colour category thus in itself takes on social importance, and hence as we have seen, becomes a source of social antagonisms. Since the white phenotype is the most highly valued in colour ideology, and the one which confers the highest social status, it thus becomes important for those who have it, to conserve it and guard it jealously (hence the strict homogamy among white Martinicans); and for those who do not have it, to get as close as possible to it by appropriate marriage strategies. Seen from this viewpoint, light 'colour' for non-whites tends to be socially advantageous and a sought-after means of upward mobility, a capital resource which has to be acquired or defended ('*sauver la race*' as they say), a resource which needs to be invested and made to grow by a 'good marriage' (namely, a marriage with someone of fairer skin than one's own, or at least with an equally fair kin). Thus, amongst the working classes a fair skin in a newborn child '*bien sorti*', one who has 'turned out right', is traditionally considered to be a guarantee of social success, a promise that he will escape from the social conditions of his parents, from the 'curse of the big black hole', as Fanon described it; hence the creole expression '*peau chappée*' (escape skin) to describe a skin of this particular hue.

In the context of a Martinican society marked by the racialization of social relations – and in parallel to what we were saying above about the need to see upward social movement concretized by a racial 'promotion' – 'whitening' therefore means social advancement. So for those coloured people who have moved up in the social class hierarchy it is a consolidation and a confirmation of that upward movement.

Thus in Martinique phenotype plays an increasing role in the definition of racial typology categories. This in turn is weakening, to a greater degree, the effectiveness in this defining process of the descent rule which, as we have already seen, has eventually become mixed up with individuals' social class.

The matrimonial strategies of the coloured lower middle class have been indelibly affected by the above class constraints, as the novelist Salvat Etchart so graphically explains:

> For generation upon generation, grandmothers, mothers, daughters and granddaughters had frantically obeyed the unwritten law, and had religiously respected the policy demanded by the situation. Since saints and priests and good husbands were white they had armed themselves to set off in the quest for a new skin, a new Golden Fleece, to take on the appearance, the semblance, the exterior, of Goodness. Resolutely they had turned their backs on the chain, filth and ignorance, which are black. Learning their lesson well, they had decided – despite themselves – that only whiteness is attractive and moral, beautiful and virtuous ... the colour of daylight. Racism is too weak a word to define this phenomenon of constant yearning. Prejudice, no matter how strongly felt, would not have been enough to give the Misses Alicante this silent enduring fervour. No. It was more a question of an underlying plan, a nebulous aspiration. It was the disquieting phase of a war in which the manoeuvres were as vicious, deadly, deceitful and cunning as those of a battle. It was pillaging and looting. Each matrix retained its share of selected seed. Servitude reigned and reigns still over wombs.[24]

The continued existence of phenotypical differences is not therefore a matter of chance but is socially conditioned by the strategies we have just mentioned. It forms the subject of social management (which fully justifies the reference to phenotypes being a capital resource when given status by colour ideologies). French West Indian societies 'are permanently managing a biological phenomenon, namely that of the transmission of a certain number of discriminating characteristics, *in much the same way that others manage the transmission of family property from one generation to another.*'[25]

Quite evidently, the presiding logic of the dynamics of classification that make up the strategies mentioned is that of differentiation. Within this logic, being classified to the best advantage means, for each individual, 'being recognized as not belonging to the group that the colour hierarchy indicates is the one just below his own'[26] and, particularly for those of 'mixed blood', being differentiated from the black group from which they nevertheless originally came. This explains the situation of mulattos who, rejecting their black African, and therefore slave, origins (after all 'the memory of slavery dishonours the race, and the race perpetuates the memory of slavery')[27] try to come to terms with their phenotype by inventing some ancient Carib ancestry in place of their African slave origins and, more generally, accounts for the traditional negrophobia in the French West Indies, which Fanon analyzed in so masterly a fashion in *Peau noire masques blancs*. From this it is clear that the increasing significance of phenotype in racial classification only finds its full expression in a sort of falsified respect paid to the descent rule, by means of manipulation of the principle of filiation.

## *New deal, old logic*

Today the drawbacks of the designation of the French West Indies as overseas departments (economic recession and increased unemployment, the failure of land reforms, the growth of inequality, mass emigration) have destabilized the idea that these islands are a part of France. A national consciousness is beginning to arise in Martinique, and in Guadeloupe too, and the independence platforms of new, but minority nationalist organizations are gaining increasing sympathy. Traditional colour ideology which is inextricably linked with assimilationist ideology (colour ideology is to race what assimilation is to culture, French culture being a sort of cultural 'whitening') has been affected by this political change. Not because the schema of raciological thought that this change implies (and which throughout their history has been internalized by French West Indians) has become ineffective, but because the scale of values that it proposes has been, to some extent, turned on its head. Via a logical process, of which analysts of race will be well aware, namely that of stigmata inversion, blackness is today a strong feature in the political and cultural life of the French West Indies. 'The black stain has today become a sign of autochthony'.[28] Black consciousness, which has existed for decades now, and its attempt to rehabilitate negro values, is a product of this turnabout. But it must also be pointed out that this reversal is above all the work of a small number of intellectuals and militant political figures, which does not give us the right to suppose that their views are widely shared. Also it exists primarily within the context of the political and cultural relations between France and the West Indies, which does not therefore mean that the colonial colour ideology no longer operates among French West Indians in their relations with one another.

The racialization process within society has, at least to some degree, shaped its value system, but its principles still exist. It is that racialization which has transformed, in the minds of a great many political figures, the national opposition between the French and the West Indians into a racial split between whites and blacks shown by the fact that the serious political clashes which have taken place in the French West Indies since the 1960s have culminated in a series of race riots in which the metropolitan French and their property have increasingly been the principal targets. Nationalism has thus often coincided with black fundamentalism and this has brought about a withdrawal into identity groups, which in turn has bred all kinds of intolerance and sectarianism.[29] In particular it has created a strong desire for homogeneity, which has given rise to the idea that the negroes of Martinique (and also of Guadeloupe) are the only authentic Martinicans (or Guadeloupeans) or at least that they are direct descendants of African slaves. The descent rule (with its various manipulations), in conjunction with the phenotype rule, then comes into its own.

# Notes

1  R. Bastide, *Les Amériques noires,* Paris, Payot, 1968, p. 21.
2  C. Wagley, (ed.) *Races et Classes dans le Brésil rural,* Paris, UNESCO/Gallimard, 1952, p. 12. See also by the same author 'On the concept of social race in the Americas' in D.B. Heath and R.N. Adams, (eds) *Contemporary Cultures and Societies of Latin America,* New York, Random House, 1965.
3  See P. Crépeau, *Classifications raciales populaires et métissage: essai d'anthropologie cognitive,* Centre de Recherches Caraïbes de l'Université de Montréal, Montreal, 1973.

4   We have borrowed the terminology for these rules from Pierre Crépeau (see P. Crépeau, *op. cit.*).

5   M. Leiris, *Contacts de civilisations en Martinique et en Guadeloupe*, Paris, UNESCO/Gallimard, 1955, p. 161.

6   On this distinction see O. Nogueira, 'Skin Colour and Social Class' in V. Rubin, (ed.) *Plantation Systems of the New World*, Pan American Union, 1959.

7   'Stereotypes are generalizations which are not based upon logical reasoning but on hearsay, rumours, anecdotes, incomplete evidence, and limited experience.' (O. Klineberg quoted in M.C. Munoz, *Le Développement des stéréotypes ethniques chez l'enfant, approche psychosociologique*, Ph.D. thesis, Paris, Ecole Pratique des Hautes Etudes, 1973, p. 6).

8   Cf. H. Hoetink, *The Two Variants in Caribbean Race Relations: A Contribution to the Sociology of Segmented Societies*, London, New York, Toronto, Oxford University Press, 1967. See also F. Fanon, *Peau noire masques blancs*, Paris, Editions du Seuil, 1952, where it is stated that 'c'est en référence à l'essence du Blanc que l'Antillais est appelé à être percu par son congénère' (p. 152).

9   See by the present author *Races et Classes à la Martinique*, Paris, Editions Anthropos, 1979.

10  From a well-known song, the words of which Michel Leiris reproduced in an article in *Les Temps Modernes*, in February 1950.

11  'On est blanc comme on est riche, comme on est beau, comme on est intelligent' (F. Fanon, *op. cit.*, p. 61).

12  See by this author *Races et Classes …, op. cit.*, pp. 229–30.

13  Those freed while slavery still operated, as opposed to those 'new freemen', freed when slavery was abolished.

14  In which a biological signifier and a social signified are superimposed. On race as a sign see the now classic work by Colette Guillaumin: *L'Idéologie raciste. Genèse et langage actuel*, Paris, Mouton, 1972.

15  J. Zobel, *La Rue Cases-Nègres*, Paris, Editions des Quatre Jeudis, 1955, p. 104.

16  Quoted in F. Fanon, *Peau noire …, op. cit.*, p. 127.

17  Cf. M. Leiris, *op. cit.*, p. 138.

18  There is an old Brazilian saying which goes even further: 'A rich negro is a white man.' Quoted in D. Pierson, *Negroes in Brazil, a Study of Race Contact in Bahia*, Chicago, Chicago University Press, 1944, p. 155.

19  P. Crépeau, *op. cit.*, p. 37.

20  See by this same author *Races et Classes …, op. cit.*, pp. 94–7, and for similar results with regard to Haiti, M. Labelle, *Idéologie de couleur et classes sociales en Haïti*, Montreal, Les Presses de l'Université de Montréal, 1978.

21  Which is why I.R. Buchler sees in the multiplication of racial typology categories what he calls a '*gapping mechanism*', defined as 'any structured social device that serves to decrease the social distance between two groups interacting on grounds of social and economic inequality, by which individuals may theoretically pass from one socio-economic category to another, excluding the polar categories', I.R. Buchler, 'Caymanian Folk Racial Categories, *Man*, 1962, LXII, p. 185, quoted in P. Crépeau, *op. cit.*, p. 20.

22  This same determination to differentiate is also manifest in the tendency by the coloured lower middle classes in Martinique to 'blacken' members of the working classes; see by the present author *Races et Classes …, op. cit.*, pp. 99–100 or, as Pierre Crépeau puts it 'to reverse the process of racial assimilation with a view to maintaining their social superiority over the social classes beneath them', P. Crépeau, *op. cit.*, p. 40.

23 J.L. Jamard, 'Réflexions sur la racialisation des rapports sociaux en Martinique: de l'esclavage biracial à l'anthroponomie des races', *Archipelago*, 3–4 June 1983, p. 60.

24 S. Etchart, *Le Monde tel qu'il est*, Paris, Mercure de France, 1967, pp. 95–7.

25 J.L. Bonniol, 'Phénomènes de racialisation dans l'affirmation identitaire' in *Vers des sociétés pluriculturelles: études comparatives et situation en France*, Paris, editions de l'ORSTOM, 1987, p. 196 (the italics are ours).

26 J.L. Jamard, *art. cit.*, p. 62.

27 A. de Tocqueville quoted in M. Leiris, *op. cit.*, pp. 166–7.

28 J.L. Bonniol, *op. cit.*, p. 198.

29 On this point see M.C. Lafontaine, 'Le Carnaval de l'Autre – à propos d'authenticité en matière de musique guadeloupéenne', *Les Temps Modernes*, 'Antilles', 441–442, April–May 1983, pp. 2126–73, and also M. Giraud, 'Crispation identaire et antisémitisme en Martinique: le cas d'Antilla', *Traces*, 11, 1984, pp. 129–51.

# CHAPTER 6

## The Declaration of the Treaty of Maastricht on the ultra-peripheral regions of the Community: an assessment

*Emmanuel Jos*

The 'Treaty on European Union' signed in Maastricht on 7 February 1992 includes, in addition to its various articles, 17 protocols and 33 declarations appended to the final Act.[1] These international undertakings are the outcome of negotiations which began in Rome on 15 December 1990 and ended in Maastricht on 11 December 1991. Amongst the declarations, we find, in twenty-sixth position, one on the 'Ultra-peripheral Regions of the Community'.

This declaration resulted from the pressures exercised on the French government by the interparliamentary group representing the overseas departments (DOM). The government initially seemed satisfied with the existence of article 227§2 of the Treaty of Rome, as interpreted by the Hansen Decree, implemented in particular by way of the adoption of the programme of options specific to the distance and insularity of the DOMs (POSEIDOM). At the end of October 1991, the government was tending towards favouring a simple unilateral declaration by France affirming, as an attachment to the Treaty, the need to take into consideration the individuality of the DOMs. Under pressure from the DOM deputies, French diplomacy proposed a common declaration to its partners which was finally adopted.[2] A brief two-paragraph text, the declaration constitutes a synthesis of the spirit in which the member states intend to approach the specific position of the so-called 'ultra-peripheral' regions.

From the perspective of parliamentary or popular ratification of the Treaty, it was important to be able to indicate the political will to take account of the particular problems of the territories concerned. There was an opportunity not to be missed for winning over the necessary support. The existence of the declaration has made it possible to highlight the advantages of the principle of rightful application of the Treaty and of the derived right as well as the principle of the right to specific measures.

Eligibility to the structural funds of the Community constitutes a major argument in the matter of the advantages of an ultra-peripheral region statute. The oft-mooted comparison is that of the amount of funds received by the DOMs in relation to the amount conceded to the African, Caribbean and Pacific States (ACP). M. Jean Crusol was already pointing out in 1987 that the annual per capita transfer for the DOMs was 583 F and only 31 F for the ACPs.[3] Community officials have had occasion to stress that the DOMs, which only represent 0.5 per cent of the Community population, are nevertheless receiving 2 per cent of its loans between 1989 and 1993.[4] Moreover, in the name of rightful application, the DOMs are able to demand the advantage of common organizations for markets within the agricultural sector, which makes it possible to enjoy Community preference for certain produce. This is what the banana-growers are demanding, among other things. The reaffirmation of rightful application, which was already one of the recognized merits of the Hansen Decree, thus provides the opportunity of stressing the advantages of integration.

In contrast, in a context where the fear of unequal competition (which risks destroying what remains of the economy in the DOMs) or the dread of integration-dilution (which risks destroying local identity) have made the imagery of the wolf (the symbol of a predatory Europe)[5] very popular, it was important to be able to reassure the various peoples by clearly stating that such fear and dread were without foundation. This is because the Community, recognizing the particular problems of the ultra-peripheral regions, was prepared to take specific measures in their regard. Had it not in fact adopted the POSEIDOM programme?

The YES in favour of ratifying the Maastricht Treaty largely won the day in the DOMs in the referendum on 20 September 1992: 67.40 per cent in French Guiana, 67.46 per cent in Guadeloupe, 74.30 per cent in Réunion and 70.13 per cent in Martinique. This contrasts strongly with the narrow YES result throughout metropolitan France (51.04 per cent against 48.95 per cent). The YES voters thus concluded that the DOMs were satisfied with a Treaty which recognized their rights without undermining their individualities.

What are we to think, then, of the massive abstention which exactly parallels the rate of participation in metropolitan France (81.37 per cent in French Guiana, 73.35 per cent in Réunion, 83.37 per cent in Guadeloupe and 75.47 per cent in Martinique)? The YES voters have regarded it as reflecting the electorate's customary attitude in the case of European elections. At the same time it indicated the difficulty of being faced with a text which has not been sufficiently explained. Whatever the case, in their opinion, it could not convey refusal of Europe.[6]

The declaration on the ultra-peripheral regions thus helped to bring in votes during the referendum campaign, and as such had a degree of political impact. It emerges from the legal analysis, however, that it has a limited impact, due less to the legal form adopted than to the content of the text. The provisions concerning the ultra-peripheral regions were not included in the body of the Treaty, nor even in any of the protocols, but in a common declaration attached to the final Act. Does this mean that this declaration is devoid of any legal power?

One might be tempted to place the declaration in the category of 'non-conventional acts in question' which Michel Virally states are international texts devoid of legal impact.[7] Their instigators have no international responsibility to comply with them and they cannot form the subject of jurisdictional redress. They need not be introduced into national legal orders and cannot be invoked before national courts. By way of example, it is relevant to mention the European Council resolution regarding which the Constitutional Council, in its decision of 29 December 1978, concluded that it was a matter of a declaration of a political nature which did not come under the application of articles 52 and 53 of the Constitution.

On the other hand, one could consider, on reading the various declarations attached to the final Treaty of Maastricht, that the will exists amongst the instigators of the Treaty to make genuine international undertakings of these texts. Some of them appear indissociable from the treaty in so far as their contents are expressed in a normative fashion, providing essential information in respect of applying the contractual provisions themselves. Such is the case, for example, of the declaration (No. 2) relating to the nationality of a member state.[8] It is stated that this matter is governed 'solely with reference to the national law of the state concerned'. Here is a provision which cannot have force of law through the courts in the event of a dispute. This is equally true of many other subjects broached in the declarations. Some of them even cover elements of procedure for the running of institutions. In contrast, other declarations have a very general and very vague content which renders them simple declarations of intent. This is the case, for example of the declaration (No. 3) relating to monetary co-operation with other countries.

It would prove difficult to sort out the normative declarations from the declarations of intent in the process of ratification. Thus the

Treaty, the protocols as a whole, and the declarations have been submitted for ratification. The important thing, therefore, is to know whether or not the content of each declaration constitutes a normative statement. Nevertheless, the form of the declaration is limited within itself. In effect it cannot allow an essential principle which would not be contained within the body of the Treaty to be affirmed. The declarations may specify but not introduce changes. They are subordinate to the essential rules contained in the treaty. On these grounds, the declarations remain secondary and in essence refer to the provisions of the Treaty itself.

With regard to the declaration on the ultra-peripheral regions, its inadequacies reside partly in its form but especially in its content, on two counts in particular: on the one hand, the concept of an ultra-peripheral region is ambiguous and, on the other, the legal system to which it refers is unsatisfactory.

## An ambiguous qualification

The concept of an ultra-peripheral region certainly makes it possible to emphasize the development handicaps which are common to a number of Community territories, but it entails an obvious risk of fusion.

### Confirmation of a concept

The regions involved in the declaration are explicitly named. It concerns the DOMs (French territories), the Azores and Madeira (Portuguese territories) and the Canary Islands (Spanish territories). The conference qualifies these regions as ultra-peripheral. The term is not new. Already in 1973, awareness of their individualities had encouraged the more underprivileged maritime regions of Europe to group together in order to defend their interests more efficiently before Community authorities. Thus, the Maritime Peripheral Regions Conference (CRPM) came into existence at Saint Malo. It has a permanent structure based in Rennes. In 1980, an island commission was created within it. The CRPM, a non-governmental organization, was behind the initiative which enabled the creation, in 1985, of the Assembly of the Regions of Europe. It plays a role in the Consultative Committee of the Regional and Local Communities within the European Community.

The entry of Spain and Portugal into the Community high-

lighted the existence, within the body of peripheral regions, of territories in still more underprivileged situations, whence came the
usage of a new concept – ultra-peripheral. This concept has become
popular since 1986 and has entered the Community vocabulary. In
that year, an inter-services group was created at the initiative of
President Delors and given the task of globally studying all matters
dealing with the integration of the ultra-peripheral regions within the
Community.

In 1987, the Commission indicated its wish to find an appropriate framework for responding to the problems of these regions. A
POSEIDOM was worked out, then adopted, after many trials and
tribulations. And, within the context of Community initiative programmes, an operational programme called REGIS was adopted in
favour of the ultra-peripheral regions. At the time of the Treaty of
Maastricht negotiations, the expression was already widely in common use. The Treaty, by its declaration, formally sanctions the concept. Thus is recognized a particular category of 'problem' regions, in
addition to the general category of backward regions, industrial
regions on the decline, agricultural regions, urban regions with problems, and frontier regions.[9]

Certain 'problem regions' are characterized by the stating of
indicators such as a threshold percentage for the Community average
in regard to GDP or unemployment rates. The ultra-peripheral
regions are identified by factors which further exacerbate their structural backwardness. These factors are of a geographical, climatic and
economic nature.

At the geographical level, the declaration in the first place
acknowledges the great distance involved. This takes on greater or
lesser significance depending on how far away the respective metropolitan territories are situated: the archipelago of the Azores is
1,500 km from the Portuguese coast; the archipelago of Madeira is
900 km away; the Canaries are 1,050 km south-west of Spain;
Martinique and Guadeloupe are 7,000 km from France; French
Guiana is 7,500 km away; and Réunion is 10,000 km away. Then
comes insularity, which is in fact a common characteristic of these
territories, with the exception of French Guiana. However, this territory is in fact very isolated in relation to its continental neighbours.
There is also the modest surface area of each region, which varies:
2,333 km$^2$ (252,000 inhabitants) for the Azores; 796 km$^2$ (272,000
inhabitants) for Madeira; 7,273 km$^2$ (1,500,000 inhabitants) for the
Canaries; 2,512 km$^2$ (570,000 inhabitants) for Réunion; 1,705 km$^2$
(345,013 inhabitants) for Guadeloupe; 1,110 km$^2$ (350,579 inhabitants) for Martinique; 90,000 km$^2$ (100,000 inhabitants) for French

Guiana. Most of the territories concerned are generally rugged in relief. With respect to climate, the intention of the declaration is to stress the hazards and not the normal situation which, on the contrary, is a tourist asset. The tropical territories are sometimes subject to devastating inclemencies such as cyclones. These natural catastrophes can, in a very short period of time, cause major destruction of infrastructure, buildings and industries, built up through several years' hard work. Economic dependence on a limited number of products is evident in all the regions. The growing of bananas and tourism are the mainstays of the economy for most of them. The declaration notes that the exacerbating effect of these geographical, climatic and economic factors results from the fact that they are constantly present and that there is an accumulation of them.

## The risk of fusion

The grouping with the other territories classed within the category of ultra-peripheral regions is without doubt the result of administrative convenience for the Commission. Moreover, as a group rather than as individual countries, these territories are in a stronger position to have the states to which they belong defend certain interests in Brussels. As a group, the states concerned carry more weight against their partners. The strategy of ultra-periphericity is thus not without its use. But there is a risk of fusion. In fact, the different territories concerned retain specific juridical qualities which should not be overlooked.

We see, firstly, that the DOMs are not eligible for the economic and social cohesion fund created by protocol No. 15 of the Maastricht Treaty. This fund is reserved for 'member states whose GNP is less than 90 per cent of the Community average', which excludes France (and therefore the DOMs), but applies to Portugal (and therefore includes Madeira and the Azores) and Spain (therefore the Canaries). The DOMs are, however, affected by the policy of economic and social cohesion stated in article 130A of the Treaty, which aims to rectify the backwardness of the least privileged regions. The way of doing this is to double the structural funds. However, it must be emphasized that the faculty for the various territories to participate in the international negotiations concerning them is not the same. Non-existent for the DOMs, it exists to a certain extent for Madeira in view of the unusual nature of its status within the Portuguese territories as a whole.

The socio-historical data are not the same for the DOMs as for the Portuguese or Spanish territories. The DOMs, situated within the developing tropical regions, possess geographical, historical and ethno-cultural links with their neighbours which the Azores, Madeira and the Canaries do not have. This is reflected by a relatively developed facet of regional co-operation in the POSEIDOM which is not found, for good reason, in similar measures proposed for the Canaries and Madeira.

The territories also do not have the same geopolitical situation. The DOMs are excluded from the sphere of application of NATO and the Schengen accords.[10] This, moreover, illustrates the dissociation between the territorial spheres of application of the treaties and their personal field of application. DOM nationals, as French citizens, can be incorporated into the French army and mobilized to enable the realization of an operation carried out within the framework of the combined European military command (UEO). Conversely, the member countries of the alliance are not obliged to employ collective self-defence in the case of an attack on French territory in the DOMs. The geographical position of the Portuguese and Spanish territories is different, they do not involve the same exclusions.

These few examples show that the category of ultra-peripheral regions does not support identical legal positions, hence the risk of fusion. The legal system of the DOMs has its own specific qualities. How should they be appraised?

## An unsatisfactory legal system

M. Christian Kert notes in his report that the jurisprudence of the Official Journal of the European Communities (CJCE) results in 'an unsatisfactory situation characterized by Court intervention case by case, with the major disadvantage of maintaining legal ambiguity for all peoples in respect of which it was not applied'. He goes on by stressing:

> There is no doubt that these legal uncertainties have contributed to a poor perception of the European challenges and of the opportunity they represent for the DOMs. The adoption of POSEIDOM, by unanimous decision of the Council, is certainly providing some guarantees as far as the specific qualities of the DOMs are concerned, but it only has decisional value and is subject to being abrogated

by another. The idea has thus gained ground, especially amongst our elected colleagues from the DOMs, to formally affirm this specific quality in the EEC Treaty. The European Council of Maastricht was therefore going to make it possible to finally lift the last legal ambiguities.[11]

In reality, when the Declaration contents itself with an abbreviated reiteration of the preambles of the POSEIDOM, it shows evidence of a lack of originality, and moreover it could not let it be forgotten that the fundamental legal basis of the Community status of the DOMs is, and remains, article 227§2 of the EEC Treaty. The European Council of Maastricht can only therefore 'finally lift the last legal ambiguities' by clarifying article 227§2 itself.

## The declaration's lack of originality

The content of the declaration is none other than the reiteration, word for word, of certain preambles (2, 5 and 6) of the decision to set up the POSEIDOM. The first paragraph of the declaration, besides the qualification that it confirms, diagnoses the development handicaps of the ultra-peripheral regions. Paragraph 2 of the declaration states the guidelines on Community action towards the ultra-peripheral regions.

The Hansen decree of 1978 already maintained that: 'the provisions of the Treaty and the derived law must be rightfully applied to the DOMs ... it nevertheless being understood that it is always possible to subsequently provide for specific measures with a view to meeting the needs of these territories.'[12] The POSEIDOM, having reiterated the aforementioned statement of the Hansen decree, added for its part that the specific measures may be adopted 'so long as there is an objective need to take such measures'. The declaration reiterates this phrase.

The second sentence of paragraph 2 recalls the POSEIDOM notion that the measures taken must reconcile two requirements:

– because these territories form an integral part of the Community, it is therefore advisable to implement the objective of the internal market;
– because they have an unusual localization (tropical developing regions for the DOMs), it is necessary to acknowledge the regional reality.

Lastly, the aim of the action, affirmed in the first place by the POSEIDOM, and then by the Maastricht Declaration, is to catch up on the average economic and social level of the Community.

It turns out that the reiteration of several preambles has only led to important statements being put to one side. The POSEIDOM further emphasizes, for example, that the implementation of the internal market in the DOMs may 'in particular force adjustment to general Community rules in so far as they do not take sufficient account of the specific realities of the DOMs'. This is to recognize the legitimacy of specific measures not only in the form of structural assistance but also in the regulatory sphere. It is further explained that 'the implementation of this programme should result in the adoption of legal acts, by the Council or the Commission as the case may be, some of which may apply solely to the overseas departments and others only relating to them in passing in texts of general impact'. The preambles of the POSEIDOM also recognize the existence of 'constraints of a permanent nature'. They also stress the need to seek the most appropriate forms for a greater liberalization 'within the framework of the partnership with the local authorities'.

The declaration could also have been able to bring in changes by integrating new aspects, such as the culture, for example. The cultural dimension carries great importance in the DOMs in search of an identity.[13] So long as the Community restricted itself to the economic dimension, one was able to consider that the exclusion of the cultural dimension of development of the DOMs could be justified. But ever since the Treaty of Maastricht instituted a Community in the wider sense and made explicit reference to culture in article 128, it became possible to point out the will of the Community to foster the full development of the DOMs in all its dimensions, including the cultural ones.

It is pertinent to note that article 131 of the Treaty of Rome maintains that the association aimed to steer the inhabitants of the Overseas Departments and Territories (PTOM) 'towards the economic, social and cultural development they are expecting'. The cultural dimension was therefore included in the concept of development. With regard to the Lomé IV agreement, article 4 refers to global development founded on the social and cultural values of the ACP states. Furthermore, section XI is dedicated to cultural and social co-operation. We can read there in particular that 'the human and cultural dimension must pervade all sectors and be reflected in every development project or programme'. The objective of integral development was worth reiterating for the DOMs; such lack constitutes one of the regrettable gaps in the declaration.

# A missed opportunity to clarify article 227§2

The only real basis for Community status of the DOMs resides in article 227§2. This 3-paragraph article is the outline of a differentiation justified by one essential aim: to foster the economic and social development of the DOMs. But it concerns simply an outline which increasingly reveals its inadequacies. According to the decree of the Community Court of Justice, pronounced in connection with the Legros affair on 16 July 1992, which to some extent clarifies the Hansen decree of 10 October 1978, the specific quality of the Community status of the DOMs can be résuméd as follows:

> In respect of those provisions of the Treaty which are not listed in the first line of paragraph 2 of this article, it is always possible to subsequently provide for specific measures with a view to meeting the needs of these territories.[14]

Thus, the particular and general provisions relating to the free circulation of goods, agriculture (with the exception of the provisions concerning the Common Agricultural Guarantee and Guidance Fund (FEOGA)), the liberation of services, rules of competition, safeguard measures (articles 108, 109 and 226) and institutions cannot be the subject of specific measures. Conversely, the provisions dealing with the free circulation of people and capital, freedom of establishment, the taxation system, transport policy, social policy, the FEOGA, the European Investment Bank (BEI), etc... can be the subject of specific measures. This device calls forth a number of reflections and remarks.

Today, to foster economic and social development in the DOMs is to move from a consumer economy to a production economy; it is to battle against unemployment which is reaching worrying proportions (30 per cent); it is to promote greater social equality. But as we have noted above, development must also be cultural in scope.

The first fact is that article 227§2, like the declaration on the ultra-peripheral regions, ignores the cultural dimension. The second is that, taking into account the constraints quite rightly diagnosed by the Community, the question arises: should one exclude the possibility of specific measures in the key sectors such as free circulation of goods, services or agriculture? In actual fact, the specific measures applied by the POSEIDOM for the most part concern agriculture[15]... Hence the persistence of a degree of legal insecurity.

The competitiveness of the DOMs cannot come simply from aid measures backed up by the structural Funds. Protection is essential, for example, to enable the emergence of local industry. If we take the case of the *Octroi de mer*,[16] we observe that its reform has made it possible to tend towards greater conformity with Community law by taxing locally-produced goods equally. But one wonders whether the reform is at present fully compatible with Community requirements. In fact, there are provisions for exemptions for paid delivery by producers operating in the DOMs. The criterion of the provenance of the product is therefore accepted in respect of eligibility for exemptions. The Legros decree recalls that

> a tax levied on a product from another member state does not constitute a tax with an effect equivalent to a customs duty, but internal taxation under article 95 of the Treaty if it comes under a general system of domestic taxes which systematically perceives categories of products according to objective criteria applied regardless of where the product comes from (decree dated 3 October 1981, Commission/France, 90/79, Rec. p. 283 point 14).

According to the decree, should the exemptions also be allowed by reason of certain objective criteria rather than place of production? In order to get out of the difficulty and to legalize the *octroi de mer* as an instrument for developing the local economy, would it not be necessary for the Council to be able to have the right to also take specific measures on the provisions stated in paragraph one of article 227§2? To be still more precise, we need to consider the significance of the expression 'specific measures'.

Firstly, it is necessary to recognize that the possibility of specific measures exists for all the territories in the Community. With regard to the DOMs, how far does the possibility of exemptions and particular measures extend? Article 227§2 is hazy on this point. Its terms are particularly vague since it only mentions the 'conditions of application' specified by the Council.

As for the procedure to be followed, the POSEIDOM considers that 'the Treaty has not provided for the powers of actions required for the adoption of the present decision and that it is therefore advisable to resort to article 235 of the Treaty'. This justified the reference to this article in the certifications to the text. That is to say, article 227§2 is inadequate by itself to be used as a legal basis and to specify the procedure to be followed for adopting the necessary measures in certain domains. Does not the obliged recourse to article 235 rob the status of the DOMs of its originality since it is a matter of a common law provision?

An improvement to the drafting of article 227§2 or else the

addition of a special protocol is thus proving essential in order to provide a more clearly differentiated legal situation for the DOMs in the Community. Will France's partners understand it? Will they accept it? And at what cost?

## Notes

1   Commission et Conseil des Communautés Européennes –, *Traité sur l'Union Européenne*, office des publications officielles des Communautés Européennes, 1992, p. 253.

2   See *Rapport d'information*, filed by the Délégation de l'Assemblée Nationale pour les Communautés Européennes on *L'Europe et les départements d'outre-mer*, presented by M. Christian Kert, no.2 603, recorded on 7 April 1992, p. 21. France's initial position was due to her fear at seeing her acquisitions called into question and to the possible proliferation of demands for special dispensations or preferential treatment for other regions.

3   Jean Crusol, 'Bilan et perspectives de l'intégration des DOM à la Communauté Economique Européenne (1957-1992)', *Questions sur l'administration des DOM*, Décentraliser Outre-mer, Economica et PUAM, 1989, p. 485.

4   See statement by M. Ciavarini-Azzi, President of the Inter-services Group, *France-Antilles, Martinique*, Thursday, 5 November 1992, p. 4. It is worth pointing out that France is, on net balance, in credit in relation to the Community.

5   The reference here is to the smash hit of the 1990 Carnival in Martinique, 'Le Grand Méchant Loup' by Djo Desormo.

6   See results and comments in *France-Antilles Martinique*, Monday, 21 September 1992, pp. 6–7.

7   Michel Virally, 'the distinction between international texts having legal impact amongst their instigators and those texts devoid of it', Ann.IDI, 1983, pp. 166–257 and 328–357.

8   DC 78–100 dated 29 December 1978 Rec. 38.

9   Yves Doutriaux, *La politique régionale de la CEE*, PUF, Que sais-je? no. 2 587, 1991, pp. 36–9.

10  Article 5 of the WEU (UEO) concerns attacks *in Europe*; NATO's article 6 establishes the territorial field of application of the treaty as continental Europe and the North Atlantic *'to the north of the Tropic of Cancer'*; article 138 of the agreement on application of the Schengen accords of 19 June 1990 provides for the agreement to apply only to *the European territory of the French Republic*.

11  *Rapport d'information* quoted in note (2), pp. 20-1.

12  CJCE, 10 October 1978, p. 1806.

13  On the cultural issue, one may refer to the research by M'Consultants carried out on behalf of SODEMA in May 1990 and March–April 1991, under the heading: *Etude sur les mentalités des Martiniquais face aux enjeux de développement*.

14  Decree dated 16 July 1992, case C-163/90, point 8.

15  See Danielle Perrot, 'Marché intérieur des DOM et marché communautaire', AJDA, special Overseas issue, September 1992, pp. 586–92.

16  The *octroi de mer* dates back to 1866 and gives the Conseils Généraux of Martinique and Guadeloupe the right to raise duties on non-French imports into the islands. It is scheduled to disappear under the provisions of Maastricht.

# CHAPTER 7

# The French Antilles and the wider Caribbean

*Maurice Burac*

Guadeloupe, Martinique and French Guiana are located in the Caribbean area, one of the most fragmented in the world. It is an area composed of territories of variable size, insular or continental, endowed with very different social, economical and political structures. Strongly influenced by the colonial system, these countries maintain privileged relationships, either with their former mother countries, merged in the European Community, or with the United States.

In order to fight against underdevelopment and foreign dependency, the private sector, political parties, labour associations, then local governments were engaged very early in regional co-operation, following the failure of experiments in political union. The former British colonies, by their number and the similarity of their problems, were the first to be organized in order to answer this real need. The founding of institutions such as the Caribbean Free Trade Association, then the Caribbean Community including the Caribbean Common Market, the Caribbean Development Bank, the Organization of Eastern Caribbean States or the University of the West Indies, encouraged many territories in their continuing struggle against underdevelopment and economic and even political fragmentation.

Because of their political and economic status characterized by a high degree of dependency on their mother country, Guadeloupe, Martinique and French Guiana, former French colonies, overseas departments since 1946, contributed much less to the development of a regional solidarity with their neighbours. Soon, they were isolated with very limited trade with their immediate environment, despite undertakings from the Caribbean Community and afterwards the private sector and the Caribbean Commerce and Industry Association.

During these past few years, in order to break up their regional isolation, Guadeloupe, Martinique and French Guiana have increased their relations with neighbouring countries. This new trend has also been favoured by the association of the former British and Dutch colonies in the Caribbean area with the EC, after the signature of the Lomé Convention and by a broader commitment from the private sector, of the French government and local political assemblies.

## Regional solidarity in the Caribbean area: The English-speaking West Indies

The colonization of the Caribbean by European powers, Spain, Great Britain, France and Holland, led to the formation of four geopolitical groups having relatively few ties between them, notably during periods of war. Decolonization was followed by the founding of new states, about thirty of them, keeping privileged relationships with their mother countries or creating more and more bonds with the United States, the richest American territory. Due to their political, economical and social situation, these states had to increase their trade, both with their traditional and new partners and between themselves, which led progressively to a co-operation and even, in certain cases of the English-speaking West Indies, to a relatively high level of integration. Because of their proximity and a similar economy, their history and related cultures, and their overall poor conditions, these territories engaged in a number of experiments of political unity as an important movement of economical, social and cultural co-operation.

English-speaking islands failed systematically in their attempts at political unity. The failure of the Leeward Islands Federation (1674–1798 and 1871–1956) and above all the failure of the British West Indian Federation (1958–1962) left a deep impression on the political and labour leaders as well as on the populations concerned.

After the dissolution of the Federation, the government leaders of Barbados, British Guiana (Guyana), Jamaica, Trinidad and Tobago, met, in July 1963, in Port of Spain, to hold a first convention and examine matters of common interest. The discussion dealt with various questions such as commerce, communications, emigration to Great Britain and to the United States, economic and technical assistance, and the University of West Indies.

The responsible authorities came to an agreement and requested increased assistance from Great Britain and the United States, and set up a working group in order to study the operating problems of the Shipping Company (WISCO). They agreed to request amendments to the British law on integration and to study modalities of assistance on behalf of West Indian migrants settled in the United Kingdom. On the other hand, they agreed to consult together regularly on their future policy and on matters dealing with tourism, air transport, the university, all of which had been the reason for calling the convention originally.

The Port of Spain convention became the basis of co-operation and strong regional integration which were subsequently confirmed by the founding of the Caribbean Free Trade Association (CARIFTA), in May 1968, followed by the Caribbean Development Bank (CDB), in October 1969, the Caribbean Community (CARICOM), including the Caribbean Common Market in July 1973, and the Organization of Eastern Caribbean States (OECS), in July 1981.

Unlike the Caribbean Community which is composed of English-speaking members only, the CDB is open to third countries. At first, only sixteen regional members received loans and two non-regional members, the United Kingdom and Canada were included. It increased in size, notably with the admission of Venezuela in 1973, of Colombia in 1974, of Mexico and Anguilla in 1982 and of France in 1984. The Caribbean Development Bank tends essentially to promote co-operation and economic integration between states, and see to it that the poorest ones may be particularly taken care of.

The Caribbean Free Trade Association having been replaced by the Caribbean Community, co-operation has been accelerated between the member countries with regard to health, education, meteorology, agriculture, tourism, fishing and transport. Much foreign aid coming from organizations such as the International Monetary Fund, the European Community, or United States, Canadian and international institutions, was enlisted in order to facilitate CARICOM interventions.

The English-speaking countries, except when the Caribbean Community was operating, had few institutionalized exchanges with France and its West Indian departments: Guadeloupe, Martinique and French Guiana. Only since 1970 has their relationship become active, with the signature of the agreements of Lomé. Since then, little by little, the three French departments started to get to know their neighbours better and to discover progressively their West Indian way of life.

# Guadeloupe, Martinique, French Guiana: Territories isolated from their environment in the past

## Political causes

Colonial antagonisms, over the centuries, between the European powers, caused the French Antilles populations to be opposed to those of the British West Indies as well as to the Spanish and Dutch West Indies. The extension of European conflicts to the Americas deeply divided the populations, mostly when they were often required to defend the geopolitical and geostrategic interests of their respective colonial powers. Language barriers reinforced the isolation of the French territories. Indeed, the use of the Creole language, the temporary occupation by France of British colonies, the temporary British occupation of Guadeloupe or Martinique, favoured relationships, notably between the two territorial units of Dominica and St Lucia. But, on the whole, each large geopolitical entity resided in its natural area. The French colonies, less numerous and more sparsely populated, surrounded by English-speaking or Spanish-speaking territories, suffered much more from their isolation. The distance of Haiti from the French colonies in the south, the demographic economic underdevelopment and the marginalization of French Guiana, due to its penitentiary, contributed also to limit trade inside the French-speaking Caribbean area.

Much more integrated into France, with regard to politics, Guadeloupe, Martinique and French Guiana were very different from the British and Dutch Caribbean colonies, particularly since 1870. Electing their representatives and senators who sat in the French parliament, the populations of these territories were more politically, administratively and judicially assimilated to the European French, especially since the transformation of these colonies to overseas departments, in March 1946, then into region-departments in 1982. The possibility of organizing a larger political region including Guadeloupe–Martinique–French Guiana, did not get unanimous approval from the representatives of these three departments, though this did not prevent the implementation of a co-ordinated relationship with the neighbouring countries.

As French departments, Guadeloupe, Martinique and French Guiana, which are also integrated into the EC, benefit from numerous transfers of public funds which allow local authorities to answer the various needs of their populations. On the other hand, these region-departments benefit from the possibility of having their inhabitants emigrating freely to France, thus improving the local employment market, and more generally the living conditions of the resident populations. These positive factors explain the vertical relationship with France, leaving little room for major horizontal trade between these departments and their Caribbean and American neighbours. As a result, there is a very strong European feeling on the part of local politicians, and a lack of interest, even some kind of contempt, towards the other Caribbean countries and their people.

It must be said that for a long time political parties and local unions have been and remain simple appendices of larger French organizations. Anxious to defend their local interests, strongly linked to metropolitan or European institutions, political élites very often remain more interested in European and African problems, due to their cultural or ideological affinities, than in the Caribbean and American problems.

Political divisions are also a reality in the French departments of the Caribbean. With the system of departmentalization, political relations are much more vertical between these territories and France than horizontal between the same departments. Colonial antagonism and traditional insular individualism often interfered in any political harmonization between Guadeloupe, Martinique and French Guiana. The refusal to found a single Antilles–French Guiana region, rich in a human potential of 700,000 inhabitants and likely to offer considerable economic development is explained by this.

## Economic consequences

The trade of Guadeloupe, Martinique and French Guiana with other Caribbean countries is very restricted, especially if it is compared with that developed with France and the EC. Year after year, exports from the islands to the free zone (France and overseas departments) reach three-quarters of total sales. Exports to the Caribbean area were 1.06 per cent and 1.37 per cent of the total amount for Guadeloupe and Martinique in 1987. They were practically nil for French Guiana. Trade was mostly with the United States–Puerto-Rico, Trinidad and Tobago, St Lucia and Dominica.

Imports from these three territories come essentially from the free zone, i.e. 50 per cent to 75 per cent. Those coming from the Caribbean area – United States–Puerto Rico, Trinidad and Tobago, Venezuela, the Dutch Antilles – remain insignificant in some years.

The similarity of agricultural products coming from the surrounding countries makes them direct competitors, which is a serious obstacle to trade. Oil supplies, when they come from Caribbean countries, diminish the European imports quota. This overall picture is only different for the islands of St Martin and St Barthélemy, with their free port statute inside the department of Guadeloupe favouring trade with Caribbean and American countries. The United States represents the principal supplier in St Barthélemy. Purchases coming from France and other European countries: food stuffs, consumer goods, equipment facilities, energy needs, considerably exceed exports in value. The covering rates are therefore very low, ranging from 11 to 20 per cent according to the departments. The weakness of exports to the Caribbean area is due to the economic system in this area, characterized by a very limited domestic demand. To this must be added the protectionist policy of the CARICOM states, including the OECS members, which, by their 'negative lists' prohibit imports without licence. Another limiting factor is the preference of the Caribbean countries for the United States market with the CBI plan. At the end of 1980, imports were coming first from the United States (40 per cent) then from the United Kingdom (7 per cent), the German Federal Republic (5 per cent), from Japan and Canada (4 per cent). France has only 2 per cent trade with these countries. As far as Caribbean exports are concerned the United States remains the first customer, with 45 per cent of supplies, followed by Canada (5 per cent), the Netherlands and Japan (4 per cent), Norway and GFR (3 per cent). The quota destined to France is less than 2 per cent of the whole.

## Limited cultural exchanges

In Guadeloupe and Martinique the Creole population is confronted by both an increase in foreign West Indian immigration (Haitians, Dominicans) and a steady European immigration, specially French. At the same time, United States cultural influence is becoming more and more perceptible in the French Caribbean departments as a whole. French Guiana, with its diverse ethnic composition, is facing a special cultural situation. The presence of Amerindians, a limited number of Creoles, fast growing communities of Haitians, Brazilians, Surinamians, West Indians and French, the development of the Kourou space station and the success of the services system attract many, often illegal, immigrants from surrounding areas.
Even if the former French colonies are linked by their common

French language direct exchanges remain limited. Cultural co-operation with other Caribbean populations has been hindered by the Europeanization of Guadeloupe, Martinique and French Guiana. With the recent political changes in Haiti large-scale actions have been studied and decided with a view to systematic co-operation with that country in the fields of education and medicine. These types of exchanges often remain insignificant, except in short-term circumstances such as requests for assistance, at the time of natural catastrophes, or within projects planned by the French government.

The DOMs' cultural isolation with regard to the surrounding Caribbean countries has been accentuated by the fact that no real effort has been made to learn foreign languages, particularly English, Spanish and Portuguese. The systematic application of metropolitan school programmes to Guadeloupe, Martinique and French Guiana, without any particular adaptation or reference to the Caribbean environment, is yet another obstacle to developing exchanges.

Despite very positive action conducted by organizations like the association INTERCA, for youth exchange and the learning of foreign languages, the populations of the DOMs, are, on the whole, unable to communicate with their non-Creole-speaking neighbours. This is true for both teachers, politicians and business managers. Conversely, the CARICOM countries have failed to develop the teaching of French in their schools, since trade with France and its Caribbean possessions is negligible.

So, despite their belonging to the same Caribbean archipelago and their geographic proximity, populations from different cultural blocs are often ignorant of each other, with the exception of fishermen who, from an early period, established ties with their counterparts in the neighbouring islands. Unable to speak to each other, not very informed of the daily life in the neighbouring countries, Guadeloupe, Martinique, and French Guiana still remain marginalized with regard to culture. The relative indolence shown by DOM businessmen, in their search for American markets, is explained by this negative aspect of their cultural heritage, and causes them always to give priority to the European markets with which they are most familiar.

## Obstacles to population movement

The lack of organic relationship between Guadeloupe, Martinique and French Guiana, on the one hand, and the surrounding

Caribbean countries, on the other hand, is a considerable impediment to regional exchanges. Large organizations dealing with the Caribbean and Americas' regional co-operation, like CARICOM, OECS, the American States Organization, Central America Common Market, the Treaty of Amazonian Co-operation, have no institutional relations with the American French departments. France alone is their interlocutor for any matter concerning Guadeloupe, Martinique and French Guiana.

In recent years, Caribbean countries of the ACP have, consequently, emphasized the difficulties encountered by their citizens to obtain visas to Guadeloupe, Martinique and French Guiana. Indeed, while Europeans, EC members, and people coming from the United States do not require visas, foreigners, like citizens from Latin America, are submitted to a compulsory visa, whatever the length of their stay. Entering Guadeloupe and Martinique is a difficult undertaking for creolophone St Lucians because of the DOMs' sensitivity with regard to the employment market on migratory problems. Also, fearing a massive Brazilian and Surinamian migration into French Guiana, French authorities do not grant any visa exemptions. However, clandestine immigration occurs across the French Guianese borders.

Another factor limiting exchange of people and trade between countries in this area is insufficient means of communication. Air and sea transport of passengers and goods serve France and Europe, North America and South America. For a long time, the Leeward International Air Transport Company regularly served the Eastern Caribbean islands. Its limited capacity was reinforced with the addition to the network of Air Guadeloupe and Air Martinique, branches of Air France.

At present, inter-Caribbean airlines fly only 15–16 per cent of the traffic between Pointe-à-Pitre and Fort-de-France airports. However, the air and sea networks remain insufficient because of the mediocre amounts of traffic.

Charges for intra-Caribbean travel, by air or by boat, are often exorbitant. The inadequacy and cost of postal transport and telecommunciations between DOMs and the surrounding Caribbean countries and the Americas are real handicaps. Mail, departing from Guadeloupe, Martinique and French Guiana, often transits through France, before being dispatched to its final American and Caribbean destinations.

## New dispositions for a broader regional co-operation

In February 1981, in Pointe-à-Pitre (Guadeloupe), there took place the first '*Contacts Euro-Caraïbes*', initiated by the Chamber of Commerce of Guadeloupe, French Guiana and Martinique. Representatives from Caribbean countries, signatories of the Lomé Convention, of countries and overseas territories of EC government members, of the Committee of European Communities, and of development organizations participated in this meeting which allowed the parties concerned to stress the obstacles to regional co-operation.

The third Lomé Convention, known as Lomé III, operating during the period 1985–90, opened new perspectives to DOM–ACP countries' trade. The plenipotentiaries of member states and the Community, and those of ACP States, issued a common declaration on co-operation between countries signatory to the Lomé III and the PTOM and DOM. This declaration is a part of the annex VII of the Convention. It was calling for a larger co-operation in the Caribbean.

Strongly supported by the EC, in the face of the United States' Caribbean Basin Initiative (CBI) and the Canadian assistance plan to CARICOM countries (CARIBCAN), the Chambers of Commerce and Industry of the DOMs integrated in CAIC, launched a second '*Contacts Europe-Caraïbe*', in April 1987 in Fort-de-France, to strengthen regional co-operation. Nearly 400 participants from the private and public sectors representing countries participating in Lomé III, PTOM, DOMs, and EC countries, as well as foreign observers, summed up the action undertaken since 1981. Forty recommendations were issued in the economical, social, cultural, medical and technical fields, in order to contribute to development in this part of the world. Concurrently, many businessmen on the spot met to conclude particular agreements.

Recommendations concerned co-operation between the ACP states, PTOM and DOMs, commercial promotion, trade, tourist development, transport, telecommunications and free zones, training, research, mutual knowledge of rules and customs in business relations, medical co-operation at times of natural catastrophe, cultural and sports co-operation.

### Other interventions in the private sector

Other initiatives were taken in the course of the past 15 years by socio-professional groups in Guadeloupe and Martinique, in particular by the Chamber of Commerce in Guadeloupe. Following a bid by the Secrétariat aux Affaires Economiques of OECS, this institution was trusted with the responsibility of a technical assistance programme and training, aiming at improving craftsmanship in six islands, all of them OECS members.

Many firms located in Martinique and Guadeloupe have (through their Chambers of Commerce) multiplied market surveys, in order to trade, set up business in the neighbouring countries or create joint-ventures with private partners. As a result, these contacts allowed the DOM contractors to be better known in the area. Investments by Martinicans in St Lucia, St Vincent and the Grenadines, Dominica or Trinidad and Tobago, have been increasing regularly, both in industrial production and in commerce and tourism.

In recent years, in order to face the disastrous economic consequences predicted from the Single European Act, producers in the DOMs met those neighbouring countries which belonged to the Convention of Lomé. These two groups, exporting identical products to the EC markets, realized their common interest in co-operating. Banana producers, meeting in Martinique, signed an agreement in September 1991, in order to reinforce their solidarity on the European banana market. The objective of the agreement was the fight against any attempt to dismantle national market organizations profitable to bananas coming from the Caribbean, which might provoke their elimination, by admitting low-cost bananas from third countries.

## EC initiatives

The European Community is inclined more and more to favour rapprochements between DOMs and OCT and ACP countries located in the same geographic area. It tends to arrange specific steps allowing the DOMs to be better integrated in their regional environment. The Lomé Convention and the DOM Programme of Specific Options to Distance and Insularity (POSEIDOM) adopted by the EC on 22 November, 1989, serve as a legal and financial frame to these applications. Appendix VII of the Third Lomé Convention, contents of which have been included in Appendix 32 of the Lomé Convention, states explicitly that the EC must support any co-operation initiatives that are undertaken between ACP, OCT and DOMs.

## A larger commitment from the French State

### French government interventions until 1989

Co-operative plans undertaken by the government have been relatively numerous since 1984–7. Assistance regarding civil protection is shown by the emergency aid given to the regional countries that have been victims of natural catastrophes, notably hurricanes. Dominica, Montserrat, and St Kitts-Nevis, much affected by hurricane Hugo, were able to benefit from French assistance initiated from Guadeloupe and Martinique.

Co-operation regarding security, police and customs was especially developed with surrounding countries. Political co-ordination between France and other Caribbean countries has been necessary, since 1989, to fight drugs. The third and fourteenth inter-Caribbean customs conventions in 1977 and 1991 which took place in Martinique were approved by the French state.

As of 1976 and 1984, first Haiti, then the Lesser British West Indies OECS members benefited from various plans carried out within the co-operation plan of development. French interventions in Haiti after the collapse of Duvalier's regime were variable, due to the instability of the different governments.

A mission of co-operation responsible for bilateral development schemes, was set up in Castries (St Lucia) in 1984 with partners such as Antigua-Barbuda, St Kitts-Nevis, Dominica, St Lucia, St Vincent and the Grenadines, and Grenada. Agreements to co-operate have been drawn up with some of these countries, since December 1987, along with the formation of the first joint commissions.

Financial resources coming from the Ministère de la Coopération et de la Caisse Centrale de Coopération Economique provide grants from the Fonds d'Aide et de la Coopération (FAC) which passed from 20 million francs in 1984 to 150 million francs in 1988. They are used to improve rural development, the habitat, productive infrastructures, the promotion of small firms, cultural and linguistic programmes, notably the teaching of French and the diffusion of French culture and techniques.

Government interventions through its Ministry of Foreign Affairs amount to 15–20 million FF per year, since 1987. They aim at developing the French presence in the Caribbean area and Cuba, and concern the Dominican Republic, Jamaica, Trinidad and Tobago, Surinam, Barbados and Guyana. These financial resources are often devoted to the teaching of French, and some other cultural, scientific and technical schemes. The result of these different actions remains limited, since the creation of a real French politics of regional co-operation in the Caribbean is recent, going back to a delegation sent in 1988 by the Ministry of Foreign Affairs and Co-operation. Only in August 1989, was it possible to discuss co-operation with Surinam.

## The conference in Cayenne

On 5 and 6 April 1990, the French government organized in French Guiana, with the prime minister Michel Rocard, a conference in Cayenne, in order to present his new doctrine regarding regional co-operation between Guadeloupe, Martinique and French Guiana and their neighbours. Among the participants at this important meeting were Jacques Pelletier, Minister of Co-operation and Development, Louis le Pensec, Minister of DOM-TOM, Madame Edwige Avice, Minister Delegate to the Secretary of State, the Minister of Foreign Affairs, and the French diplomatic corps in the Antilles–French Guiana.

At this conference, the prime minister expressed his government's new objectives: to help developing direct relations between AFD and their neighbours, in order to strengthen the political decentralization in these region-departments; to extend French influence in this part of the world; to promote a real co-operation for development and see to it that Europe ceases to appear as a threat in the context of the 1993 Single Act, to Guadeloupe, Martinique and French Guiana. On the other hand the prime minister stressed the government's willingness to ensure the fullest possible development of the overseas departments and territories in their regional environment, putting an end to a traditional colonial practice of isolation. In short, the French government, clearly breaking with the past, was calling Guadeloupe, Martinique and French Guiana to take into account their future in the Caribbean area, in the Americas, and to organize the best co-operation possible with their neighbours.

Many financial resources have been released by the French government in order to implement the new regional co-operation. Everything suggests that these measures, implemented by the French government, should favour regional co-operation in the Caribbean area. The recent and effective participation of France in the ASO conference on commerce and industry in Miami at the end of each year, its contribution to the Caribbean Action Plan for the Environment set up within the United Nations Programme for Development, and its admission to the Caribbean Development Bank, give it a stronger presence in the area. The Caribbean partners are, for their part, very satisfied with the French assistance added to that of the United States, the Commonwealth and Canada.

## New population trends

Up to 1970, with the high degree of assimilation of Guadeloupe, Martinique and French Guiana into France and the underdevelopment characterizing the neighbouring countries, no room was left for regional co-operation. The rise of nationalism in the three DOMs, contesting departmentalization-regionalization, gradually modified this state of mind. As a result of the persisting economic crisis in the AFDs, the economic and social failure in the 1980s, followed by many migrants' return to their department of origin, the commitment of the government towards a regional co-operation, as well as the consequences of the Lomé Conventions, led the populations to question the development strategies of their countries. Another factor raised more questions in Guadeloupe, Martinique and French Guiana: the meaning and consequences of the 1993 European Single Act.

Until 1981, French politics in the West Indian departments were strongly contested by autonomists and supporters of independence. Seen from Paris, Basse-Terre, Fort-de-France or Cayenne, the opposition political representatives were often considered as 'the ones wanting French money but not the French'. With a new socialist President of the Republic, the political arena had to be modified in France and in the AFDs. The autonomist opposition became the new majority in Guadeloupe, Martinique and French Guiana.

As a result of the economic crisis of the 1980s, more and more unemployed migrants came back to their countries of origin, often influenced by the increase of racism in France. Then, at the same time, in these departments, metropolitan French immigration was developing, adding to that of Haitians and Dominicans to Martinique and Guadeloupe, and of Surinamese and Brazilians to French Guiana. Even if the government and political parties, supporters of departmentalization, dispelled as much as possible people's anxiety, anti-European feeling was shown to be on the increase, mainly in Martinique, where economic conditions and social contradictions are the most difficult.

The assertion of such anti-European feeling was followed by a new interest in the West Indian world by an increasingly substantial élite. With the rise of their standard of living, people were more inclined to travel abroad, for touristic, professional and cultural visits. After discovering Paris and 'la métropole', French West Indians of all ages discovered with more and more enthusiasm the Lesser Antilles, St Lucia, Dominica, Barbados, Antigua, St Maarten, Trinidad and Tobago, Puerto Rico, the Dominican Republic, Haiti, even Cuba. Increasingly, the American continent attracts visitors from AFDs, notably the United States, with Florida as a major stopover point, but also Venezuela and Canada, to cite only the most frequented destinations.

The presence of numerous immigrant communities coming from other countries in the area, supporting public demonstrations on behalf of the struggle of the Caribbean people, gradually made the AFD populations aware of the political, economic, social and cultural problems in the Caribbean and the American world. None the less, Guadeloupe, Martinique and French Guiana remain today relatively cut off from their American environment, even if several positive factors show the populations' willingness to be more sensitive to the West Indian and American way of life. Caribbean countries, conscious of the DOM's limited political and judicial capacity for developing their economic, social and cultural needs, developed direct contacts with the French government and thus the EC, rather than with the other overseas departments.

The recent world turmoil, with the collapse of the European socialist bloc and the strong request for assistance from the countries newly-converted to economic liberalism, risk, however, compromising the willingness of the French government to strengthen this regional co-operation. This regional co-operation is further in doubt given that the Caribbean countries are themselves facing considerable development problems.

ACP    African, Caribbean and Pacific States
AFD    American French Departements
CARICOM    Caribbean Community
CARIFTA    Caribbean Free Trade Association
CBI    Caribbean Basin Initiative
CDB    Caribbean Development Bank
EC    European Community (now EU European Union)
FAC    Fonds d'Aide et de la Coopération
OCT    Overseas Countries and Territories
OECS    Organisation of Eastern Caribbean States

# CHAPTER 8 | West Indians in France

*Alain Anselin*

Beginning in 1945, France used unqualified labour to fuel the 30 'glorious years' of economic expansion that followed. Up until 1975, wave upon wave of immigrants arrived in France, coming from Mediterranean Europe, from the Maghreb and from former black African colonies which France (after having modified their frontiers) had just restored to their former independence, and completed the generalized use of female labour in order to satisfy the needs of the French economy. Between 1962 and 1975, two million jobs were created in this way, representing 10 per cent of the active population of France.

The policy of encouraging emigration from the West Indies, set up by France in the early years of the Fifth Republic, first with the help of Departmental Labour Agencies, and shortly afterwards by a state agency, the Bureau pour le Développement des Migrations des Départements d'Outre-Mer (BUMIDOM), is essentially no more than one important aspect amongst others of French labour policy. It is only secondarily that it forms part of French demographic policy, its purpose being to check and regulate the population explosion in the West Indies by means of contraception (which, quite correctly, was welcomed by women) and of emigration (which transferred the population surplus in the West Indies to a France still suffering from the negative demographic effects of the war years).

Four successive plans, from 1961 to 1981, determined the volume of emigration and its distribution in the labour-deficient sectors of the French economy: construction, metallurgy, the care industry (towards which male emigrants were directed), hospitals, national organizations, and domestic service (towards which female emigrants were directed). As early as 1958 official commissions were studying the installation of the system and setting up the apparatus responsible for recruitment of labour in the overseas departments. A network of link organizations was established, and a series of regulations drawn up to control the system's dealings with its various partners, be they individual 'migrants' or public service enterprises. Transit centres, staffed essentially by women, were established to complement the reception service provided by the Adult Training Programme (FPA).

For 20 years the four national plans fixed on an unchanging quota for emigrants that the BUMIDOM attained as early as 1965: 2,500 people per island per year, in other words 5,000 emigrants annually for the two islands, Martinique and Guadeloupe, combined. As early as 1965, again, the number of persons emigrating under the aegis of BUMIDOM exceeded the number emigrating spontaneously on their own initiative and came to represent 60 per cent of the total outflow of emigrants.

The France of the 1960s exported to the sugar plantations of its 'American departments' the modern urban lifestyles born of its postwar prosperity. Three indicators, with no link between them other than the movement of history that determines the social and economic phenomena they express, are enough to suggest the profound mutation undergone by Martinique and Guadeloupe in the 1960s and 1970s: declining sugar exports, emigration, and the increasing number of cars. A rural, colonial world quickly vanished, unable any longer to sustain an active human population. An Old World – France – was rejuvenated by the population that it took from its 15-year-old overseas departments and exported to them lifestyles and consumer patterns that the ensuing 15 years would establish there in an irreversible manner.

Beginning in 1965, Martinican sugar exports fell by 25 per cent, collapsing to zero in 1975 (89,000 tonnes exported in 1963; 62,000 in 1965; 2,000 in 1974). At the same time, close to 50,000 Martinicans left the island for France, half of them under the aegis of BUMIDOM. Emigration replaced sugar on the list of exports and became the principal 'product'. The sugar islands became repositories of labour, condemned to economic and demographic decline. Transfers of public funds, which provide the islands with their income, were devoted to consumer products and transformed the islands into a huge market for French goods. Between 1965 and 1975, the number of cars imported into Martinique matched the number of people 'exported': 55,000 'entries' as against 50,000 'departures'. This means that throughout these 10 years, for every four Martinicans who left the island, five cars were imported. Under slavery a man was worth less than a mule: today he is hardly worth a car. Goods arrive, human beings depart. The island is increasingly impoverished, but the level and style of life it accepts disguise its economic collapse.

After 1975 the global crisis led France to accelerate its policy of modernization, above all the conversion of its old labour-based economy into an economy based on technology and geared to an ever increasing rate of productivity. The structure of employment in France was radically altered, the tertiary sector being the principal beneficiary of the movement that emigration from the West Indies followed and faithfully reflected. Millions of jobs were created in this sector over 20 years but were scarcely able to make up for those lost by industry and were insufficient to absorb the tens of thousands of young people who come on to the labour market each year. Demand for jobs increased more quickly than openings became available. The role of unemployment in France doubled in 10 years and reached 8.4 per cent in 1982; the rate of unemployment amongst emigrants increased threefold to 12.7 per cent. West Indian emigrants no longer arrived in a prosperous country with scarcely more than 200,000 unemployed, but in a society in crisis with more than 2,500,000 out of work. The unemployment rate amongst emigrants who had arrived since 1972 rose in consequence to 20.1 per cent in 1982.

From 1975 onwards, the world crisis led BUMIDOM to restructure its activities, to reduce the number of professional placements and to give precedence to bringing families together. When, at the end of 1981, BUMIDOM ceased operation, it brought to their conclusion a labour policy and a population policy that had laid the foundations of a new community in France: West Indian emigrants. In 20 years, from 1961 to 1981, it had established an employment policy that continues to be followed since its demise and had been responsible for the installation of 84,572 of the 192,632 West Indian-born people in France enumerated in the 1982 census, in other words 43.90 per cent of the total.

Most of the active population that BUMIDOM conveyed to France had a precise economic destination, a place reserved for them in the productive or service sectors. The programme of professional training that was advanced as an article of faith in the media affected no more than 12 per cent of arrivants. Those whom BUMIDOM installed in France, at the completion of its programme of professional insertion and regrouping of families, were fated to remain in low-grade jobs in a restricted number of economic sectors.

It is difficult to see, in 1992, how the island economies, unproductive, dependent and with little diversity, could reabsorb in the future returning emigrants who have been trained by the thousand to perform low-skill tasks: postal (18,000 plus) and hospital (15,000 plus) workers, public sector employees, domestic workers, typists and office workers.

Table 8.1

| Activity | Number | Per cent |
|---|---|---|
| Installation with training by: | | |
| FPA | 8,988 | 10.63 |
| Others | 2,038 | 2.41 |
| Installation without training | 29,678 | 35.09 |
| Demobilized soldiers | 11,187 | 13.23 |
| Regrouping of families | 32,681 | 38.64 |
| Totals | 84,572 | 100.00 |

Source: Bilan de l'activité du BUMIDOM au 31 décembre 1981.

Socio-professional concentration has as its corollary geographic concentration: the emigrant community lives where it works. Two-thirds of West Indians in France live in the Parisian region. Half of its members are distributed amongst ten *arrondissements* in Paris and in 20 or so suburban districts: Sarcelles, Bobigny, Aulnay-sous-Bois to the north of Paris, and Créteil to the south.

The West Indian community is inscribed, as it were, contrapuntally in the major changes to which France has been driven in its quest for rejuvenation amid the global crisis. The emigrant community is a community of the young and active within an ageing society. Six out of ten of its members are active, as against four out of ten within the host society. The proportion of senior citizens amongst West Indians is forever declining (8 per cent in 1975, 3.6 per cent in 1982), whilst it continues to rise in French society as a whole. West Indian emigration represents a transfusion of new blood into an ageing society: one West Indian in three was aged between 25 and 34 in 1982, more than one in two (57 per cent) between 15 and 34, as against one in three for French society as a whole (31.5 per cent). Its high proportion of women (51 women for 49 men) combines with its youth to transform what was originally a migration of producers into a migration of reproducers.

The youthfulness of the West Indian community is not, however, rewarded with any collective advance in society. The West Indian community seems to be following the general movement of the French host society, and appears to be contributing to remedying its economic and demographic deficiencies. But the gap that separated them in 1960 had grown still wider by 1990. The number of West Indians in senior administrative positions has increased fourfold during the last 30 years, but the proportion in such positions has fallen from 20 per cent of the total active population to 10 per cent. At the same time, the number of unskilled workers has increased eightfold, the number of office workers tenfold. But the fact that office workers now make 30 per cent of the total active population (as against 20 per cent 30 years ago) does not mean that the West Indian community as a whole has moved forward in society. Its socio-professional movement in France has not been vertical but lateral: people have changed jobs, not their position in society.

*Table 8.2  Socio-professional distribution of active West Indians in France*

| Category | Year | | |
|---|---|---|---|
|  | 1962 | 1975 | 1982 |
|  | % | % | % |
| Management | 21.5 | 14.0 | 12.0 |
| Office workers | 19.0 | 28.7 | 29.2 |
| Unskilled workers, service personnel | 46.5 | 49.7 | 53.2 |
| Police, army | 13.0 | 7.6 | 5.6 |
| Total | 100.0 | 100.0 | 100.0 |

*Source:* INSEE.

The West Indian community has been subject, especially since 1975, to two simultaneous but contradictory movements, one taking the form of an ascension and integration within the wider society involving an ever diminishing proportion of its members, the other consisting of a 'relative decline and marginalization' that is stressed in official reports by the Inspection Générale des Affaires Sociales.

Education reproduces and amplifies this social dynamic. Children from emigrant families are twice as likely to go to *lycées professionnels* (secondary modern schools) than French children who are more than twice as likely to proceed to sixth form level as West Indians. Children from the lowest socio-professional categories follow the least prestigious courses in education, and three-quarters of West Indians in France belong to the lowest socio-professional categories.

The relative decline in the community's economic and social situation is reinforced by the nature of the spontaneous movement of migration which took over from the diaspora of the 1960s. This dropped on to a shrinking French labour market the rejects and failures of an educational system which keeps a growing majority of young people enmeshed in the islands without resolving the problem of job outlets on the spot. By the year 2000, people will be leaving later and with a better education, but they will still be leaving, and perhaps for destinations other than France.

Since 1975, official studies have noted the declining educational and vocational qualification of 'spontaneous migrants' and the dangers of an increasing marginalization that awaits them. But if, since 1975, the unemployment rate amongst West Indians in France has doubled, rising from 6 per cent to 12 per cent, it still remains three times less than the rate in Martinique and Guadeloupe where it is around 35 per cent for the whole of the potentially active population, but around 50 per cent for young people between 15 and 24. Such young people have thus tended to move from the country with the highest rate of unemployment to the country with the lowest and to take the traditional path of the diaspora that links the two poles of the system: Guadeloupe and Martinique in the Caribbean, France in Europe.

Three decades have sufficed to make of the West Indian emigrant community a 'third island' embedded in the very heart of Europe. Close by virtue of history and numbers to the West Indian communities in Britain and the Netherlands, and neighbours with whom it forms the archipelago of exile. This archipelago of 1,200,000 people is approaching the end of the twentieth century in the suburbs of London, Paris and Amsterdam where a third of these new 'islanders' were born.

As far as the West Indian community in France is concerned, 1980 represented the end of an era, the last years of which favoured female emigration and the regrouping of families, and established the conditions for a demographic vitality which created a whole new second and, already, a whole new third generation, both increasingly numerous. Integration in the wider society continued, dictated by employment which dispersed the same members of community into a range of often precarious executive positions. The community became stretched between the two extremes of the social hierarchy, concentrated and numerous at the bottom, dispersed and without real weight at the top.

In the 1980s a new era began. It was, first of all, the era of the myth of the return, a myth fostered by subsidized periods of leave established by law in 1978 in a growing number of professions. It was the era of a mini-diaspora. The ANT, which succeeded BUMIDOM in 1981, sought, along with the regions, to draw and organize a current of migrants back to the overseas departments (whether the 'migrants' had been born there or not). It was a current characterized by its competence and professional experience, with a view to filling the gaps in skilled employment that had been ascertained in the West Indies and to promoting a Caribbean labour policy based on regional development projects.

It was the era when installation in France became a definitive reality, accompanied, as its necessary complement, by the setting-up of a mass of associations and other organizations which became the focus for the assertion of cultural and social identity, culminating in the right of periodic return (established in 1978) and in the creation, in 1986, of the carnivals of Paris and Marseilles. The development of religious phenomena, such as attendance at Protestant or 'West Indian' churches and recourse to *quimboiseurs* (obeah-men), underlines the moral and psychological fragility of these 'definitive migrants' who have difficulty in taking control of their lives in a context which is legally favourable to them, but unfavourable from a social, economic, cultural and human relations viewpoint and which is further impaired by the rise of racism.

The increase in petty or moderately serious delinquency amongst the younger members of the community, and the decline in trade union membership – already low – amongst its older members, appear to indicate the growing marginalization of the community as a whole.

The 1980s witnessed the emergence of new forms of political practice which affirm at one and the same time West Indians' right to a separate identity and their full membership of French society. People listen to the West Indian radio stations that have appeared in the last ten years and which broadcast the same musical programmes that can be heard in the islands. People also listen to news bulletins that come directly and on the same day from Martinique and Guadeloupe: political life in the islands has ceased to be a distant myth.

Finally, people participate directly in the political life of France. Some vote, though not yet in large numbers, but above all people become candidates and get elected to municipal councils. Political life has ceased to be a distant mythical realm in which one delegates to others the task of looking after one's material interests. The West Indian has become an immigrant who uses his or her political rights.

The community is affirming the independence of its political life at the very moment when it is becoming more conscious of the links that bind it to its countries of origin, Martinique and Guadeloupe.

# CHAPTER 9

# Women from Guadeloupe and Martinique

*Arlette Gautier*

Studies undertaken in the 1950s about West Indian women mostly centred on their roles as mothers and sometimes as tradeswomen.[1] In order to compensate for this deficiency, an in-depth research project has compared the totality of women's roles in the English-speaking West Indies.[2] In the French West Indies information is much more fragmentary[3] even though the census, and especially the employment surveys, permit analysis of the relationship of women to their work and to the family. Moreover, while literary studies are not in short supply, political analysis rarely takes into account West Indian women.

## Women's employment: exclusion for some, discrimination for others

The decline of agriculture and its incomplete replacement by a state subsidized economy (*transferts publics*) have been accompanied by a change in women's occupations, but also by an increase in unemployment.

### From farmers to employers and teachers

Throughout history, although women have performed important and productive activities, the value of these efforts has for the most part not been recognized since they were practised within the family without any monetary compensation. In the West Indies, the insufficiency of men's wages and the large number of single-parent families have often led women to work for wages and even to become dock workers.[4] In 1954 in Guadeloupe, for example, 39.6 per cent of women worked in agriculture; 28.3 per cent in dressmaking, fashion, lingerie, hat making, weaving, mattress making or in wickerwork; 12.5 per cent were servants; and 10 per cent were in trade.[5] These occupations represent 80 per cent of women's occupations surveyed and 60 per cent of them are in the productive sector. Since the 1930s, women farmers often worked only two to three days a week for salaries that barely allowed for the upkeep of their families. During the rest of the week, and between harvests, these women would iron, do washing or work in a trade. This underemployment, in both its visible (low work hours) and invisible (low wages) manifestations, is a persistent reality of West Indian life. Even though the percentage of women's activity was above 37 per cent, it is sufficient to read the childhood memoires of Patrick Chamoiseau from Martinique[6] to see that, although women exercised a variety of productive occupations, the multiplicity of these poorly compensated jobs made them difficult to measure by census takers.

The situation remained unchanged until the beginning of the 1960s when women's employment began to shrink in the agricultural sector as a result of mechanization and then because of the collapse of the agricultural sector. The clothing, weaving, etc. sectors also shrank with the introduction of ready-to-wear and other imported products from mainland France.[7] In the 1970s women's employment rose again, in part because of the multiplication of jobs in the public sector and later on as a result of its expansion in the commercial domain: development of shopping centres and of the service sector.

According to the 1986 employment surveys, the exclusion of West Indian women from the productive sectors is complete since 90 per cent work in the tertiary sector (89 per cent in Martinique), even though the total number of women in Martinique is much closer to that of men than is the case in Guadeloupe.[8] The largest category is that of servants followed by clerical workers and then teachers. Thus for every 100 women employed in Guadeloupe,[9] 18 per cent are in the intermediate professions (half are teachers, a third work in the health sector, and the rest are in social services), 8 per cent are craftswomen or shopkeepers, 7 per cent are manual labourers, 4 per cent are salaried employees, and 2 per cent are in agriculture. The remaining 61 per cent are employed half in the service sector, a third in the clerical field, and 14 per cent are in business; thus their life experiences are different. The number of hours worked in commerce is higher than that in the clerical sector even though monetary compensation is comparatively low. Women in the service sectors work only a few hours a week or for salaries of about 1500 francs per month. Approximately half work in private homes (their numbers are undoubtedly underestimated) and rarely have access to social security benefits: an especially acute problem for single mothers (a problem not experienced by workers (20 per cent) employed in the public sector). Moreoever, this category of women is especially subjected to the contempt and sexual harassment of some employers.[10]

The number of women in a profession is highest in those fields under hierarchical (masculine) control and lowest in the managerial or independent fields since 73 per cent of employees are women, 55 per cent are in the intermediary professions, and between 22 per cent and 25 per cent are found in other socio-professional categories. If both women and men have salaried positions in the private sector, men outnumber women three to one as employers; 2.3 per cent more men are independent than women which hurts salaried personnel in the public sphere. Forty-seven per cent of declared women workers are employed in the public sector, which does not guarantee, however, steady employment. The 1980 employment survey[11] demonstrates that only men have strong upward mobility: one-third of males from Guadeloupe over 40 years old quit their jobs for a higher position while women's development is more discontinuous, mobility is rare and their trajectories are often downward; their principal destination being service personnel.

*Table 9.1:  Employment status by sex in Guadeloupe in 1986*

|  | Employers | Independents | Salaried personnel public | Salaried personnel private | Salaried personnel together |
|---|---|---|---|---|---|
| Female | 2.9% | 8.1% | 47% | 41.2% | 42,976 |
| Male | 9.5% | 18.3% | 30.8% | 41.3% | 54,624 |

*Source:* 1986 Employment survey, *Femmes en chiffres*, Guadeloupe, 1988, p. 27.

The balance sheet of half a century is thus modified: one woman out of every four or five women in the work force achieved a certain professional status in the education or health services sectors within the welfare state, another quarter however work as servants. Moreover, the first group of women is often the employer of those in the second group, a situation which does not promote solidarity among women. The position of women servants and employees in commerce is often a precarious one.

## Rise in unemployment, decline in underemployment

*Table 9.2:   Types of activity in Guadeloupe and Martinique in 1980 and 1986*

|  | Guadeloupe | | | | Martinique | |
|---|---|---|---|---|---|---|
|  | 1980 | | 1986 | | 1986 | |
|  | F | M | F | M | F | M |
| Normal employment | 35.9% | 56.3% | 3.4% | 58% | 39.5% | 52.7% |
| Underemployment | 32.3% | 26% | 33% | 20% | 23.3% | 14.2% |
| Unemployed | 30.4% | 17.6% | 33% | 22% | 37.1% | 33% |

*Sources:* INSEE employment surveys. Guadeloupe 1980: Hervé Domenach; Jean-Pierre Guengant – 'L'emploi en Guadeloupe', *Dossiers Antilles-Guyane*, 8, 1984: calculated from pages 77 and 89 by adding the two surveys from March to June and from October to December 1980. 1986: *Antiane éco 7*, July 1988. Martinique: *Femmes en chiffres. op. cit.* Calculated from tables 38 and 40 on pages 41–2.

Since the first employment surveys in 1969–70, underemployment has declined while unemployment has risen as a result of the modernization of the economy (stable employment has been relatively well compensated) which, in turn, has diminished the attractiveness of the traditional sector and increased the ability of the family to sustain itself *vis-à-vis* those of its members out of work. While this evolution is the same for both sexes (except from 1980 to 1986 where underemployment rose slightly among women), women are much more affected both by underemployment and by unemployment since West Indian men enjoy a majority – although slight – in regular employment whereas this was the case for only one-third of women from Guadeloupe and for 40 per cent of the women from Martinique in 1986. This holds true for any socio-professional category since women farmers and manual labourers are twice as likely to be underemployed as men, reaching extremely high rates of 70 per cent, and women from Martinique in other categories are underemployed three times more often than men but at lesser rates: 40 per cent for women shop owners and employees, and only 15 per cent for the middle and upper level salaried personnel. For this last group, it is without doubt a question of part-time employment linked to women's family obligations, and this despite the fact that West Indian civil servants are less likely to be employed part-time than their colleagues in the metropole. This could be because it is easier and less costly to have housekeepers.

The most severe problem is unemployment which has risen continuously since the 1970s as a result of the collapse of the agricultural sector which has been relieved only in part by the tertiary sector because of the number of young people entering the work force. Thus from 1982 to 1990, 24,000 jobs were created in Guadeloupe and 17,000 in Martinique. Despite these advances, the numbers of unemployed have risen twice as fast as the creation of jobs: an expansion of three times more jobs in Guadeloupe and four times more jobs in Martinique would have been necessary to offset the rise in unemployment. Unemployment hits French West Indian women of all ages harder than men since a quarter of the men are unemployed compared to more than a third of unemployed women. Unemployment represents not only a problem at the entry level of the work force but is a persistent reality throughout French West Indian women's work life. The duration of unemployment is often extended, as between 15 per cent and 17 per cent of the women out of work (those looking for jobs) have been unemployed from one to two years and half of them for more than two years. The duration of unemployment is longer in Martinique. This particularly high level of unemployment of French West Indian women is explained both by their exclusion from the productive sectors and from the small number of liberal professions, and by the preference given to men in the work place.

*Table 9.3:* Unemployment rates by age and sex within the workforce of Guadeloupe and Martinique in 1990 (percentages)

|  | 15–19 | 20–24 | 25–29 | 30–34 | 35–39 | 40–44 | 45–49 | ENS |
|---|---|---|---|---|---|---|---|---|
| **Guadeloupe** | | | | | | | | |
| Female | 73.1 | 61.3 | 50 | 37 | 28.1 | 22.2 | 19.2 | 37.2 |
| Male | 69 | 48.6 | 33.8 | 21.5 | 16.7 | 13.6 | 12.6 | 25.9 |
| **Martinique** | | | | | | | | |
| Female | 72.3 | 64.2 | 50.6 | 38 | 26.5 | 20.2 | 17.8 | 36.2 |
| Male | 69 | 54.2 | 38.3 | 24.9 | 17.9 | 14.6 | 12.8 | 28.4 |

*Source:* INSEE – CENSUS.

In general, the notion of the contribution of salary favours males in the work place: men feed a family while women work for their own comforts. This point of view, already criticized in industrial countries, is even more so in the French West Indies where a little less than a third of families with children are headed by single mothers. Thus the rate of unemployment among these women, which was a third in 1954 and 1961, has since risen to more than half. The rise in unemployment is therefore linked to the collapse of women's traditional occupations that took place before women had acquired family allowance rights in 1975. These single mothers have only the family allowances on which to survive and these have proved to be highly insufficient as we shall see.

## Incomes

The fact that women earn less than men is a universal phenomenon in which the gap varies in time and place. In the French West Indies, legislation provides for three levels of minimum compensation: civil servants earned 6,000 francs in 1986 (in fact only half of the salaried positions in the public sector earn that much while 15 per cent earn less than the minimum wage); the salaried personnel in the private sector received less than 4,000 francs, a sum many salaried personnel do not even receive; the allowance for domestic workers was not even 2,400 francs per month. In Martinique in 1986 half of the women received monthly payments of less than 4,500 francs whereas half of the men received more than 6,000 francs. In Guadeloupe, the distribution of incomes is more even, however, 32 per cent of the women receive less than the minimum wage compared to 26 per cent of the men. The gap in the distribution of allocations is especially noticeable above the 6,000 franc level. In the French West Indies as elsewhere, compensation paid to women is less because they are in lower paying occupations and because they earn less than men even when they are in the same occupation. Thus, according to the 1980 employment survey in Guadeloupe, if the compensation paid to women farmers was 100, men farmers earned 105, salaried agricultural workers earned 188, employees earned 156, lower-salaried staff earned 158, craftsmen and shop owners earned 188, service personnel earned 233 (this group is made up of taxi drivers, caretakers, and those who work in the cleaning services). In fact women from the ages of 15 to 39 earn only 85 per cent of what men earn and women from the ages of 40 to 59 earn even less: only 71 per cent since they benefit little from promotions (thus 91 per cent of women in lower-salaried staff positions stayed at the same level compared to 64 per cent of the men), and because some young women had access to better paying positions in the public sector than did their elders. All the same, if women employees (excluding domestic activities) and those in salaried positions earned less than did their male colleagues, they earned more than those women in other categories.

Moreover, the 1986 statistics in Martinique indicate clearly that the inequality of remuneration for women carries over to the educational level where the gap diminishes only for those salaries above the minimum allowance in the public sector with equal or superior educational qualifications. Thus, men who have not completed elementary school are two times more numerous than women at that level to receive more than the minimum allowance in the public sector while at the high school graduate level, 80 per cent of women from Martinique and 91 per cent in Guadeloupe received this compensation.

Large numbers of the unemployed turn to welfare. This is true also for older workers who have been eligible for retirement benefits since 1950, and for women whose access is more limited since they earn less in the professional occupations. Unemployment benefits have existed only since 1980. At the present time, a quarter of those unemployed do not receive any benefits because they have not yet worked and have left school before receiving their diplomas, or because they have been unemployed for over a year which is most often the case with women. Moreover, French West Indians are entitled to a guaranteed minimum revenue if they are handicapped adults (1800 francs per month), single parents (since 1978) or without any other sources of income (since 1989). Many more women than men receive these allocations because of their exclusion from the work place: 15,000 in Martinique and 16,500 in Guadeloupe. Parents are entitled also to certain allocations for their children but these benefits, although they have recently been raised and should be adjusted again before 1992 so that their value is equal to those in the metropole, are far from adequate to compensate for the price of raising children.

Forming a large marginal class within their society, 80 per cent of French West Indian women are either excluded from the work force, in occupations whose positions are precarious, or are earning very low wages. Do marriage and motherhood represent alternative solutions for these women?

## West Indian women and family life

The debate on family relations in the West Indies has focused on the mother at the expense of the more current approaches involving the sociology of the family, for example the study of homogamy or, more recently, the study of domestic production. Moreover, the large drop in the birth rate encounters certain limitations within the lower working class sectors.

## Matrifocal families

The term 'matrifocal', created by Raymond Smith in the 1950s[12] has been used in at least three different ways: 1) the family domain for three generations (grandmother, her daughter(s), and their children); 2) the domicile of a single mother and her children, which has come to be known as 'single-parent'; 3) a household where, even if a man is present, his role is overshadowed by that of the mother.

According to the world fertility survey of 1975, the first type of household made up only a little more than 3 per cent of all households (including those without children) in the French West Indies.[13] However, censuses in Guadeloupe show that from 1954 to 1974, between 16 per cent and 18 per cent of households headed by women living with children less than 15 years old, were headed by women who were more than 60 years old and who could not therefore have been their mothers: they raised by themselves or with their own children their grandchildren or children who had been left in their care. In 1982 this percentage was 11 per cent: possibly access to benefits for single mothers has allowed these mothers to live alone with their children.

As for single parents, Charbit[14] has shown that the nuclear family is in the majority throughout the Caribbean, although single parent families represent a quarter of the families with children in Martinique and a third of those in Guadeloupe, three times the rate for those same families in the metropole. The analysis of censuses taken in Guadeloupe since 1954 shows that the proportion of families headed by women has changed little, declining from 30 per cent in 1954 to 26.2 per cent in 1967 and then rising again after this date (before the creation of family allowances) to 28.6 per cent in 1982. One is struck by the stability of the large numbers of single parent households, even though the French West Indies have undergone considerable social transformations, and by the lack of impact of family policies which were suspected at first of artificially stimulating the rise in nuclear families, and since 1975, of causing their decline.

Single mothers belong to the most underprivileged classes. In Guadeloupe in 1982, half of the single mothers were out of work. For those with jobs, 35 per cent held salaried positions in agriculture, 30 per cent were manual labourers, 25 per cent were farmers and domestic workers, 12 per cent were lower-level civil servants and

10 per cent belonged to liberal professions. Moreover, 69 per cent of single mothers did not finish elementary school compared to 50 per cent of the married women. Employment and education are thus two resources encouraging married life. The lifestyle of single parent families is worse than that of couples: half of all single mothers live in one or two rooms with only one child compared to only a quarter of couples with one child; 53 per cent of single mother's homes lack modern necessities (running water, bathroom, toilet) compared to 39 per cent of couple's homes. According to a 1988 survey of 95 lower-class families living in Pointe-à-Pitre and in the town of Côtesous-le-vent, women become single parents due to their lack of knowledge about contraception, to the difficulty in setting-up a household (a problem which is more acute in rural areas), and because they have been abandoned; only 18 per cent have preferred to leave violent or unfaithful men. Never have they chosen to have babies alone; these results could be different in the case of the more rare privileged women.

Sixty per cent of all single mothers are not married. Celibacy, which in 1990 involved a quarter of women from Martinique and 29 per cent of women from Guadeloupe between the ages of 50–54, a time when celibacy becomes permanent, is especially prevalent among those women in the most underprivileged classes. Contrary to the experience in France, the most educated women marry as often as men, and to spouses with less education. Working women most often marry men belonging to lower socio-professional classes. The number of single women, however, at least when they are young, either living with a man or maintaining friendly relationships with men without living with them, has increased in Martinique from 1968 to 1976, reaching 24 per cent of the women in the ages between 15 and 49 compared to 17 per cent in Guadeloupe. These increases took place before women had access to family allocations as single mothers.[15] Moreover, the higher death rate among men and the fact that they remarry more often than women after divorce or the death of their spouses explains why the majority of women are not married between the ages of 35 and 59. The percentage of women still married between the ages of 60–74 is not more than 43 per cent; thus married life proves to be relatively short for West Indian women.

The third meaning of the term 'matrifocal', that attributed to it by R.T. Smith, goes back to the centrality of mother-children relations and to the loss of interest by men who live mainly outside the home with their friends or mistresses. The sociologist and linguist Dany Bébel-Gisler[16] from Guadeloupe confirms and lends legitimacy to this analysis, as well as France Alibar and Pierrette Lembeye-

Boy's 63 extremely poignant narratives, collected in *Le Couteau seul.*[17] Thus Leonora's (a country woman from Guadaloupe described by Bébel-Gisler) two spouses, were ladies' men leading lives for the most part in the 'lolos' (small boutiques where men meet especially to talk while drinking rum and playing dominoes) instead of in the home.

A woman has always to be ready to cook for her companion regardless of the hour, if not he will often consider it normal to beat her.[18] A man's frequent absences from the home do not keep him from dominating it. Moreover, the employment situation that makes married life a necessity for many women and the large number of West Indian women without spouses do not favour the position of women within marriage or with relation to the fidelity of men. It would seem, however, that the situation is changing in the middle classes and among the young.[19] An extensive survey, one including the privileged sectors, would be necessary in order to grasp these transformations.

Given this situation, one can understand that a West Indian woman overinvests in the child who should give her the affection that she does not always receive within the couple. Childrearing remains rather strict, however, and the father, if he is present, is generally in the position of authority. Half of the women inhabitants of Guadeloupe surveyed did not find it unusual to take out a belt to 'teach the child respect', a practice which truly terrorized some children.

## A different mobilization of women's occupations according to the socio-professional categories and to the islands

In 1990 the income tax returns of salaried workers in the private sector, of farmers, and of fishermen (excluding civil servants and independent workers), showed that 57 per cent of the couples in Martinique had only one source of revenue compared to 86 per cent of the couples in Guadeloupe within the same categories. This inequality undoubtedly comes from the higher rate of underemployment in Guadeloupe. The situation differs according to the professional standing of the spouse: thus in Guadeloupe in 1980, 75 per cent of the spouses of civil servants and of clerical employees carried out occupations that were compensated (at 90 per cent within this category) compared to 40 per cent of the spouses of domestic servants, of farmers or of salaried farm workers. At the same time in

Martinique in 1986, members of the liberal professions and of the higher-salaried staff positions primarily married among themselves, while the same phenomenon holds true for the employed and those unemployed. On the other hand, more than 40 per cent of the manual labourers and of the employees, as well as more than half of the men from other categories, married women out of work. These marriages thus reinforce social inequalities since privileged households often have both partners employed.

The wives and mothers living alone, labelled 'out of work', dedicate themselves to their children and to domestic production, a situation which may stem from the difficulty these women have in finding work, from the fact that rural mothers cultivate a garden, and from the lack of household appliances, a problem which further increases the housework. In fact, even though lodging conditions have clearly improved, not only since 1954 but even more so between 1982 and 1990, 20 per cent of housing in Guadeloupe and 14 per cent of housing in Martinique still do not have running water, electricity and half are not linked up with sewer systems. Moreover, only 58 per cent of the housing in Guadeloupe is equipped with washing machines compared to 53 per cent in Martinique, and there are very few launderettes. Again, social differences are important since in 1985 in Guadeloupe the rate with washing machines varied from 27 per cent for the farmers to 86 per cent for civil servants and those in the liberal professions. The importance of the differences in household appliances leads one to assume that housework varies greatly among social classes, even more so since those who are the best equipped can also benefit from the work of servants, which also helps to avoid the question of the division of domestic work for the husband. For all women, though, the work involved in raising a family has been reduced with the decline in birth rates.

## The incomplete revolution of fertility

In the 1950s, a French West Indian woman had on average 5.5 children. This number rose slightly in the 1960s, reaching 5.8 in Guadeloupe, and then rapidly declined reaching within 15 years a level of 2.3 for Martinique and 2.6 for Guadeloupe. The decline has been slightly more rapid and pronounced in Martinique. One can imagine the implications of these changes (the decrease in family size by three children) in the life of French West Indian women. Explanations of this decline vary. For Charbit and Léridon[20] this decline could be explained by the diffusion of the metropolitan model of smaller families which continued to be at variance, at the time of their survey in 1975, to the tradition of high birth rates in the islands: thus 24 per cent of the women surveyed living in Martinique and 29 per cent of those women living in Guadeloupe have no idea about the desirable number of children although 30 per cent felt that they have had too many children. According to Poirier,[21] the economic transformations linked to the collapse of productive activities have modified the foundations of the post-slavery family economy and therefore the 'demand' for children (even more so as the infant mortality rate has greatly decreased). This was the case in 1960 for the new middle classes and in the 1970s for the other categories whose relative size has since declined. Thus single mothers from underprivileged social backgrounds would have more children since they contribute much more to the family revenue (40 per cent of the total family revenue for farmers and salaried farm labourers over 40 years old) than children from nuclear families where women heads of household came from socially privileged classes.

It might be suggested that this is confusing the effect with the cause since women in these milieux complain especially about not having known earlier about contraception. For Dagenais and Poirier,[22] it is a question of the desire of West Indian women, who for a long time had been using ineffectual, if not dangerous, local methods of birth control (various herbs, pineapple preparations), to have access to new family planning centres. In our opinion, these various interpretations complement rather than contradict one another. They do not take account of, however, one important factor, namely that pregnancy in general is much more of a burden for women than for men especially since men rarely participate in the upkeep (in the case of single parents) or in the upbringing (in the case of nuclear matrifocal families) of the children. Until the 1960s, the only available means of contraception (withdrawal, condoms) depended on the goodwill of the male, who seemed rarely to use them. In fact a large number of unwanted children are born, especially to single mothers. In our opinion, the belated decline in the birth rate among the underprivileged classes can be explained as much by the slowness in the diffusion of an innovation like the pill as by the weak bargaining position of women, especially that of mistresses.

In 1990 the birth rate in the French West Indies was comparatively low but there was a relatively large number of births among adolescents (the birth rate among French West Indian women between the ages of 15–19 is more than 50 per cent compared to 22 per cent in France), also a group of women with high birth rates. Social workers and a part of public opinion explain this phenomenon by the desire to 'have children in order to receive benefits'. In fact, in 1988 among those women living in Guadeloupe without occupations between the ages of 30–39, at the height of their reproductive years and whose children represent the heaviest burden, 18 per cent had only one child and 28 per cent had two: half of these 'single women' can therefore be exonerated of the charge of having children for money.

In general, the women surveyed living in Guadeloupe in 1988[23] wanted two or three children (whereas the ideal number was four in 1975) to 'make up a family'. In other words that the children will surround them and give them emotional support. However, a number of these women had already gone beyond this number, for single women as well as for couples, because of a lack of knowledge about birth control methods. Thus 16 per cent of rural women had had their first child when they wanted compared to 29 per cent of the couples and 36 per cent of the women from Pointe-à-Pitre. Two variables are essential: first, place, because the city allows the dissemination of information, and secondly, age. A number of unwanted pregnancies resulted from the first sexual encounter where no precautions were taken. Thus more than a third of the rural women questioned had their first child before the age of 17, and none had wanted them. Youth aggravates the lack of information problem as much as parents who often refuse all sexual education so as not to 'encourage this vice' in their daughters.

A third of the couples and of single women in Pointe-à-Pitre compared to 45 per cent of the rural women did not use contraception even though they did not want children. Two-thirds of those who did not use contraception did not know about it, while the remainder of women were afraid of its side effects, of cancer or of becoming sterile. Failures of contraceptives are equally numerous: 45 per cent of the couples and of the single mothers in rural towns, 30 per cent of mothers without spouses in Pointe-à-Pitre. A few single women do not accept well sporadic sexual relations, especially as they would have wanted children but under different conditions: with a spouse and a job. Moreover, more than 10 per cent of the women were not able to have the abortions they had wanted, half of them for monetary reasons. As for the men, they do not feel contraception is their obligation in the case of relationships with mistresses even when they have relationships with minors. In fact, judicial action is rarely taken against them. A few older men are against their wives using contraceptives.

The media plays a large role in misinforming the public by spreading false notions about the pill. Women not using contraceptives have rarely completed elementary school (57 per cent of women in Guadeloupe in 1982), a fact that makes them particularly receptive to the distortions of the popular media. Doctors rarely take the time to contradict these myths or to explain the real functioning of birth control methods; the unwillingness of some is especially pernicious in rural areas where it is difficult to find a more understanding doctor. The state also played a role in perpetuating the misunderstandings since, until 1990, information about the advertisement of contraceptives was illegal. Thus, women could not read a different type of information in the women's publications.

Exclusion from the work place, the demands of domestic production, a birth rate whose decline is recent and unequal are all factors influencing West Indian women's access to public life.

## Women in public life: many voters, few elected

Although French West Indian men have been able to vote since 1870, women could not vote until 1946. At this time, 33 per cent of the women in Martinique voted compared to an average voter turnout of 36 per cent, although no women were elected and it was necessary to wait until 1983 to have the first woman (de Grandmaison) seated next to men at the regional council. In Guadeloupe, however, Eugénie Eboué (Socialist Party) was elected to the constituent Assembly of 1945 followed by Gerty Archimède (Communist Party) who was elected to the National Assembly from 1946 to 1951. It was necessary to wait for Lucette Michaux-Chevry (Socialist Party and then Rassemblement for the République, RPR) and then the Guadeloupe Party (Parti guadeloupéen) which she founded, before a woman deputy from Guadeloupe was elected again. Michaux-Chevry would even become President of the General Council and then Secretary of State for the French-speaking countries in the government of Jacques Chirac, the first woman from an overseas department nominated in a government and the first 'person of colour' since 1932. The success of a few personalities in Guadeloupe should not make us forget, however, that the situation is very similar in the two islands (Table 9.4).

In 1970 women represented only 3 per cent of the 62 political and economic leaders surveyed by Murch;[24] in 1987 women made up 15 per cent of the elected West Indian officials although for the most part they were at the municipal council level. At the higher levels (general and regional councils, mayors) women represent only 4 per cent and 1.5 per cent of the elected officials in Guadeloupe and

Table 9.4: Elected officials in Guadeloupe and Martinique broken down by
sex, for 1987

|  | General council | | Regional council | | Mayors | | Municipal councils | |
|---|---|---|---|---|---|---|---|---|
|  | F | % | F | % | F | % | F | % |
| Guadeloupe | 2 | 5 | 3 | 7 | 1 | 2 | 160 | 16 |
| Martinique | 2 | 5 | 0 | 0 | 0 | 0 | 143 | 17.6 |

Source: Regional Council, Femmes en chiffres op. cit. Guadeloupe: 52.
Martinique: 46.

Martinique respectively. There is only one woman for every four
deputies and no women senators.

French West Indian women's polit-
ical power would seem, therefore, not to have evolved except for
their rise to power in the municipal councils and for the fact that a
few women are mayor's deputies in the large communes (like Robert
in Martinique). These changes seem to indicate that West Indian
women are slowly gaining confidence and that they are obtaining a
working knowledge of politics. In France women make up 5.5 per
cent of the deputies, less than in 1945. Women's progress has been
noticeable, however, in the independent countries of the Caribbean:
in 1971 women made up only 4 per cent of the leaders from the
English-speaking West Indies whereas today 9.7 per cent of the
deputies are women, 11.7 per cent are senators and 4.5 per cent are
ministers.[25]

It has been asked whether West Indian women vote differently
from men. In 1981, a newspaper accused women from Martinique of
lacking dignity because they would have voted for the right because
of family benefits and especially benefits linked to single parents,
issues repeatedly denied by the right.[26] In the absence of electoral
surveys, explaining the votes and determining the reasons for them
are nothing but conjecture. If women had really voted for the right,
this could be explained, as was the case in France in 1981, by the fact
that they are more numerous and older than the men and that they
have been compensated less often and are not in socializing occupations. In France, since the massive integration of women into the
work force, the women's vote has changed profoundly and they are
now more to the left than are the men. Moreover, it is necessary to
point out that the benefits for single women are highly criticized and
stigmatized whereas other benefits do not raise such indignation, for
example the cost-of-living bonus which raises the salary of civil servants sent to the overseas departments by 40 per cent compared to

those in France, regardless of whether an increased productivity justifies it. Beneath the criticism – usually made by men – of benefits for single women, there may well lie a fear of the degree of autonomy, however limited, that such benefits confer on the women concerned.

In 1965 associations in favour of birth control were created by women and doctors in order to allow West Indian women to choose the number of children they wanted, thereby permitting a certain liberation of women. In Guadeloupe the association 'Maternité Consciente' has always been controlled by women whereas the associations in Martinique have been controlled by men. These associations have run into strong opposition, especially from the Communist Party (adhering to the party line issued from France), but also from spouses who received visits from social workers with machetes in hand. Later on, however, the Union of Women in Guadeloupe and Martinique, who were close to the Communist Party, led a movement to sensitize and inform women through their press and through their legal actions. Thus the Union of Women in Guadeloupe organized a demonstration against the killing of five women by their partners and has taken legal action in cases of rape and violence against women. In Pointe-à-Pitre the communist-controlled city hall has opened an information centre, 'Solitude', maintaining a legal crisis centre which often deals with these problems. An autonomous women's movement has not emerged, perhaps because the action of feminists in France has led to the abolition, at least on paper, of the most flagrant injustices.

French West Indian women, after having experienced the great disadvantages (at least in political life) of numerous pregnancies, suffer from desocialization through exclusion from the work force or by a scarcity of jobs. Women from the middle classes who benefit from steady employment, especially in the public sector, and from the use of servants who free them in part from a double work day, would be better suited to enter political life, as they are beginning to do at the municipal council level. But these women run into other obstacles: when it is not a problem of the all-consuming lifestyle of single parenting, it could be the sexism of spouses who want to control their movements, as well as that of political parties who grant only to men the right of permanent employment within the party, or it could be because some newspapers continually attack the social rights of mothers without questioning those benefits going to men. Thus, there can be no equality and therefore major participation of women in power without taking into account motherhood, a burden only for the mothers but an enrichment for the entire community.

# Conclusion

French West Indian women have experienced a large number of transformations within the last half century which have given them a relatively high standard of living within the global community: an acute decline in mortality, as much in the general population as for children; a decline in the birth rate; a rise in the level of education; and improvements in living conditions. Other areas are more negative: continued male domination manifesting itself through violence and the weak political representation of women. The economic and social evolution has allowed the development of a creole middle class which 20 per cent of the women reach because of their occupations. These women have benefited from all the positive factors and have achieved economic independence, even though they are discriminated against at the level of salaries and of jobs. On the other hand, the large majority of West Indian women have not benefited from the progress in education or in living conditions and are excluded from, or marginalized within, the work force thus reducing their chances of forming couples and impairing their negotiating position within the couple.

The comparison of the two islands shows that they share essentially the same characteristics. Martinique, however, is slightly more 'modern' in certain respects: underemployment for women is lower (28 per cent compared to 33 per cent in Guadeloupe) but unemployment is higher as is the proportion of nuclear families. On the other hand, more women from Guadeloupe have attained fame, whether in the literary field or in politics, a fact which could be related to a more entrenched history of fighting for women's interests, especially at the level of associations.

## Notes

1 Huguette Dagenais, 'L'apport méconnu des femmes à la vie économique et sociale aux Antilles: le cas de la Guadeloupe', *Anthropologie et sociétés*, 8, 2 (1984), pp. 179–88.
2 Pat Ellis (ed.) *Women of the Caribbean*, Zed Books, 1986.
3 For further information, consult France Alibar and Pierrette Lembeye-Boy, *Le Couteau seul. La Condition féminine aux Antilles* (Editions Caribéennes, 2 vols., 1981–2; the special numbers on French West Indian women of *Nouvelles questions féministes* (9–10, 1985) and *Les Dossiers de l'outre-mer* (82, 1986); and the statistical surveys *Femmes en chiffres: Martinique* and *Femmes en chiffres: Guadeloupe* published by INSEE-SERAG in 1988 and 1989 respectively.
4 Cécile Celma, 'Les femmes au travail en Martinique (17e–20e siècles): première approche', *Les Dossiers de l'outre-mer*, 82 (1986), pp. 24–31.

5 INSEE, *Résultats statistiques du recensement général de la population des départe-ments d'outre-mer effectué le 1er juillet 1954*, Imprimerie nationale/Presses univer-sitaires de France, 1956.

6 Patrick Chamoiseau, *Antan d'enfance*, Hatier, 1990, pp. 69–70, 159.

7 Huguette Dagenais and Jean Poirier, 'L'envers du mythe: la situation des femmes en Guadeloupe', *Nouvelles questions féministes*, 9–10 (1985), pp. 53–83.

8 In Guadeloupe 55,000 men work compared to 42,700 women, while in Martinique the numbers are 48,300 and 46,500 respectively.

9 *Femmes en chiffres: Guadeloupe* (INSEE-SERAG, 1989), p. 27.

10 Michel Laguerre, *Urban Poverty in the Caribbean. French Martinique as a Social Laboratory* (Macmillan, 1990), pp. 77–95. See also Arlette Gautier, *Politique familiale et familles monoparentales en Guadeloupe* (ASD/CNAF, 1989).

11 Jean Poirier, *Structure sociale, modes d'organisation familiale et baisse de la fécon-dité en Guadeloupe (1954–1982)*, Collection de thèses et mémoires 23, Université de Montréal, 1989, pp. 150–8.

12 Raymond T. Smith, 'The Matrifocal Family', in *The Character of Kinship*, Jack Goody, (ed.) Cambridge University Press, 1973, pp. 121–44.

13 Yves Charbit and Henri Léridon, *Transition démographique et modernisation en Guadeloupe et en Martinique*, Presses universitaires de France, 1980, p. 30.

14 Yves Charbit, *Famille et nuptialité dans la Caraïbe*, Presses universitaires de France/Institut National d'Etudes Démographiques, 1987.

15 Charbit and Léridon, *op. cit.*, p. 45.

16 Dany Bébel-Gisler, *Léonora. L'histoire enfouie de la Guadeloupe*, Seghers, 1985.

17 See France Alibar and Pierrette Lembeye-Boy, *Le Couteau seul. La Condition féminine aux Antilles* (Editions Caribéennes, 1981–2).

18 Three quarters of the married women from the Alibar and Lembeye-Boy sample had been beaten by their husbands (Alibar and Lembeye-Boy, *op. cit.*, Vol. 2, p. 68).

19 Alain and Catherine Jacquet, 'Les freins socio-psychologiques à l'évolution de la condition féminine en Guadeloupe', *Les Dossiers de l'outre-mer*, 82 (1986), pp. 111–20.

20 Charbit and Léridon, *op. cit.*, p. 172.

21 Poirier, *op. cit.*, p. 213.

22 Dagenais and Poirier, *op. cit.*, p. 67.

23 Gautier, *op. cit.*, pp. 105–35.

24 Alvin Murch, *Black Frenchmen. The Political Integration of the French West Indies*.

25 Maurice Satineau, *Contestation et politique aux Antilles. Les élections de 1981*, L'Harmattan, 1986, pp. 55–6.

26 Ellis (ed.), *op. cit.*, p. 13.

CHAPTER 10

# The idea of difference in contemporary French West Indian thought: Négritude, Antillanité, Créolité

*Richard D.E. Burton*

When Martinique and Guadeloupe[1] became departments of France in 1946, they were, despite the long-standing Francocentric orientation of their mainly coloured middle class, profoundly different in cultural terms from the *mère-patrie* into which they would henceforth be assimilated politically. This cultural distinctiveness rested on, and was sustained by, an economic infrastructure which, in the case of Martinique, had consistently been in credit from 1905 onwards and would remain so until two years after departmentalization.[2] Earnings from the export of sugar, bananas, citrus fruit and rum regularly exceeded the cost of imports from France. Peasant agriculture and fishing met the basic food needs of the local population, most clothes, shoes and furniture were made locally, and the testing circumstances of 1940–43, when the Vichy-dominated islands were effectively severed from the outside world by an American blockade, had demonstrated the ingenuity with which Martinicans and Guadeloupeans could, when necessary, use local resources to replace the products – soap, for example, or rope – which they had traditionally imported from France.[3] The *habitation* and peasant holding together formed the matrix for the colonial culture which, with variations from country to town, and across the class-colour spectrum, was undoubtedly creole – that is, an autochthonous creation, combining a diversity of elements (principally European and African, but also Indian and Amerindian) in a manner that is entirely distinctive, entirely *sui generis* – rather than a set of African 'survivals' or a mimetic version of the culture of metropolitan France.

The Creole language – a signifying system composed, very crudely, of a preponderantly French-derived vocabulary married to a syntax and morphology of basically African origin – may be seen as paradigmatic of the creole culture as a whole. Neither 'African' nor

'European', but a dynamic synthesis of both with, above all, a defining identity of its own, it existed in a state of tension with the dominant French language which the coloured middle classes, together with upwardly mobile blacks, sought to master along with the French humanist culture to which it gave access. While the hostility towards Creole relayed by the republican school (and by middle-class households) is not to be doubted, Roland Suvélor has argued that the relationship between Creole and French in colonial Martinique and Guadeloupe was not, in terms of everyday living, as inherently conflictual as a widely-held contemporary view would have it.[4] French and Creole, he claims, each had its culturally allotted space, with speakers shifting with ease and agility from one code to the other as context and circumstance demanded, creating a situation in which, despite the 'official' antagonism between them, the two languages in effect complemented rather than clashed with each other.

The very disparagement of Creole preserved its distinctiveness as a signifying system, protecting it from the kind of infiltration by the structures and vocabulary of standard French that is so widely attested in the contemporary French West Indies. 'Officially' banished from the middle-class household, Creole was in fact used by adults amongst themselves and by children amongst themselves, though rarely, according to Suvélor, for cross-generational communication where French was the norm. French may have been the language of power and prestige, but Creole was used on a day-to-day basis with ease, pleasure and, if Suvélor is right, with a marked absence of the anxieties and penalties generated by its use in the creolophobic context of the classroom. The relationship of French and Creole, in this presentation, was one of parallelism rather than of conflict, with each preserving its separate identity and function, held apart as they were by the ideological valorisation of the first and the corresponding devalorisation of the second. Outside the Francocentric middle classes and those who aspired to join them, contact with the dominant language would be rare indeed: here *créolophonie* reigned with only marginal interference from standard French.

The linguistic parallelism evoked by Suvélor may be extended to cover the colonial culture as a whole. That culture was undoubtedly split between a valorised French status to which members of the middle classes aspired (without forsaking every aspect of the creole culture) and a devalorised creole stratum to which the vast majority of the islands' population remained confined (without, however, remaining wholly immune to aspects of the dominant culture). The *béké* élite preserved the freedom and power to inhabit simultaneously or alternately either the French or their own variant of the creole culture. As with language, so with religion, family structure, diet, dress, entertainments, and so on: if that which was French (or perceived to be so) was systematically elevated above that which was creole, the very devalorisation of the creole stratum had the paradoxical effect of preserving its integrity. But, though 'officially' opposed one to the other, the French and the creole components of colonial culture were, in practice, contiguous rather than antithetical. Participation in the rituals of the Catholic church, for example, did not exclude recourse to *quimboiseur, dormeuse* or *gadedzafé*, no more than the official promotion of religious or civic marriage stood in the way of the mass of the population forming kinship relations far removed from the French ideal of the nuclear family. The French and the Creole were undoubtedly unequal, but at least they were *different*, and the relationship between them may, partly because of that difference, have been less conflict-ridden, and above all less anxiety-generating, than many modern conceptualizations of colonial society are inclined to admit.[5] To say this is in no way to idealize colonial Martinique and Guadeloupe as, ironically, many contemporary nationalists are, in their hostility to departmentalization, prone to do. Creole culture had its roots in the world of the *habitation*, but the foundation of that world was the gross exploitation of labour, not least that of women (the *amarreuses*) and children (the *petites bandes*). Perhaps the creole culture only preserved such vitality in colonial Martinique and Guadeloupe because the vast majority of the islands' population was denied material and educational access to the French culture above it.

Colonial Martinique and Guadeloupe were, then, unequal (both in their internal structure and in their external relationship to France) but, in some fundamental way, *different*. The *départements d'outre-mer* or *régions monodépartementales* that they have become are, in theory, and increasingly in fact, the equal of any 'hexagonal' department or region, but they are widely perceived as having lost, or to be inexorably in the process of losing, that margin of otherness without which no human community can exist as a separate entity. Political assimilation has been accompanied, in a way that its instigators surely did not intend, by a massive assimilation not of French culture (or selected aspects of it) but by French culture as an undifferentiated totality.[6]

The agricultural base on which the traditional creole culture was founded has been eroded beyond all possibility of restoration, leaving that culture – where it survives at all – increasingly bereft of any anchorage in the actual lived experience of contemporary French

West Indians and, as such, subject to a fatal combination of folk-lorization, exoticization and commodification. The modern French West Indian is, it is often argued, as much a spectator of his or her 'own' culture as the average tourist. 'Culture', like everything else in Martinique and Guadeloupe today, seems to be for consumption rather than actively produced in a living human context. At every level – most noticeably in language, dress, diet and kinship patterns – the otherness of the French West Indies has, since 1945, and particularly since the mid-1960s, been subject to the pressure of homogenization as French goods, French thought-patterns, French lifestyles, and not least, the French language itself, have swept into areas of life hitherto reserved to the autochthonous culture. But it is not just lifestyles that are subject to increasing standardization.

The wonderfully variegated Antillean landscape is itself succumbing by the day to what the increasing number of Martinicans and Guadeloupeans who care scathingly call *bétonisation*: the remorseless spread of concrete in the form of hypermarkets and housing developments, *résidences secondaires*, motorways and service roads, hotels and marinas across the countryside and beaches of the two islands. On every front, both within and without, what Edouard Glissant has called '*le Divers*' (the Different) appears to be retreating before the inexorable advance of '*le Même*' (the Same), creating the threat of 'cultural genocide' – an expression Glissant used in a widely read article published by *Le Monde diplomatique* in 1977[7] – to set beside the threat of demographic 'genocide by substitution' of which Aimé Césaire was speaking balefully at much the same time. The present chapter takes as its theme the attempts by different 'schools' of French West Indian thinkers to conceptualize the phenomenon of Difference and, hopefully, to protect its various manifestations from the multifarious 'creolocidal' pressures to which it is allegedly subject. Three principal theories of Difference – *Négritude*, *Antillanité* and *Créolité* – are discussed, the focus being on Martinique (where each of these theories has received its fullest elaboration), while the sometimes very different preoccupations of Guadeloupean thinkers are examined in counterpoint to the *idées force* that it is my principal concern to elucidate.

## Négritude and its critics

Originally formulated in Paris in the 1930s, and receiving fuller elaboration in the pages of *Tropiques* during the period of Vichyist control of Martinique, the ideology of Négritude predates the departmentalization of Martinique and Guadeloupe and in many ways responds to a different set of problems than the later concepts of Antillanité and Creolité, which are essentially counters to the processes of cultural homogenization released by political assimilation in 1946. But the affective core of Négritude, as later, of Antillanité and Creolité, is anti-assimilationism. Through it, a group of French-educated intellectuals, most notably Aimé Césaire, Léon Damas and Léopold Sédar Senghor, sought before all else to affirm their difference in the face of the reductive universalism to which their formation, relaying and reflecting the reductive universalism of the whole Republican-Jacobin tradition in France, had exposed them from early childhood onwards. This difference they formulated in essentially racial-ontological rather than historical-dialectical terms. In both colonized individual and colonized society, a surface of imposed or acquired Frenchness was held to conceal and hold temporarily captive an 'African' or 'black' substance or essence which it was the task of Négritude as combined theory and practice to release and bring to fruition. When it came to defining the 'African' or 'black' essence, the Négritude writers turned, *faute de mieux*, to European concepts of the primitive, particularly as expounded in the work of Lucien Lévy-Brühl, and to ideas of the 'African' (or 'Negro' or 'black') personality contained in the writings of European Africanists such as Leo Frobenius and Maurice Delafosse. This primary recourse to the Other for a definition of Self is proof, in the eyes of its critics, of Négritude's underlying 'heteronomy'.[8] It is seen not as a counter-discourse to assimilationism but as a sub-discourse within it which, even as it consciously challenges the dominant ideology, tends unconsciously to reproduce and perpetuate its underlying thought-patterns. Négritude is held both to counter but, more profoundly, to continue the universalist or essentialist assumptions of the assimilationist discourse that is its primary target. To the essence of Frenchness it opposes a putative essence of blackness or Africanness and, in so doing, fails to escape the transcendent, anti-historical terms in which assimilationism itself is formulated. Above all, Négritude may invert a stereotypical European definition of blackness and black culture, divesting it of its overtly racist character and transforming the negative into the positive, yet the underlying structure of that definition is retained. Négritude in this view merely substitutes one alienating definition for another and, to that extent, enmeshes the black African or West Indian still more tightly in the assimilationist problematic or scheme of things even as it seems to release the repressed and repudiated black 'essence' within him.

Such criticisms of Négritude are by now the common currency of debate in both Francophone Africa and the French West Indies[9] and would, in general, be accepted both by French West Indian Marxists (who were amongst the first to formulate them in the early 1960s)[10] and, more recently, by proponents of the counter-theories of Antillanité and Créolité. It is indeed true that the insertion of Négritude in the French West Indian context raised problems of a kind that do not seem to have arisen in the case of Afrique Noire. These problems relate in part to the political complexities of, especially, Martinique and in part to the difficulties of applying, without serious distortion, a universalist theory of blackness (as Négritude, at least in its earliest formulation, undoubtedly was) to societies like Martinique and Guadeloupe. The latter, as a result of three centuries and more of sustained physical and cultural *métissage*, are certainly not – whatever else they are or may be – 'African' or 'black' in the immediately verifiable way in which Senegal, Guinea or Côte-d'Ivoire may be said to be.

Ironically, as we shall see, Négritude, especially as embodied in the person of Aimé Césaire, has had the worst of both particularist and universalist worlds. Its race-based particularism brought it into conflict first (in the 1950s) with the class-based universalism of the French Communist Party and its local supporters and then (in the 1960s and 1970s) with the class-based internationalist analysis of the new – principally Trotskyist – French West Indian left. Then, beginning in the late 1970s, it was Négritude's own brand of 'particularist universalism' – the belief in the existence of a global 'black culture', even of a universal 'black essence' – that came under attack from proponents of the new ideas of Antillanité and, in the later 1980s, of Créolité. Having defended 'black' or 'African' particularity against the threat of French universalism, Négritude now stood accused of denying the West Indian-ness of Martinique and Guadeloupe, their complex creole particularity, in the name of a simplistic generalizing black universalism. To the elucidation of these and related complications the remainder of this section is devoted.

The context in which Négritude was originally formulated in the 1930s owed more to the anti-rationalism and organicism of the right than to the dialectical materialism of the left, but it was as a man of the left – specifically as communist mayor of Fort-de-France and communist deputy for Martinique – that its leading French West Indian proponent, Aimé Césaire, came to the fore in 1945–6. The circumstances of Césaire's 'recruitment' by the Martinican branch (as it then was) of the PCF remain obscure, but Césaire must have seen – but presumably thought he could override – the potential conflict between the race-based particularism of Négritude and the class-based universalism of the strongly assimilationist political formation he had now joined. Césaire would henceforth be committed to the proposition that French West Indians were at once 'French' politically and 'non-French' in cultural, psychological and affective terms. The pursuit of political assimilation would, ideally, go hand in hand with cultural and spiritual dissimilation from the metropolitan model. When, in 1956, the tension between universalism and particularism became too great, Césaire opted for the particular, broke with the PCF and, two years later, launched his own political party, the Parti Progressiste Martiniquais (PPM). But the form of particularism espoused by the new party was a notably muted and mitigated one – autonomy not independence – as though even now Césaire was unable to break clearly with the universalist (i.e. effectively French) assumptions he owed to his formation within the Republican-Jacobin tradition.

Throughout the 1960s and 1970s, Césaire and his supporters, harried from the right by the stalwarts of departmentalization and from the far left by out-and-out *indépendantistes*, strove in vain to reconcile the competing claims of the particular and the universal, coming close to an *indépendantiste* position in the late 1970s, yet forever failing, at the last, to break out of the assimilationist mind-set in which they had been formed. And so no doubt they would have remained, spread-eagled in a manner classically French West Indian between the Different and the Same, had not the victory of the left in the French elections of 1981, and the subsequent policy of regionalization, permitted at least a pseudo-solution, in the form of the *région mono-départementale*, to the endemic problem of the particular-universal. In the course of the 1980s, the PPM was able to establish itself as the hegemonic force in Martinican politics, drawing support from certain sections of both old right and new (or new-ish) left. However, the notable advance of Alfred Marie-Jeanne's Mouvement Indépendantiste Martiniquais (MIM) in the regional elections of October 1990 and March 1992, and in the legislatives of March 1993, suggests that the age-old question of the Different and the Same has only been fudged, and not resolved, by the so-called moratorium on discussions of the island-department's status that Césaire unilaterally declared in the wake of the left's electoral victory in 1981.

As Césaire moved through what, in his 'moratorium speech' of May 1981, he called his 35 year journey in the political wilderness from bondage in the house of communist assimilationism to the 'oasis' of socialist-inspired regionalism,[11] so the content and meaning of Négritude in its Martinican expression shifted along with him.

Under the influence of Marxism, it shed first its mystical Senghorian trappings and, contrary to the criticism routinely levelled against it, in fact moved some way from the notion of a transhistorical black 'essence' to which, in *Cahier d'un retour au pays natal* (1939), Césaire had given such memorable expression. In historicizing his concept of Négritude, Césaire also to some extent West Indianized it, though in his analysis of French West Indian culture he still tended to privilege the undoubted continuities between Africa and the Caribbean over the no less real discontinuities brought about by slavery. But if West Indian culture was no longer seen simply as a set of 'Africanisms', African 'survivals' or 'reinterpretations' of African cultural forms, neither was much prominence given to the non-African – European, Indian, Amerindian – components in its make-up. At the same time, little emphasis was placed on the multiple processes whereby all the constituent elements of West Indian culture interacted with each other and were transformed – creolized – into something neither 'African', 'European' or whatever but seized of its own inalienable West Indian quiddity. This preference for the 'pure' (the 'African' or the 'European') over the 'impure' (the creole) is nowhere more evident than in Césaire's attitude towards the Creole language itself. Although, in the interview with Jacqueline Leiner that serves as a preface to the 1978 re-edition of *Tropiques*, Césaire denies that Creole is a 'patois', he goes on to describe it as a 'neo-French language, or, if you like, a neo-African language',[12] thus sidestepping, it could be argued, the actual creole character of Creole itself. Moreover, in stating that 'I have never imagined, not for one second, that I could write in another language [than French]' and that 'for me, writing is linked to French and not to Creole, and that's all there is to it',[13] Césaire has, in the view of many of his creolophile opponents,[14] been guilty of exactly the same kind of creolophobic prejudice as the assimilationist educational system itself. His hostility to writing in Creole (and, it would seem, to written Creole as such) is evidence, in this analysis, of his failure, for all his talk of Négritude, Africanité and the like, truly to 'decolonize' his mind and break free of the straightjacket of the republican-universalist problematic in which he was brought up. Thus for the prominent creolophile novelist Patrick Chamoiseau, the fact that a play like *La Tragédie du Roi Christophe* (1963) treats a West Indian theme is not sufficient to make it a West Indian play, for all the evident goodwill of its undoubtedly West Indian author:

> [The play] liberates, it raises the consciousness, but … how French it is! […] Its French is not ours. Its sentences do not

breathe like ours, our mouths will have difficulty in articulating them. In order to be at ease in them, the actor will have to become French, articulate in a French manner, think French [...] Césaire treats the situation detached from the specific Haitian context (*en dehors du particulier haïtien*), with the arms of the universal seen through a European lens.[15]

Of course, this criticism contains rigidities and unexamined assumptions of its own. It is quoted here as evidence of how readily Césaire, seemingly the arch anti-universalist, is now seen as reproducing the underlying episteme of the very universalism his works appear to denounce.

Part of the problem, of course, is that since Césaire and the PPM have implanted themselves as the controlling force in local politics, so Négritude, or a modified version of it, has moved from being an oppositional to a quasi-hegemonic discourse. Given the close relationship of the PPM and the French Socialist party, Négritude has, in a very real sense, been recuperated by the universalist tradition (now, paradoxically, presenting itself in a decentralizing, regionalizing guise) that it originally set out to contest. In the contemporary Martinican context, Patrick Chamoiseau has argued, Négritude is no more than 'an assertion of officialized difference' (*une revendication à la différence officialisée*): 'merely to proclaim a difference that is recognized by the masters is no longer so much resistance as a form of hypnosis'.[16] The 'officialization' of Négritude since 1981 has, critics argue, fundamentally changed the meaning of the annual PPM-sponsored Festival Culturel de Fort-de-France which, when it was inaugurated in 1971, was explicitly intended to counter the Francocentric cultural discourse and practice sponsored by the French government-funded Centre Martiniquais d'Action Culturelle (CMAC). In 1976, the PPM-controlled municipal council of Fort-de-France set up its own 'counter-cultural' organization, the Service Municipal d'Action Culturelle (SERMAC) which provided, and still provides, a permanent base for the kind of 'autonomist' Négritude-inspired cultural activities favoured by the PPM. So long as the PPM remained in opposition to the political status quo, SERMAC itself played a creative oppositional role on the local cultural scene, but, as, once again, Patrick Chamoiseau, has argued,

> The arrival of the [French] socialists in power, in 1981, has neutralized the cultural discourse of the Mairie of Fort-de-France. France, which has always more or less denied it, now officially recognizes a distinct West Indian identity

(*l'identité particulière antillaise*). The cultural discourse of the Mairie has become in some way 'official'.

The consequence, according to Chamoiseau, is that 'the Festival is no longer heretical, it doesn't upset anything, it doesn't spatter people's consciousness' (*il n'éclabousse aucune conscience*).[17] By the time of the 1990 Festival, the SERMAC was as much part of the assimilationist-regionalist establishment as the CMAC, bringing, in the name of Nelson Mandela, the Ballets Maliens, Howard University Jazz Orchestra and ... Molière to the less than ecstatic public of Fort-de-France.[18] Its directors shuddered at the mere mention of the words 'Antillanité' or 'Créolité', little artistic production of significance took place under its aegis, and its increasingly dated Afrocentric discourse had ceased to engage anyone but the accredited *grangreks* of the PPM. As Martinique moves towards the perils and opportunities of 1992, it is, ironically, beneath the smokescreen of 'Difference' defined *à la Césaire* that the island is being drawn inexorably into the clutches of the Same.

## The diversity of the Different: the idea of Antillanité

From the early 1960s onwards, a new way of envisaging French West Indian identity began to be articulated by a number of Martinican thinkers. In contrast to Négritude's stress on the retention of African cultural forms in the Caribbean, this new thinking dwelt rather on the creation, out of a multiplicity of constituent elements, of a specifically West Indian cultural configuration to which, in time, the name 'Antillanité' came to be given. It seems to have been René Ménil, a former collaborator of Césaire on *Tropiques* and, unlike him, a member of the local communist party after 1956, who, in an article entitled 'Problèmes d'une culture antillaise' published in the Parti Communiste Martiniquais' journal *Action* in September 1964, first clearly formulated the idea of a West Indian specificity (*spécificité antillaise*) that would enjoy such success in the years that followed. French West Indian culture, he wrote, is

> neither African, nor Chinese, nor Indian, nor even French, but ultimately West Indian. Our culture is West Indian since, in the course of history, it has brought together and combined in an original syncretism all these elements derived from the four corners of the earth, without being any one of those elements in particular.[19]

Originally intended (or so it would seem) as a PCM counter to the PPM's doctrine of Négritude, the idea of a West Indian specificity was positively received in a variety of Martinican political-intellectual circles. It was, in particular, refined, elaborated and extended by the Groupe de Recherches de l'Institut Martiniquais d'Etudes which, headed by Edouard Glissant and bringing together a diverse and talented group of thinkers (Roland Suvélor, Michel Giraud and Marlène Hospice amongst others), published the results of its discussions and research in the regrettably short-lived journal *Acoma* (1971–73). The concept of Antillanité is not, however, confined to any one intellectual grouping or political formation. Indeed, its strength – and also perhaps its weakness – is that it is so malleable a concept that virtually everyone in contemporary Martinique, from departmentalist 'dinosaurs' to militant creolists and ultra-leftist separatists, proclaims the 'specificity' of French West Indian culture and the French West Indian psyche. As indicated above, the idea of Négritude has itself been perceptibly 'Antilleanized' under the influence of the rival concept. The fullest formulation of the concept of Antillanité is to be found in the work of Edouard Glissant and it is to his *Discours antillais* (1981) and *Poétique de la Relation* (1990) that the interested reader is referred for an elucidation and elaboration of the ideas briefly expounded here.[20]

Like Négritude before it, Antillanité is in the first place an assertion of Difference in the face of the encroachments of the Same. The whole of Glissant's theoretical work, in particular, may be seen as a sustained polemic, conducted in the name of 'le Divers', against the claims of the 'universal', to which a succession of derogatory epithets are attached in a more or less routine fashion: 'abstract', 'sublimated', 'reductive', 'generalizing', and so on.[21] For Glissant, 'the preoccupation with the universal is the alienated reverse side of the uniquely western pretension to exercise universal control'. It follows therefore that the keystone of any defence of the particular must be a 'firm opposition to any ideology of "universal culture" '.[22] Where Antillanité differs most markedly from Négritude is in its conception of the constitution of 'le Divers'. Whereas for Négritude, the Different was monolithic (because essentially 'African' or 'black') in character, 'le Divers' in the thinking of Glissant and his followers is itself diverse, complex, heterogeneous. It is made up not of a single substance or essence but of a multiplicity of relations, a constellation of forces held in place by a complex process of attraction and repulsion. In contrast to Négritude's obsession with the 'pure', Antillanité makes of *le métissage,* understood both culturally and, presumably, racially, a supremely positive, indeed constitutive, principle.[23]

Creolization itself is seen as 'unlimited *métissage*',[24] a *combinatoire* of diverse cultural materials that can never be halted, fixed or tied down, forever in the process of renewing and transforming itself. If Négritude's idea of Difference is closed, fixed and monosemic, 'le Divers' is, in contrast, open, mobile and polysemic. Whereas Négritude shares with assimilationism an essentially 'extroverted' or 'heteronomous' orientation (i.e. it looked outwards to 'mother Africa' for its models and values, just as assimilationism looked to the distant *mère-patrie*), Antillanité looks both inwards (to Martinique and Guadeloupe) and outwards (to the Anglophone and Hispanophone Caribbean and, more broadly, to meso-America as a whole) in its quest for self-invention and transcendence. One of the major advances made by Antillanité is that it has in some large measure shed the regressive, matrocentric orientation common to both assimilationism and Négritude.[25] It is less a quest for origins than a project for the future.

All these considerations are summed up in the opposition that Glissant draws in *Poétique de la Relation* between 'root-identity' (*identité-racine*) and 'relation-identity' (*identité-relation*).[26] By 'root-identity', Glissant designates univocal conceptions of identity, those modes of thinking that would assign a single origin, a single root, to a given individual or group. 'Root-identity' may be highly complex, like the tree that is its fullest expression, but it is always ultimately a mono-identity which functions by exclusion: not for nothing does Glissant go as far as to speak of a 'totalitarian root'.[27] 'Relation-identity', on the other hand, designates an open, multidimensional, polyvalent conception of identity. Refusing the idea of a single root or origin, it conceives identity as an archipelago or constellation of signifieds, none of which enjoys primacy over the others and whose unity lies not in the fact of possessing a single source but in the complex of gravitational forces that hold them in relation to each other. Taking over the distinction made by Gilles Deleuze and Felix Guattari in their *Mille plateaux* between root and rhizome (i.e. a bulb or tuber) as images of two antithetical ways of thinking the world,[28] Glissant is perhaps the first major French West Indian thinker to break away from the obsession with origins and rootedness that marks traditional Caribbean discourse (and above all the ideology of Négritude) towards the idea of free-floating, multiplicitous growth whose supreme image, in the Caribbean context, is the mangrove swamp:

> Submarine roots: that is floating free, not fixed in one position in some primordial spot, but extending in all directions in our world through its network of branches.[29]

With *Le Discours antillais* and *Poétique de la Relation*, French West Indian thought has undergone an epistemological shift of major importance: identity is no longer imagined as a single tree rooted in the landscape (as it is in such classics of West Indian literature as Césaire's *Cahier d'un retour au pays natal*, Jacques Roumain's *Gouverneurs de la rosée* and Jacques Stephen Alexis' *Les Arbres musiciens*)[30] but as a tangled, proliferating growth, without beginning or end, containing within its myriad recesses infinite possibilities of interactive transformation. Négritude's concept of identity is ontological, that of Antillanité ecological. We shall return to this crucial image of the mangrove in our discussion of Créolité.[31]

## Guadeloupean counterpoint

Approaches to the question of Difference in Guadeloupe have diverged in certain significant respects from those current in Martinique, not least because there was no Guadeloupean equivalent of the 1956 split in Martinique within the local communist party and, consequently, less immediate need to clarify rival positions on such crucial issues as the relationship between class and race and the racial (or other) basis of a putative Guadeloupean identity. There being, in addition, no Guadeloupean equivalents of, say, Aimé Césaire or Edouard Glissant, definitions of identity have, on the whole, been simpler there than in Martinique and perhaps for that very reason more effective and certainly more widely diffused. The idea of a 'Guadeloupean nation' commands much broader support than that of a 'Martinican nation' in the sister island and, while there is certainly no unity amongst the autonomist-independentist groups in Guadeloupe, there do exist substantial areas of agreement as to what constitutes 'Guadeloupéanité', which is certainly not the case amongst their counterparts in Martinique. On the other hand, if Guadeloupe has produced no theoretical construct of the subtlety of Antillanité or Créolité, it has, through the writings of women such as Simone Schwarz-Bart, Dany Bébel-Gisler and Maryse Condé, raised the question of *female* identity in the French Caribbean with a directness and perceptiveness which, thus far, has not been matched in Martinique. In addition, the question of Indianité has been thrown into sharp focus in recent years – not surprisingly since one in six Guadeloupeans are of Indian origin, as opposed to one in thirty Martinicans. If Guadeloupe bulks less large than Martinique in a study of the question of Difference in the French West Indies, it may be, paradoxically, because, for a whole range of historical, cultural and political reasons, it possesses a stronger sense of national identity than the sister island.

If there is a key to the different way in which the question of identity has been approached in Guadeloupe, it may lie in the fact that, unlike its Martinican counterpart, the local communist party not only suffered no major internal split in the 1950s but has retained a dominant position in local politics as the principal voice of the autonomist alternative to departmentalization.[32] With no-one of Aimé Césaire's personal and intellectual force to promote it, the idea of Négritude had little influence amongst Guadeloupean communists who, even after they separated from the PCF to form the Parti Communiste Guadeloupéen in 1958 (adopting an autonomist political position at the same time), continued to think along much the same class-based, assimilationist lines as before, giving priority to real or imagined class solidarity between Guadeloupean and French workers (and between black and Indian workers in Guadeloupe) over questions of racial or national particularity. Accordingly, when independentist formations like the Groupe d'Organisation Nationale Guadeloupéenne (GONG) began to challenge both departmentalism and autonomism in the 1960s, they tended to do so in the name of 'race' rather than of 'class'. In contrast, their equivalents in Martinique – whose principal target amongst the autonomist parties was the 'race-based' PPM rather than the 'class-based' PCM – were more inclined to speak the universalist language of class rather than the particularist dialect of race and to leaven their commitment to Martinican nationhood with a large measure of internationalism. Thus, while Martinican independentists were denouncing Césaire and Négritude for 'proposing to us a false and consequently alienating African identity',[33] it was precisely in the name of Africanité and a radicalized version of Négritude that their equivalents in Guadeloupe were mounting their attack on departmentalists and autonomists alike. Though the language of class has certainly not been jettisoned, it is clear that for GONG and for later independentist groups such as the Union pour la Libération de la Guadeloupe (UPLG) and the Mouvement pour une Guadeloupe Indépendante (MPGI), 'blackness' or 'African-ness' are seen as essential components of 'Guadeloupéanité', raising obvious problems as far as the department's substantial Indian minority (not to mention its significant 'petit blanc' population) is concerned. As most sections of the Martinican ultra-left began, in the late 1960s, to move away from Négritude-style thinking,[34] it was towards a version of Négritude, heavily caparisoned in the language of French *gauchisme*, that their Guadeloupean equivalents turned in their struggle against departmentalism and the 'socialo-communists' of the PCG.

For Guadeloupean nationalists, the African-ness that is believed to constitute the core of Guadeloupéanité is expressed most fully through Creole and through the *gros-ka*, the African-derived style of drumming which is systematically opposed in much nationalist discourse to the allegedly 'French', 'assimilated' or 'doudouiste' music of the *biguine*.[35] The defence of Creole began significantly earlier in Guadeloupe than in Martinique and is associated principally with the name of Dany Bébel-Gisler who, in a series of works of which *Langue créole, force jugulée* (1976) is typical, advanced a number of theses that have since become the common currency of 'glottopolitical' debate in the French West Indies. The relationship between French and Creole is a 'colonial' one based on a fundamental and inevitable antagonism, Creole is a language of resistance, the core of the repressed cultural identity of the Guadeloupean people, the political liberation of Guadeloupe from France is inseparable from the liberation of Creole from French, and so on. As we shall see, many of these ideas will be taken over in the 1980s by the Créolité 'school' in Martinique, but with one crucial difference. Whereas the Créolité school will stress, precisely, the Creole (i.e. syncretic) character of Creole, Bébel-Gisler was, as late as 1989, arguing that Creole is 'the umbilical cord binding us to Africa, to others, to ourselves'.[36] In other words, Creole is not, as it has become in the theory of Créolité, the basis for a non-racial West Indian identity but rather the expression par excellence of the underlying African-ness of Guadeloupéanité.

Similarly, in systematically opposing 'African' *gros-ka* to French *biguine*, nationalist discourse has, in the view of the leading (and by no means pro-departmentalist) Guadeloupean musicologist Marie-Céline Lafontaine, been guilty of simplifying and distorting Guadeloupe's complex musical heritage and, in the name of an illusory African-ness, denying precisely what is most creative about it, namely its capacity to bring and blend together disparate musical materials into something uniquely and quintessentially Guadeloupean.[37] In the course of the 1980s, the *gros-ka* was promoted by the UPLG's significantly named Radio Tambour as the very essence of Guadeloupéanité, resulting, in the words of one (again by no means anti-nationalist) commentator, in a 'fetishization' of the instrument[38] that denied the complexity of Guadeloupe's cultural heritage and, in particular, alienated the substantial Indian minority whose support was vital if the independentist cause was to have any chance of success.[39]

It is hardly surprising that, as nationalist discourse beat the *gros-ka* with ever greater vigour, so many Indians would feel the need to foreground *talom* and *matalon* (Indian drums), not (except in the case of a tiny minority) with any separatist programme in view but rather to secure their place in Guadeloupean society by underlining the Indian contribution to its culture. The defence and illustration of Indianité is one of the most important developments in contemporary Guadeloupe.[40] At the present time, Guadeloupean thought still seems preoccupied with the problems of 'origins' and 'roots' which, under the influence of the concept of Antillanité, many Martinicans now seem to have moved beyond. The vociferous defence of Creole does not, in short, seem to have fostered a sense of the Creoleness of French West Indian cultures as a whole, the guiding inspiration of the theory of Créolité in Martinique to which we now turn.

## The Créolité debate

The idea of Créolité – most fully formulated in the manifesto *Eloge de la Créolité* (1989), the joint work of Jean Bernabé, Patrick Chamoiseau and Raphaël Confiant – is located within the general problematic of Antillanité, the ideas and example of Edouard Glissant being constantly invoked as an essential part of reference.[41] Créolité continues Antillanité's attack on 'false' universalism in the name, now, of 'Diversalité'.[42] It insists, like Antillanité, on the necessary complexity of identity in the (French) Caribbean ('the very principle of our identity is complexity')[43] and, in general, develops Antillanité's polemic against the 'fixist', essentializing character of the discourse of Négritude in favour of a way of thinking that is altogether more mobile, open (Créolité is indeed 'defined' as an 'open specificity' [*une spécificité ouverte*] )[44] and, above all, non-racial in character:

> In multiracial societies such as ours, it is urgent that we abandon the habitual raciological distinctions and that we resume the custom of designating the people of our countries by the one term that, whatever their complexion, behoves them: Creole. Socio-ethnic relations within our society must henceforth be conducted under the seal of a shared creolity (*une commune créolité*), without that obliterating in any way whatsoever class relations and conflicts.[45]

Whereas Négritude's essentially racial definition of identity, as well as sidestepping the whole question of *métissage* in creole societies, implicitly (and sometimes explicitly) denies, or qualifies, the West Indian-ness of people of non-African origin, Créolité, like Antillanité, is at pains to include all autochthonous groups – African, European, Indian, Chinese, Lebanese – in an ecumenical definition of creoleness. There has been a notable effort to demarginalize the Indian experience in the French West Indies and to stress the contribution of 'Indianité' to the creole mosaic.[46] In addition – and sometimes in the face of fierce criticism from rival schools of thought – Créolité readily admits the integral West Indian-ness of white West Indians, insisting, for example, that the white Guadeloupean-born poet Saint-John Perse – the first West Indian writer to have won the Nobel prize – is every bit as 'creole' in his inspiration, vision and style as the black Martinican Aimé Césaire.[47] Créolité locates the key to West Indian-ness not in 'race' nor even in 'culture' but in language. To be West Indian is to speak Creole, and vice versa. Créolité is at one and the same time (though with differences of emphasis from thinker to thinker) a *prise de position* on the question of the Creole language, a literary practice, a way of conceptualizing not just West Indian culture(s) but also cognate cultures elsewhere (notably Réunion and Mauritius) and, beyond that, a theory, extrapolated from the (French) West Indian instance, of cultural *métissage* as a global phenomenon of increasing importance. But the Creole language itself is the paradigm of creolity, and it is with recent controversies concerning its nature, status and vocation that our discussion of the strengths and weaknesses of Créolité as theory and practice of Difference can best begin.

   In the mid 1970s, a number of academics at the Centre Universitaire Antilles-Guyane, most but not all of them French West Indians, formed the Groupe d'Etudes et de Recherches de la Créolophonie (GEREC) which, through its publications *Espace créole* and *Mofwaz*, brought a wholly new vigour and passion to the study of Creole and, more broadly, of cultural creolisation in the French West Indies. It propelled the question of Creole to the forefront of local intellectual debate, whence it flowed out to engage significant sections of the population as a whole: teachers, educationalists, journalists, broadcasters and, not least, politicians and others involved in the unending debate on the status of the French West Indies. Two issues dominated the group's discussions. First, there was the question, often tackled but never satisfactorily resolved, of creating a single orthographical system that could adequately transcribe Creole into written form. Should the orthography of Creole keep as close as possible to that of French (the so-called etymological system) or should it, rather, be rigorously based on phonetic principles and so create the greatest possible distance (*déviance maximale*)[48] between the acrolect (French) and the basilect (Creole)?

The second, allied, question concerned the relationship between acrolect and basilect and the problems caused by the emergence, under the multiple pressures of assimilation, of a whole range of interlectal forms. These were variously known as '*français créolisé*', '*créole francisé*', '*français régional*' or '*antillais*', '*langue antillaise*' (or '*martiniquaise*' or '*guadeloupéenne*'), '*frantillais*', '*francole*', '*fréole*' or, most pejoratively, '*français-banane*'.[49] This is a problem between what had, prior to departmentalization, been the clearly differentiated linguistic levels of standard French and standard (i.e. basilectal) Creole. It was the perceived threat of decreolization that gave the GEREC's discussions of Creole and, more broadly, of creole culture their particular intensity and brought about rifts within the group which, as ever in the French West Indies, had, and continue to have, immediate political resonances and consequences.

In the course of the debate on the problem of orthography and the status of the interlectal forms between standard French and basilectal Creole, two rival positions emerged which, invidiously, but, in the highly charged context of French West Indian intellectual life, inevitably, became associated with the personalities of their two leading proponents: Jean Bernabé in the case of the 'radical' position, Lambert-Félix Prudent in that of the 'moderate' counter-position.[50] While the 'radicals' stand for the maximization, through the use of the phonetic principle, of the orthographical distance between French and Creole and for the defence of basilectal Creole against morphological and lexical infiltration by French (even to the point of favouring the creation of Creole neologisms (*pawol nef*) such as *latouwonni* and *tirèdpotré* for French *environnement* and *photographe*[51], the 'moderates' advocate an orthographical system which combines phonetic and etymological principles. They are notably more tolerant towards emerging interlectal forms, arguing that the relationship between French and Creole is less one of opposition (*diglossia*) than of a continuum of over-lapping linguistic forms over which the majority of French West Indians move with relative ease and assurance.

Not surprisingly, these differences are coupled with, and are directly expressive of, sharply contrasted political positions. The desire of the radicals to 'autonomize' Creole *vis-à-vis* French[52] and to counter where possible the growth of an interlectal '*français-banane*' is symptomatic of their *indépendantiste* political stance. By contrast the moderates' determination to preserve the orthographical links between French and Creole, and their openness towards interlectal exchanges between the two codes, is a translation into linguistic terms of their desire to preserve links with France and the French in other spheres of life and of their commitment to continuing economic, cultural and other exchanges between the metropole and its overseas departments.

'Radicals' and 'moderates' are both strongly creolophile, but the kind of Creole, and the associated concepts of creolity and creolization, to which they are committed differ sharply. The radicals seek to preserve the difference of basilectal Creole against acrolectal penetration by French as a prelude to, and preparation for, eventual political separation from France. Their stance against decreolization, and their commitment to the principle of *déviance maximale* in writing Creole, expose them to the charge of wishing to conserve a rigid 'hyperbasilectal' Creole that few, if any, French West Indians actually speak any more and which virtually no-one, outside the inner circle of the GEREC, is capable of reading without first – and usually with great difficulty – oralizing the phonetically transcribed text. For their part, the moderates, in their tolerance of interlectal convergence between French and Creole, may by favouring, willy-nilly, the eventual disappearance of Creole as a distinct signifying system, hastening, by their very openness, its 'glottophagic' absorption by standard French. On the one hand there is that threat of ossification and impoverishment in an exclusivist defence of Difference at all costs, on the other the threat of dissolution of the Different in the Same – precisely the same threats, in other words, that, in the present French West Indian context, are inseparable from the independentist and regionalist-assimilationist positions respectively.[53]

The theory of Créolité emerged from the radical wing of the creolist movement, but there are significant differences of emphasis, indeed possibly differences *tout court*, amongst the three signatories of *Eloge de la Créolité*. The manifesto insists on the need for an 'annihilation of false universality, monolingualism and purity', on the heteroclitic internal structure of the Creole 'diversality' that is contrasted to it and on the impossibility of ever fixing or defining the 'maelstrom of signifieds' that constitute the 'kaleidoscopic totality' that is Créolité.[54] The whole contemporary world is said to be 'evolving towards a condition of creolity' (*le monde va en état de créolité*),[55] that 'new dimension of man, of which we are the prefiguration in silhouette'.[56]

It is at this point that a number of tensions begin to emerge between the theory of Créolité and the actual practice of its leading proponents. First, Bernabé's resolute defence of basilectal Creole against interlectal corruption appears to run against the open, progressive, innovative quality attributed to Créolité itself. The product of a myriad human-cultural-linguistic exchanges, Creole (and, by implication, creole cultures more generally) is apparently to be 'frozen' at a particular stage of its development and denied the possibility of entering into further combinatory interaction with other cultures. Second, while the interlect is said by *Eloge de la Créolité* to represent a 'danger of surreptitious but terribly effective alienation',[57] it is precisely the interlectal space between standard French and basilectal Creole that Chamoiseau and Confiant have invested and exploited so imaginatively in the literary works they have published in France, thereby earning a more or less open reprimand from their fellow signatory.[58]

Moreover, though Créolité is in theory oriented towards the future, what is in practice celebrated in its name – the *djobeurs* in Chamoiseau's first novel *Chronique des sept misères* (1985), the *conteur créole* in its successor *Solibo Magnifique* (1988), the *épicerie créole* evoked in his recent account of his childhood in the Fort-de-France of the 1950s, *Antan d'enfance* (1990) – has disappeared, or is in the process of disappearing, swallowed up, like basilectal Creole itself, in the monolithic, monolingual, monocultural world being progressively installed by integral assimilation in its regionalist guise. Prospective and progressive in theory, Créolité is in practice often retrospective, even regressive, in character, falling back, in a last desperate recourse against decreolization, into the real or imagined creole plenitude of *an tan lontan* of Martinique and Guadeloupe as they were before the 'fall' of departmentalization or the massive disruptions of the 1960s. There is a danger, in short, that Créolité may itself fall prey to the trap of universalism and essentialism so vigorously denounced in the *Eloge*. The dread suffix -'*ité*' is always capable of injecting what Barthes called the 'virus of essence' into even the most dynamic historical concept, and there may be grounds, as the theory's intellectual progenitor, Edouard Glissant, has recently indicated, for preferring the verbal expression *créolisation* to the abstract and nominal *créolité* which, he cautions, runs the risk of regressing towards the 'generalizing Négritudes, Francities and Latinities' against which it protests so vociferously.[59]

A striking feature of Créolité is its close association with the burgeoning Martinican ecological movement ASSAUPAMAR,[60] and it is an ecological image, the mangrove swamp, that Jean Bernabé has himself put forward as a remedy to the threat of rigidification and re-essentialization to which the theory and practice of

Créolite are undoubtedly exposed. The *Eloge* 'defines' Créolité as a 'mangrove of potentialities' (*une mangrove de virtualités*)[61] in which, as new forms are being born, so others die, in which everything interpenetrates with everything else and in which, by definition, nothing can be defined or fixed.

The same image is used by Patrick Chamoiseau in a report on the 1990 meeting of the international creole association Banzil Kréyol, to evoke the relationship between the basilectal Creole defended by GEREC and what he disarmingly calls the 'natural Creole', incorporating a host of interlectal and acrolectal forms, actually spoken by the majority of French West Indians.

Describing GEREC as 'a kind of Creole super-ego' (and Jean Bernabé as the 'Pope of Creole'), Chamoiseau, following Bernabé, speaks of basilectal Creole and standard French as of two contiguous mangrove swamps linked by an intermediary mangrove where interlectal exchanges between basilect and acrolect take place and where 'natural Creole', an *Kréyol mitannyé,* is constantly in the process of being formed and reformed, combining and recombining elements drawn from the other two mangroves into ever-changing syncretic patterns. In this presentation, the three mangroves are essential to each other's continuing vitality; they must somehow both be kept apart, each preserving its own identity, and maintained in communication with each other lest they stagnate and are drained of life, at which point, like so many actual mangrove swamps in Martinique and Guadeloupe, they will succumb to *bétonisation* by and in the name of the Same. According to Chamoiseau (again he is repeating Bernabé's argument), this ecological model opens up a whole new way of imagining the relationship between basilect, interlect and acrolect:

> To think of the linguistic space [of the French West Indies] as an eco-system avoids a great deal of sectarianism, and opens the way for beneficial interactions. GEREC will henceforth seek to put this ecology of languages into practice. The basic principle is that there exists in Martinique, for the reasons that we know and with the imbalances that we know, an ecological niche for Creole and an ecological niche for French. And that these niches have their place in the Caribbean linguistic eco-system, an eco-system which, in its turn, is coiled up in that of the world as a whole. To think in this fashion makes it possible to understand that the defence of Creole is inseparable from the defence of all other languages; that the collapse of one language

would impoverish all the others; that to kill off French would curiously diminish the vitality of Creole; and that the question of Creole must be thought through in conjunction with the political, economic and the cultural ecosystems of the region, in a state of openness towards the Caribbean as a whole, and in the presence of the rest of the world.[62]

The ecological model thus offers at least the possibility of fruitful interactions between the Different and the Same in which the identity of each would be preserved while permitting a third interlectal space – the space which, culturally and linguistically, the majority of French West Indians actually inhabit – to develop and thrive between them. If Créolité is to avoid the pitfall of nostalgic essentialism to which Négritude in time fell prey, it must, without turning its back on the cultural and linguistic basilect, open itself out towards the intercultural domain where without question the most dynamic and creative developments in the French West Indies are currently taking place. On the evidence of Chamoiseau's article, its leading proponents are well aware of this need, and are actively engaged in making the necessary adjustments of theory and practice.

## *Conclusion:* Les Marrons de la Différence

We have, therefore, three principal ways of thinking Difference in the contemporary French West Indies: the pre-modern (Négritude), the modern (Antillanité) and – when it resists its penchant for nostalgia – the post-modern (Créolité).[63] Identity as monad, as relation, as mosaic;[64] as root, rhizome and mangrove. But can any of these constructions of Difference ultimately resist the relentless advance of the Same across the physical, cultural and psychological landscape of Martinique and Guadeloupe? Each of the theories of Difference discussed here presupposes the existence of what Edouard Glissant calls an *arrière-pays*,[65] a hinterland, at once physical, cultural and psychological, in which individual and community can find refuge from the advancing empire of the Same, as the runaway slaves of old fled plain and plantation for the upland fastness of the *mornes*. But now the hinterland is disappearing month by month and year by year, ingested physically by *grandes surfaces*, golf courses, secondary residences and marinas, and culturally and psychologically by the remorseless spread of 'French' patterns of thinking, consuming, acting and speaking. For the would-be maroon in contemporary

Martinique and Guadeloupe[66] there is practically nowhere, either within or without, in which to live and from which to speak, that has not already in some way been taken over by the dominant discourse, so that the language of Difference is often uncannily transformed, without the speaker's knowledge, into the language of the Same, and the status quo is sustained and perpetuated by the very counter-discourse it provokes. As Edouard Glissant wrote in 1977, *'there is nothing (by way of contestation and opposition) that cannot be recuperated here by the system.'*[67]

Since Glissant wrote those words, the recuperative capacity of 'the system' has become even greater, with the implementation of the French socialist government's regionalizing policies in the early 1980s. Where once visiting ministers of the DOM spoke the language of Sameness, stressing the overwhelming Frenchness of Martinique and Guadeloupe, they have since 1982 taken over the language of (relative) Difference and routinely emphasized the need to foster the now regionalized overseas departments' 'right to be different', to promote their 'distinct cultural identity' and to take measures to ensure the 'deepening of the West Indian soul' (*l'approfondissement de l'âme antillase*),[68] stopping well short, needless to say, of the point at which separation, or even a meaningful degree of autonomy, from France might become a serious possibility. By this means not only has Négritude become, in Patrick Chamoiseau's words,[69] already quoted, 'an assertion of officialized difference', but the concept of Antillanité has also been absorbed back, in a modified form, into the dominant discourse, its insistence on the heterogeneity of West Indian identity falling in perfectly with recent assimilationist-regionalist thinking about 'la France créole'.

Even the idea of Créolité – perhaps the most radical assertion of Difference in the French Caribbean to date, given that the Creole language was always the most heavily stigmatized, and hence least readily recuperated, aspect of the creole culture – is susceptible to neutralization in the name of regionalism. Creole is now 'officially' recognized by the Diplôme Universitaire de Langue et Culture Créoles (DULCC) run by the Centre Universitaire Antilles-Guyane, some school classes are, with ministerial encouragement, taught in and on it, and the would-be subversive 'fusion' of French and Creole practised by Patrick Chamoiseau and Raphaël Confiant in their novels is regularly hailed by metropolitan critics for its 'enrichment' of French through the structures and vocabulary of Creole.

Identity is no sooner constructed in the French West Indies than it frays and dissolves back into the ocean of universalism from which it was drawn and where assimilationism, that Proteus, waits to absorb it back into itself. So long as Martinique and Guadeloupe remain politically attached to France, there seems no way of staunching this haemorrhage of the Different into the Same, and no guarantee, of course, that political independence would arrest what may be an inexorable process.

Finally, of course, the universal may not always be quite the wholly negative, wholly destructive force that almost all recent French West Indian thinking seems routinely to assume. In a series of trenchantly argued essays,[70] the Guadeloupean philosopher Jacky Dahomay, has challenged the way many French West Indian writers – he is thinking chiefly of Edouard Glissant and the authors of *Eloge de la Créolité* – automatically reject 'all verticality, all transcendence' in the name of '*le Divers*' or '*Diversalité*'. He contends rather that some, at least, of the values relayed by 'the universal' (notably those enshrined in the Declaration of the Rights of Man and subsequent international accords on human rights) are indeed universal and not to be rejected out of hand as 'abstract' or 'false' or relativized out of existence simply because they are 'imported' from France or else-where and not produced in the West Indies, for West Indians, by West Indians.[71]

Rightly stigmatizing the 'militant antidemocratism' of many *indépendantistes* in Guadeloupe (and, though he does not say so, in Martinique as well)[72] and mindful, no doubt, of Duvalierist Haiti with its grotesque parody of Négritude, Dahomay argues that 'there may exist tomorrow independent West Indian political systems, complete-ly creole (*en toute créolité*), in which human beings can be mas-sacred'.[73] French West Indians, he goes on, have always, when given the choice, preferred 'the universal' (meaning equality with other French citizens) to 'the particular' (meaning political separation from France), and there is no sign that they will in the future do and think any differently. The pursuit of equality and the pursuit of identity are, in short, antithetical in the French West Indies and, so long as this remains so, the democratic choice of French West Indians will, he says, be in favour of equality even if it entails a comprehensive loss of identity at the political, economic, cultural, linguistic and psy-chological levels.[74]

If Dahomay is right, and French West Indians always opt for (French) citizenship and equality rather than (West Indian) national-ity and identity, then the prospects for Difference, and those who would defend it, are grim indeed. The time is surely past – if it ever existed – when it was possible to posit a single identity in which all French West Indians could find themselves, whether that identity was constructed on the basis of race, culture, language or the simple fact of being born and living in Martinique or Guadeloupe. On this last point, it is no longer possible – if, again, it ever was – to draw an absolutely clear distinction between autochthonous, resident Martinicans and Guadeloupeans and so-called *négropolitains* or *zoreils noirs*, the 400,000 French West Indians living in metropolitan France (one-third of them actually born there) who regularly revisit family and friends in the DOM, bringing with them French attitudes, French lifestyles and, increasingly, French accents. French West Indians, Alain Anselin has written, no longer emigrate and return, they circulate,[75] their endless to-and-fro movement across the Atlantic and back further eroding already fragile images of self, deconstructing the opposition of 'here' and 'there', and causing the distinction of the Different and the Same on which so much French West Indian thought is based to collapse on the crowded concourses of Le Raizet, Le Lamentin and Orly/Charles de Gaulle.

For this and other reasons, any French West Indian identity must be open, flexible, complex and contradictory, and it is the great merit of the theory of Créolité to have recognized this, even though in practice it too often goes against this forward-looking intuition with a regressive attachment to the real or imagined creole plenitude of the past. Yet the very open-endedness of creole identity, if it offers endless opportunities for creative exchange with other cultures, also exposes them to absorption by and into them, and one can understand Glissant's belief in the need to 'opacify' such difference that remains in the hope of preserving it from the 'transparencies' of the universal.[76]

For the would-be-maroons of contemporary Martinique and Guadeloupe (particularly the former), there is no going back on the traces of the runaways of old. Inexorably, or so it seems, the mangroves are drying up or being polluted or drained, inexorably the monolithic world of *béton*, having conquered the plains, is now encroaching on the complex creole ecosystems of the *mornes*. There is no elsewhere, no exteriority, no *arrière-pays* for the modern maroon, no possibility of getting wholly outside the system in order to resist it.[77] All that is left is opposition from within the system, along the cracks and fissures left by the onward march of concrete. It is here, in the gaps between the Different and the Same, along the advancing edge of the plain and what is left of the *mornes*, that the modern maroon must henceforth play out a complex and ironic oppositional game.

# Notes

1 Space, and the present writer's lack of competence, make it impossible to give French Guiana the attention it deserves. For an illuminating comparison and contrast between the meanings of the word 'creole' in Martinique and French Guiana, see Marie-José Jolivet, 'Culture et bourgeoisie créoles. A partir des cas comparés de la Guyane Française et de la Martinique', *Ethnologie française*, 20, 1 (1990), pp. 49–61.

2 Roland Suvélor, 'Masques et mécanismes de la dépossession', *Le Monde Diplomatique*, 279 (June 1977), p. 19.

3 See Eugène Revert, 'L'Economie martiniquaise pendant la guerre', *Cahiers du C.E.R.A.G.*, 33 (1977), pp. 4–11. The self-sufficiency of the island economies between 1940 and 1943 is – at the cost, it must be said, of some idealization – a common topos in contemporary nationalist discourse and forms a major theme in Raphaël Confiant's magnificent novel on Martinique under the Vichy regime, *Le Nègre et l'Amiral* (Grasset, 1988).

4 Roland Suvélor, 'Regard critique sur la société antillaise', *Historial antillais* (Dajani Editions, 1981), T. 6, p. 474.

5 See, once again, Roland Suvélor, 'Eléments historiques pour une approche socio-culturelle', *Les Temps Modernes*, 441–2 (1983), pp. 2174–208.

6 For the distinction between 'assimilation of' and 'assimilation by', see Suvélor, 'Eléments historiques', pp. 2197–8.

7 Reproduced in Edouard Glissant, *Le Discours antillais* (Seuil, 1981), pp. 166–79. The present quotation occurs on p. 173.

8 For an excellent discussion of Négritude from this viewpoint, see André Lucrèce, 'Le Mouvement martiniquais de la Négritude. Essai d'analyse d'un discours idéologique', *Acoma*, 2 (1971), pp. 93–124.

9 See, for example, Alain Blérald, *Négritude et politique aux Antilles* (Editions Caribéennes, 1981) and, from a Haitian standpoint, René Dépestre, *Bonjour et adieu à la Négritude.* (Paris: Laffont, 1980).

10 See above all René Ménil, 'La négritude: une doctrine réactionnaire', first published in *Action* in 1963 and reprinted under the title 'Sens et non-sens' in Ménil, *Tracées. Identité, négritude, esthétique aux Antilles* (Robert Laffont, 1981, pp. 63–77).

11 The speech – essential for an understanding of contemporary Martinique – is reproduced in full in *Le Naïf*, 329 (3 June 1981), pp. 13–15. For an incisive discussion of the issues it raises, see Fred Constant, 'Les Usages politiques de la décentralisation dans les D.O.M. Le cas de la Martinique', *Cahiers de l'Administration Outre-Mer*, 2 (May 1989), pp. 43–65.

12 *Tropiques* (Editions Jean-Michel Place, 1978), T, 1, xvi.

13 *Ibid.*, xiii.

14 For the militant creolist Jean Bernabé Creole possesses no 'anthropological density' (*épaisseur anthropologique*) in Césaire's eyes: 'it is only the index of the Negro's subjugation and the recurrent symptom of the loss of Mother Africa' (Jean Bernabé, *Fondal-natal. Grammaire basilectale approchée des créoles guadeloupéen et martiniquais* (L'Harmattan, 1983), T, 1, p. 205.

15 Patrick Chamoiseau, 'Le Christophe de Césaire', *Antilla*, 394 (2 August 1990), pp. 6–7.

16 Patrick Chamoiseau, 'Plaidoyer pour un nouveau festival', *Antilla*, 341 (10 July 1989), p. 28.

17 *Ibid.*, p. 24.

18  See Patrick Chamoiseau, 'Quoi de neuf? ... Molière', *Antilla*, 392 (19 July 1990), pp. 9–11.

19  'Problèmes d'une culture antillaise', reprinted in Ménil, *Tracées*, 26–44. The present quotation occurs on page 32.

20  A selection of the most important texts in *Le Discours antillais* has been translated into English by J. Michael Dash under the title *Caribbean Discourse* (Caraf Books, University Press of Virginia, 1989); Dash's introduction (pages xi–xiv) is the best guide available to the complexities of Glissant's thinking. See also the specials numbers on Glissant of *CARE* (No. 10, 1983) and *Carbet* (No. 10, December 1990).

21  See *Le Discours antillais* (Seuil, 1981), pp. 14, 134, 245, 249.

22  *Ibid.*, pp. 224, 213.

23  *Ibid.*, p. 20.

24  *Poétique de la Relation* (Gallimard, 1990), p. 46.

25  On this subject, see the important and controversial essay by Jacques André, 'L'Identité ou le retour du même. Les discours sur l'identité et la configuration de la parenté', *Les Temps modernes*, 441–2 (1983), pp. 2026–37.

26  *Poétique de la Relation*, pp. 156–8.

27  *Ibid.*, p. 23.

28  I have discussed Glissant's use of the root-rhizome distinction in the paper entitled 'Penser l'Indianité: la présence indienne dans la réflexion martiniquaise contemporaine' that I gave at the Festival International de l'Indianité held at Saint-François (Guadeloupe) in December 1990.

29  *Le Discours antillais*, 134. Translation in *Caribbean Discourse*, 67.

30  Cf. Simone Schwarz-Bart's *Pluie et vent sur Télumée Miracle* and Xavier Orville's *Délice ou le fromager* amongst other examples. For a valuable discussion of the tree image in French West Indian writing, see Beverley Ormerod, *An Introduction to the French Caribbean Novel* (Heinemann, 1985), especially pp. 28–9.

31  Significantly, the mangrove frequently suggests torpor and stagnation in Césaire's poetry. See the poems 'Mangrove' and 'La Condition-mangrove' in his most recent collection *Moi, Laminaire* ... (Seuil, 1982), 25 and 30 (Translations in Aimé Césaire, *Lyric and Dramatic Poetry 1946–82*, translated by Clayton Eshleman and Annette Smith (Caraf Books, University Press of Virginia, 1990), pp. 107 and 117.

32  The PCG has recently adopted an independentist position, partly as a response to the perceived threat of 1993, partly to avoid being outflanked by the far left. None the less, its autonomist leanings remain strong, and it is not difficult to imagine it reverting to an autonomist position as and when circumstances require.

33  *Matinik*, 3 (no date (1977?)), p. 2.

34  For a discussion of this, see Richard D.E. Burton, *Assimilation or Independence? Prospects for Martinique* (Occasional Monograph Series, 13, Centre for Developing-Area Studies, McGill University, Montreal, 1978), pp. 52–6.

35  See the anonymous statement cited by Marie-Céline Lafontaine in 'Le Carnaval de '"Autre". A propos d'"authenticité" en matière de musique guadeloupéenne: théories et réalités', *Les Temps modernes*, 441–442 (1983), p. 2145: 'Even if the quadrille and biguine are played in county areas in Guadeloupe, they cannot, by virtue of their origin, their style and their assimilationist character, represent the authentic music that expresses the Guadeloupean soul in its depths.'

36  Dany Bébel-Gisler, *Le Défi culturel guadeloupéen* (Editions Caribéennes, 1989), p. 23.

37  See Lafontaine, 'Le Carnaval de l'"Autre"', p. 2144.

38  See Yves Leborgne's contribution to Alain Brossat and Daniel Maragnès (eds), *Les Antilles dans l'impasse?* (Editions Caribéennes, 1981), pp. 103–19.

39  On the exclusion of Indians by nationalist discourse, see Danik Zandwonis, 'Pas mort le racisme!', *Sept Magazine*, 599 (13 December 1990), p. 5.

40  The key contributions to the Indianité debate are Ernest Moutoussamy, *La Guadeloupe et son Indianité* (Editions Caribéennes, 1987) and Max Sulty and Jocelyn Nagapin, *La Migration de l'Hindouisme aux Antilles* (no publisher given, 1989). See also note 46 below.

41  According to Chamoiseau, 'the concept of Créolité is formulated through and with the thought of Edouard Glissant', *Antilla*, 335 (5 June 1989), 8.

42  Jean Bernabé, Patrick Chamoiseau, Raphaël Confiant, *Eloge de la Créolité* (Gallimard/Presses universitaires créoles, 1989), p. 55.

43  *Ibid.*, p. 29.

44  *Ibid.*, p. 27.

45  *Ibid.*, p. 29.

46  See above all the special number of *Carbet* (No. 9, December 1989) on 'L'Inde en Nous. Des Caraïbes aux Mascareignes'. The co-ordinator of the number, Gerry L'Etang, is close to the Créolité 'school' of thinkers. There is a certain vogue for 'Indianité' in contemporary Martinique whose implications, political and other, I discuss in the paper referred to in note 28.

47  See Henriette Levillain and Mireille Sacotte (eds), *Saint-John Perse. Antillanité et universalité* (Editions Caribeennes, 1988).

48  The term 'déviance maximale' is associated with the work of Jean Bernabé. For a full discussion of the orthographic controversy, see his *Fondal-natal*, 1, pp. 296–348.

49  The term '*français régional*' (or '*antillais*') is favoured by Marie-Christine Hazaël-Massieux, while '*langue martiniquaise*' (or '*guadeloupéenne*') is preferred by Lambert-Félix Prudent. The term '*francole*' was suggested by the Guadeloupean writer Germain William in his *Aurélien a paré le saut* (1980), an early attempt to use the interlect as a literary language; '*français-banane*' is a catch-all term, commonly used by opponents of Patrick Chamoiseau and Raphaël Confiant to describe the '*franco-créoloïde*' language of certain of their literary works.

50  For a summary of Bernabé's viewpoint, see his 'Promouvoir l'identité culturelle? Eléments d'écolinguistique et de glottopolitique appliqués aux aires créolophones' in Jean-Claude Fortier (ed.), *Questions sur l'administration des DOM. Décentraliser outre-mer?* (Economica/Presses universitaires d'Aix-en-Provence, 1989), pp. 341–52. For Prudent's viewpoint, see, in addition to his *Des baragouins à la langue antillaise* (Editions Caribéennes, 1980), 'Ecrire le créole à la Martinique: norme et conflit sociolinguistique', in Ralph Ludwig (ed.), *Les Créoles français entre l'oral et l'écrit* (Gunter Narr Verlag, Tübingen, 1989), pp. 65–80, and 'La difficile construction de la linguistique créole aux Antilles', *Nouvelle Revue des Antilles*, 3 (September 1990), pp. 3–12.

51  These examples are taken from the glossary of Creole neologisms in Raphaël Confiant's creole novel *Marisosé* (Presses universitaires créoles, 1987, pp. 139–40).

52  The expression 'autonomisation du créole' is used by Bernabé in *Fondal-natal*, 1, p. 307 in opposing phonetic orthography to its etymological rival which, he says, maintains Creole in a state of 'objective dependence on the French language'.

53  Phonetic orthography is, in general, adopted in independentist publications such as *Douvanjou*, *Magwa*, *Jougwa* and *Ja ka ta* (Guadeloupe) and *Grif an Tè*, *Kabouya*, *Antilla* and *Koubari* (Martinique) as well as by the Creole language

edition of the *Courrier de l'Unesco*, *Kourilet*. In 1988 the moderate creolists joined other anti-independentist intellectuals in establishing the *Nouvelle Revue des Antilles*; the prominent PPM (and ex-Trotskyist) mayor of Robert, Edouard De Lépine, is a member of its editorial committee and, in general, it adopts a 'regionalist' position against the independentist implications of the idea of Créolité.

54  Bernabé *et al.*, *Eloge de la Créolité*, pp. 27–8.

55  *Ibid.*, p. 52.

56  *Ibid.*, p. 27.

57  *Ibid.*, p. 49.

58  See Bernabé's contribution, '*Solibo Magnifique* ou le chant de l'oiseau-lyre' in the special number of *Antilla* (*Antilla Special*, 11, December 1988/January 1989, pp. 37–41) devoted to Chamoiseau's literary practice.

59  See Glissant, *Poétique de la Relation*, p. 103.

60  Association pour la Sauvegarde du Patrimoine Martiniquais.

61  Bernabé *et al.*, *Eloge de la Créolité*, p. 28.

62  All quotations from Patrick Chamoiseau, 'Penser créole', *Antilla*, 408 (2 November 1990), pp. 32–4.

63  For an interesting discussion of Créolité and post-modernity, see '*Eloge de la Créolité* et nouvelle modernité. Entretien avec Paul Blanquart', *Antilla*, 389 (29 June 1990), pp. 19–26.

64  See Bernabé *et al.*, *Eloge de la Créolité*, p. 53 ('l'ambiguïté torrentielle d'une identité mosaïque').

65  See Glissant, *Le Discours antillais*, pp. 166 and *passim*.

66  The theme of the maroon (whom Glissant calls 'the one true popular hero in the West Indies', *Le Discours antillais*, p. 104) and his modern equivalents or analogues – the runaway criminal (Beauregard and Marny in Martinique), the *quimboiseur*, the Rasta, the political fugitive (Luc Reinette, Henri Bernard and Humbert Marboeuf in Guadeloupe) – is to be encountered everywhere in contemporary French West Indian thought and literature. See, for example, René Louise, *Manifeste du marronisme moderne. Philosophie de l'esthétique des artistes de la Caraïbe et d'Amerique latine* (Editions O Madiana, 1990). The theme of marronnage in Glissant's work is discussed in Ernest Pépin, 'Le Personnage romanesque dans l'oeuvre de Glissant', *Carbet*, 10 (1990), pp. 89–99, and there is an illuminating comparison between Beauregard, Marny and the maroon in Marlène Hospice, *Pas de pitié pour Marny* (Editions Désormeaux, 1984), pp. 143–52.

67  Glissant, *Le Discours antillas*, p. 171 (Glissant's italics).

68  Such language was also spoken during the later years of the Giscard presidency. See Bébel-Gisler, *Le Défi culturel guadeloupéen*, pp. 182–4.

69  See note 16 above.

70  The essays in question are Jacky Dahomay, 'La Philosophie politique moderne et la Caraïbe', *Chemins Critiques* 1, 2 (August 1989), pp. 7–29 and 'Habiter la créolité ou le heurt de l'universel', *Chemins Critiques*, 1, 3 (December 1989), pp. 110–33.

71  Dahomay, 'Habiter la créolité', pp. 127 and 131.

72  Dahomay, 'La Philosophie politique', p. 17.

73  Dahomay, 'Habiter la créolité', p. 130.

74  Dahomay, 'La Philosphie politique', pp. 23–4.

75  Alain Anselin, *L'Emigration antillaise en France. La Troisième Ile* (Karthala, 1990), p. 266.

76  Glissant, *Le Discours antillais*, p. 245.

77 For the distinction between 'opposition' and 'resistance' on which this conclusion is based, see Michel de Certeau, 'On the Oppositional Practices of Everyday Life', *Social Text*, 3 (1980), pp. 3–43.

# CHAPTER 11 | French West Indian writing since 1970

*Beverley Ormerod*

During the last 20 years, it is the novel that has dominated French West Indian literature. Seldom standing free from its public or its environment, it attests to the continuing debates in the region regarding cultural and economic policies, national identity and independence. The rise of the novel has been supported by the increasing popularity of the essay, which confirms the socio-political and linguistic preoccupations of fiction (indeed, the essayist is sometimes a novelist wearing another hat). In the decade of the 1970s, most writers of fiction touched on themes first sounded by the Négritude movement: the West Indian's alienation from both Europe and Africa, with the psychological suffering and loss of cultural identity that this had entailed. At the same time, new theories were advanced concerning the economic decline and environmental predicament of the Francophone islands, and their inhabitants' long indifference to a history seen by writers as vital to the formation of a sense of nationhood. From the 1980s greater stress has been laid on the cultural solidarity of the Caribbean archipelago and on the status of Creole, while a number of earlier themes have been prolonged or explored afresh.

A further shift in emphasis, away from the novel of the individual towards that of the group or collectivity, has been apparent in recent years. Exemplifying this trend are the works of Edouard Glissant and younger authors clearly influenced by him, such as Daniel Maximin, Patrick Chamoiseau and Raphaël Confiant, whose fiction deals with the experience of clearly defined, yet overlapping social groups, and whose choice of epigraph signals the theoretical underpinning of their literary creations. Implicit in their writing is the desire to embrace and define a Caribbean identity. Occasionally intersecting with these narratives of the collectivity, through a common sense of historic lack and loss, are those novels in which Africa continues to serve as a springboard for the emotional quest of a West Indian protagonist.

There is no doubt that the dominant figure in French West Indian writing over the last 20 years has been that of Edouard Glissant. Yet so idiosyncratic is his voice that he has no close literary imitators. Through a series of theoretical works culminating in his major collection of essays, *Le Discours antillais* (Seuil, 1981), and recently reinforced by his *Poétique de la Relation* (Gallimard, 1990), he has been responsible for the formulating of a sociology of Caribbean literature, the key concepts of which have provided the impetus for much recent creative writing in the region. In his promotion of Antillanité ('Caribbeanness'), he does not look backward to Africa or sideways to France, but outward to the rest of the West Indies, divided by language but sharing a common cultural heritage: '*Toutes les Iles que vous ne voyez pas plantées dans la mer alentour et qui protègent votre tête*' ('all the islands that you can't see, standing in the sea all around, and protecting your head': *La Case du commandeur*, Seuil, 1981: 235).[1] He insists on the novelist's obligation to counteract the historical imposition of a warped and sterilizing version of the past: '*Parce que la mémoire historique fut trop souvent raturée, l'écrivain antillais doit "fouiller" cette mémoire, à partir de traces parfois latentes qu'il a repérées dans le réel*' ('Because memory of the past was too often effaced, the West Indian writer must "dig up" this memory, starting from sometimes latent traces that he has discovered in [surrounding] reality': *Discours antillais*, 133). He calls attention also to the psychic components of French/West Indian discourse and the threat to Creole, which has long been disparaged as 'folklorique', without further *raison d'être* (*Discours antillais,* 173), the unserious language of an inferior social group. This is linked to a lengthy analysis of the contact of oral and written worlds in the plantation system, a subject to which he returns in *Poétique de la Relation*. Glissant's influence is evident in younger novelists' emphasis on history, their view of contemporary society and the ways in which they experiment with the assimilation of Creole into their French texts. But his particular tone of irony, which is his chosen response to the pain of the Caribbean's brutal history, lends a unique imprint to his own work, even while, through its combination of obscurity and emotional restraint, it remains at a certain remove from a popular audience.

With hindsight, Glissant's *Malemort* (Seuil, 1975) has probably been the most influential work of the past two decades. It pioneered a way of writing about the West Indies that was not picturesque or overtly heroic, but deployed a wry compassion, tinged with an often derisive humour, in its presentation of social reality. *Malemort* was never, of course, intended to be viewed in isolation: it was the third in a series of interrelated narratives, fictional reconstructions of moments in Martinican history, which had begun with *La Lézarde* in 1958, continued with *Le Quatrième Siècle* in 1964, and was to produce two further volumes in the 1980s. But *Malemort* differed radically from its predecessors. Its first impact is through a style and structure so esoteric that the novel resembles no conventional work of social realism. Yet with a virtuoso deployment of shifting scenes and narrative voices, elliptical references, reversals of time-schemes, indeed a wilful embracing of the indirect, Glissant still voices plainly many of the socio-cultural concerns that he was to develop in his later *Discours antillais.*

*Malemort*'s leitmotif is the loss of history – the way in which a callous ruling class, through the shattering of family structures and the cavalier neglect of archives in the era of slavery, rendered virtually impossible the preservation of folk memory. Through the heads of Glissant's protagonists runs the yearning for an elusive, intangible forbear:

> *celui que dans toute autre langue que cette absence et ce manque d'ici on eût sans doute appelé l'Ancêtre et qui n'était plus qu'un vague nœud au ventre, un cri sans feuille ni racine, un pleurer sans yeux, un mort sans retour* (the one who, in any language other than this absence and this lack of ours, would doubtless have been called the Ancestor, but who was no more than a vague knot in our stomachs, a leafless, rootless cry, a sightless weeping, a dead man gone forever: 61).

Beyond this lies the author's doctrine of the hard necessity of self-knowledge, so that a West Indian identity may be forged through a willed confrontation of the fragmented, shameful past, '*l'empan de minuit qu'il eût fallu accepter de traverser pour se connaître vraiment*' ('the midnight space that we would have to agree to pass through so as to know ourselves truly': 166).

Alongside the disregard of the past, the despoliation of the Martinican countryside is perceived as symptomatic of a betrayal of national identity. At a literal level, Glissant protests against the ravages wrought by metropolitan development companies upon a landscape of once untouched beauty, the damming of watercourses and felling of the primordial forest in order to make way for the gimcrack construction of a so-called industrial zone that will bring no real benefits to the island's economy. At a symbolic level, the destruction of the land is portrayed as an act of aggression against a precious repository of the past, indeed its only true guardian. For history waits, latent, in Caribbean nature, which is filled with sorrowful reminders of slavery and repression:

> *depuis les tas d'années que les nègres pour un oui un non se faisaient fusiller sans écho ni souvenir... on peut commencer à compter à tenir la liste à dérouler le temps comme une feuille de canne tout au long de la canne avec à chaque nœud le portrait de ceux qui sont tombés* (for so many years black people had been getting shot for the merest trifle, leaving behind no echo or memory... we can begin to count to draw up the list to unfold time like a cane leaf all the way down the cane stalk and at every joint there is the portrait of those who fell: 128–9).

In his later *Discours antillais* Glissant treats the topic of a population heedless of both landscape and the past, whose indifference must be seen in the context of various alienating factors which have militated against national feeling in Martinique: the absence of agrarian reform, the repression of strikes, and above all, economic dependence on France.

The influence of certain aspects of *Malemort* has become fully evident only in recent years: the creation, for example, of the character of the *djobeur* – temporary coffin-bearer, catcher of pigs, archetypal bystander – whose drift through life, with its brief bursts of gay energy and its undermining weight of frustration, mirrors the aimlessness of a dependent country unable to agree on its long-term goals. The invention of a mode of discourse in which standard French is infused with the tone and pace of West Indian speech, and occasionally with snatches of Creole, is the forerunner of later fiction in which Creole will assume a higher profile. Glissant's habit of shunning both passion and pontificating, his preference for irony, satire and the deadpan conveying of insights, offer a new way of talking about the problem of identity:

> *Quel nègre? Qui est élu n'est pas un nègre. C'est un citoyen de la République, nous ne sommes pas des Africains. La plèbe peut noircir la nuit, elle est pour souffrir et élire* (Which black man? A man who's been elected isn't a black man. He's a citizen of the Republic; we aren't Africans. Let the lower classes blacken the night, they're there to suffer and to elect: 77).

In the fictional works roughly contemporary with *Malemort*, there are indications of a widespread feeling that political and economic dependence are tied to cultural impoverishment. Several novels of

the 1970s are built around a central character whose personal alienation is suggestive of national confusion and distress regarding cultural identity. At the beginning of the decade, Vincent Placoly
published *La Vie et la mort de Marcel Gonstran* (Denoël, 1971), an
account of an obsessive womanizer who finds it impossible to form
any but fleeting relationships; whose only fertile liaison produces a
Mongoloid child; who moves aimlessly through tawdry settings
where he is often, unknown to himself, an object of scorn.
Fundamentally a loner, yet regretting his solitude, he remains an
onlooker in life, summing himself up as *'étranger à tout et partout'*
('a stranger to all and in all places': 101). Social and spiritual exile are
also the twin conditions of Jeanne Hyvrard's unnamed protagonist in
her three novels of 1975–77 (*Les Prunes de Cythère, Mère la mort, La
Meurtritude*, Editions de Minuit). These works abound in images of
sterility, madness and violent death, which are juxtaposed with the
idea of a land usurped, denied and massacred, its Creole tongue 'colonized' or forbidden. The emotional collapse of the female narrator
parallels the archetypal situation of the land laid waste:

> *Je suis la terre défoliée. La rivière détournée. La mer
> empoisonnée. La campagne sillonnée... Je suis la terre
> qu'ils tentent d'approprier... Ils monstruent notre demeure*
> (I am the defoliated land. The diverted river. The poisoned
> sea. The furrowed countryside... I am the land they are
> trying to appropriate... They are making our dwelling
> place monstrous: *La Meurtritude*, 1977, 115).

A different paradigm of alienation occurs in those works where a
protagonist pursues a search for cultural identity through an attempt-
ed 'renewal' of African roots. Maryse Condé, in what was at the time
an unfashionably frank novel about post-independent Africa,
*Heremakhonon* (10/18, UGE, 1976), uses the persona of a vulnerable
but apparently hardboiled young West Indian woman, on a short-
term assignment in a francophone African country, to explore the
unresolved conflicts in the Caribbean psyche concerning Africa.
Condé, who had already drawn on her firsthand knowledge of Africa
for two plays in the early 1970s and who was to achieve remarkable
popular success with her *Ségou* historical novels in the following
decade, is here mainly preoccupied with the issue of political corruption. But the novel's underlying theme concerns the protagonist's
need to achieve a sense of racial and cultural wellbeing. Unable, in
the West Indies, to credit a black skin with social distinction, she is
dazzled by her African lover's aristocratic connections and sees him
as her *'nègre avec aïeux'* ('black man with ancestors') rather than as

the ruthless politician he actually is. Her motive in coming to Africa was to penetrate the mystery of '*ce qu'il y avait avant*' ('what it was like before': 27): before the slave trade, before her ancestors were torn away from Africa. However, she is baffled by African attitudes towards society and government, finding them not only incomprehensible but almost always incompatible with her own way of thinking. Forced at last to recognize that she has been led astray by a fortuitous resemblance of skin colour, she must now look beyond Africa for spiritual salvation.

The one major work of the 1970s which did not present cultural alienation as an inevitable malady was Simone Schwarz-Bart's *Pluie et vent sur Télumée Miracle* (Seuil, 1972), which perhaps owed its great critical and popular success to its statement of buoyant humanism. Deeply rooted in Caribbean folk experience, its backdrop is the same wounded, self-destructive type of community evident in other contemporary fiction. But its point of view is determined by its exceptional heroine, who enjoys a privileged role as narrator. Meeting misfortune and betrayal with a smiling, understated stoicism, Télumée conveys an illusion of control in the face of life's reverses, and instils a quiet sense of triumph into her modest resolutions of disaster. Afflicted by personal problems and surrounded by the evidence of a society gone awry, she undergoes no crisis of identity: part of her irresistible appeal is that she knows where she belongs and is content with her lot. From the outset she takes up a stance outside the arena of cultural doubt and conflict:

> *Je n'ai jamais souffert de l'exiguïté de mon pays... Si on m'en donnait le pouvoir, c'est ici même, en Guadeloupe, que je choisirais de renaître, souffrir et mourir* (I have never suffered from the narrow confines of my country... If I had the choice, it's right here, in Guadeloupe, that I would choose to be reborn, suffer and die: 11).

This novel retains a unique power to delight and persuade. But its formula of acceptance and contentment runs counter to the mainstream of contemporary Caribbean writing, and indeed, set in the early years of this century, it does not claim to be representative of the West Indies of today. It is a type of pastoral: the landscape it depicts seems idyllic in spite of its burden of hardship and sorrow, for female strength is portrayed as an overriding force that can ultimately conquer every trial. Yet after all, this idyll in which the figure of the grandmother holds a privileged place as survivor, protector, and moral guide reflects a traditional cultural pattern that has not yet disappeared from West Indian society.

Schwarz-Bart has never repeated this formula, although her readily identifiable tone, poetic and discreet, blending proverbial saying with sustained symbolism, can be found again in the poignant, oblique sadness of her short play *Ton beau capitaine* (Seuil, 1987). In her allegorical fantasy *Ti Jean L'horizon* (Seuil, 1979), she turns to the notion of rootlessness and an active search for cultural identity. Ti Jean, a hero borrowed from West Indian folklore,[2] in the course of his fabulous wanderings returns to his grandfather's native Africa, where he is utterly repudiated by his tribal ancestors because his line has been contaminated by slavery. Two models of cultural affiliation are opposed in the narrative. The hero's grandfather, Wademba, a Maroon who once fought his way out of captivity and became immortal, has faithfully, fiercely preserved an African way of life in the hills of Guadeloupe, refusing to acknowledge his real geographical situation. His grandson Ti Jean, on the other hand, transcends his experience of rejection in Africa and entrusts himself to the generosity of Guadeloupe, whose soil, he believes, is ready to welcome the exiled branches torn from a mother continent now beyond recall.

An important year for French West Indian writing was 1981. It saw the publication of Glissant's authoritative *Discours antillais*, as well as of a number of novels that picked up the most important themes of the previous decade: dispossession and alienation; the prejudices and complexes that plague colonial societies; the constraints of departmental status, and the problems inherent in the contingency of independence; the need to rescue Creole from its inferior status; and the desire to take root in one's island, which also implies the movement towards Antillanité, the sociocultural solidarity of the entire region.

Xavier Orville, in his earlier *Délice et le fromager* (Grasset, 1977), had used a fresco of folk history in the first half of the twentieth century to suggest the importance of collective memory, and, at the same time, had equated the trials of a Martinican peasant woman with the ailing state of her country, featureless, wretched and resigned. His 1981 novel *L'Homme aux sept noms et des poussières* (Grasset) returned to the topics of poverty and social injustice through a tale of lack of identity. This picaresque and fantastic work describes the adventures of a lizard changed into a man. Forced out of his community, compelled to drift (*driver*, a key word in the literature of the 1980s), this creature – whose succession of names mirrors the loss of personal identity that occurred in the Caribbean during slavery – believes he is looking for his beloved, but ends up realizing that his true quest is quite different: '*J'attendais toujours d'arriver à moi, de me trouver, de me nommer enfin moi-même*' ('I was always

waiting to reach myself, to find myself, to name myself at last': 71).
The novel's epigraph, which links it with an earlier literary age,
shows the persistence of the theme of identity: it is the dirge in
Césaire's *Cahier* for Siméon Piquine, the orphan whose birth
was never registered and whose lifelong search for his name illustrates the insecurity and disorientation that slavery brought in its
wake.

The film that the 'lizard' watches towards the end of his adventures contains two characters who incarnate contradictory impulses
of the West Indian psyche: a man who, lizard-like, sheds his skin and
looks imploringly up at the face of his father, manifested as an
African mask in the sky; and a woman who moves back and forth
frantically, like a root plunging in repeated, vain attempts to tap a
water source. The latter image underscores the notion of inability to
make contact with a meaningful past. The symbol of the rooted tree
is an important one to Orville: he has described himself as *'un
fromager profondément enraciné dans les traditions de [sa] terre'* ('a
cotton tree deeply rooted in the traditions of [his] land'), and opted
for a view of reality in which the invisible is more significant than the
visible:

> *tout arbre se prolonge d'une réalité invisible que sont les
> racines. Et peut-être que la partie la plus importante c'est
> celle qu'on ne voit pas: les racines* (every tree extends into
> an invisible reality, its roots. And perhaps the most impor-
> tant part is the one we don't see: the roots).[3]

Orville has remained faithful to a style of writing which combines the
surrealistic with the poetic, the whimsical and the burlesque.
However, his preoccupation with the crisis of identity now seems to
have taken second place to a fascination with the act of invention
itself. This interest is central to his latest novel, *Laissez brûler
Laventurcia* (Grasset, 1989), which is based on the author's relationship with his heroine, a beautiful incendiary who, in between engag-
ing in wide-scale arson throughout town and countryside,
persistently materializes by the side of her creator in order to try and
force him to recognize her autonomy. At one level literary game-
playing, at another an elaborate fantasy built upon the interplay
between sensuality and fire, the novel is also a reflection of man's
reluctance to abandon his dreams. Laventurcia is a kind of Dulcinea,
essential to her quixotic inventor – victim of his own fiction – since
without her he would be directionless and desperate: *'il est trop tard
pour faire bifurquer notre histoire'* ('it is too late to make our stories
diverge': 206).

With Maryse Condé's 1981 novel *Une saison à Rihata* (Robert Laffont), we move from the realm of fantasy to that of personal alienation and the search for a political ideal. As in *Heremakhonon*, Condé shows a West Indian protagonist failing to come to terms with Africa. Her heroine, having married an African, hopes to find in his continent a model of pride, freedom and political excellence, an example to the Caribbean. But she is merely an unwelcome foreigner living uneasily under a brutal and unscrupulous regime. Parallel with her own crisis of identity is that of her dead sister's son, the illegitimate child of a vanished Haitian, who makes desperate, futile efforts to be accepted as the African child of his adoptive father. The protagonists' despair is secondary, however, to Condé's depiction of the problems of contemporary Africa: economies in crisis, insufficient food supplies, the corruption of socialism and the shattering of traditional values and relationships.

The aspects of Africa presented here, like the type of alienation, differ from those treated in Myriam Warner-Vieyra's *Juletane* (Présence Africaine, 1982). Here is another ill-fated marriage between a West Indian woman and an African. But the heroine's personal discontent is tied to very specific cultural and religious differences: polygamy, a male-dominated society, and the all-pervasive influence of Islam. This view differs again from the romanticized Africa and the victimized heroine that were to feature in Michèle Maillet's *L'Etoile noire* (François Bourin, 1990). Set in 1943, this novel establishes a parallel between the heroine's deportatation to a Nazi concentration camp and the Middle Passage which her slave ancestors were forced to traverse. In the brutal world of Ravensbrück she is sustained by an imagined African god, through whom '*une résistance noire et sauvage vit en [elle]: la mère Afrique*' ('a black, savage resistance lived within [her]: mother Africa': 198). This is not the Africa of history, but the promised land of Césaire's *Cahier*, the talisman against alienation and the charm repelling ultimate horror. Yet another Africa, that represented by the members of an eccentric sect living in a Paris squat, offers a drug-lulled, fabulous illusion of authenticity to the West Indian protagonist of Suzanne Dracius-Pinalie's *L'Autre qui danse* (Seghers, 1989). But she dies a lonely death: it is her sister that finds a sense of identity through her passionate embracing of Martinican creole culture.

Maryse Condé's involvement with Africa was to dominate her writing throughout the early 1980s. Her historical novels (*Ségou: Les murailles de terre* and *Ségou: La terre en miettes*, Laffont, 1984 and 1985), beyond their picturesque and popular appeal, represent an ambitious project to re-live the Africa from which the black diaspora was forever cast out. Their panoramic vision speaks to the profound West Indian desire to know one's roots: at home or at court, in the markets or the fields, hunting, warring, confronting political crises or communing with the spirit world, here are the ancestors and the smells, sights and familiar sounds of a civilization whose distant traces may still be perceived in the Caribbean and North America.

Condé has pursued the fortunes of the diaspora in a steady flow of novels ranging from America's eastern seaboard in the Puritan era (*Moi, Tituba, sorcière noire de Salem*, Mercure de France, 1986) to the Panama Canal zone, California and Guadeloupe in the first half of this century (*La Vie scélérate*, Seghers, 1987). She reveals her affinity with the traditional *conteur* (story-teller) and her ear for contemporary West Indian dialogue in the rags-to-riches family saga of *La Vie scélérate* and in the multiple tales that make up the *veillée* (funeral wake) of *Traversée de la mangrove* (Mercure de France, 1989). The geographical spread of African bloodlines accounts for Condé's unusual (for a French Caribbean author) variety of settings, which frequently extend into the anglophone West Indies and the United States. Her most recent novel, *Les Derniers Rois mages* (Mercure de France, 1992), shifts from Guadeloupe to Africa and North America in a tale that illustrates, like her earliest novels, the potential for misunderstanding within couples linked by race, but profoundly divided by cultural differences.

Following an independent path from that of the school of Glissant, Condé is equally concerned with the theme of national identity, but treats it through narrative and appears to cast a sceptical eye on theory. In her portrait of contemporary Guadeloupe, race, money and social mobility are important preoccupations. Her few visionaries inspire no popular following. Political parties proliferate, but none to any effect; much energy is spent debating the moral duty of good nationalists to speak Creole.[4] Martyrs are more or less accidental, and are greeted with genuine astonishment: '*Vraiment, on peut mourir pour Lendependans?*' ('People can really die for this Independence thing?': *La Vie scélérate*, 265). Condé prescribes no solutions. Mixed with her humour is a sharp perception of the contradictions in West Indian behaviour. Her novels, responding to the public's taste for dynastic sagas, may be seen as part of the overall drive towards the formation of a Caribbean sense of history.

The prolific year of 1981 also saw the publication of Daniel Maximin's first novel, *L'Isolé soleil* (Seuil), a sort of fictional meditation on the true nature of Caribbean identity; conscious of the absence of connection between the islands, yet affirming an instinctive movement towards unity: '*Nous sommes une synthèse non harmonieuse, déséquilibrée comme un corps en fusion*' ('We are an inharmonious synthesis, unstable, like a substance undergoing fusion': 249). From a standpoint similar to Glissant's Antillanité, Maximin strives for a definition beyond the confines of the francophone islands, one that would take into account '*une histoire d'archipel, attentive à nos quatre races, nos sept langues et nos douzaines de sangs*' ('the story of an archipelago, mindful of our four races, our seven languages and our dozens of strains of blood': 7). Like Glissant, Maximin is ever conscious of the significance of history. Guadeloupe's successive struggles for freedom are honoured in this novel by the evocation of key moments from the past: the heroic resistance led by Delgrès when Napoleon decided to reimpose slavery; the defiance offered to Pétain's occupying forces during World War II; and the traumatic period of the 1960s, when the Boeing bringing back the leaders of the autonomy movement crashed on Soufrière. Written in a combination of styles – letters, a diary, memoirs, snatches of Creole and of the Ti Jean folktales; revelling in puns, word-play and veiled or open allusions to the Caribbean writers and artists of this century, the novel is loosely held together by the personalities of its young protagonists as it ranges through the West Indies, Europe and North America in pursuit of a synthesis glimpsed beyond the '*fragments d'un pluriel*' ('fragments of a plural': 311).

These same protagonists reappear six years later in *Soufrières* (Seuil, 1987), along with the same urgent desire for a meaningful synthesis of the races and classes of the Caribbean. The novel has a specific setting – Guadeloupe in the summer of 1976, when Soufrière was expected to erupt – and offers a more densely textured portrait of the island than did its predecessor. The title is a semi-serious pun, suggesting both the links between the islands (St Vincent too has its Soufrière, and beyond lies the entire volcanic chain out of which the islands rise), and a mingling of sisters and brothers (*soeurs/frères*). Behind that fusion there remains an essential separation; Maximin's work always hints at the individual solitude and suffering that have haunted the Caribbean region. But the signs are promising: the narrative's ultimate gesture of confidence is that of the old woman who has long cherished the ashes of her son, killed in Guadeloupe during a protest riot in the Vichy era, and who returns from Paris to rescue these ashes from the threatened eruption. In the end, she decides instead to throw them into the ash of the volcano, choosing to turn her face towards the future. Her gesture is implicitly related to the children's song in Creole which closes the novel, and which promises that the needle of hope, using the thread of the days, will mend destiny.

Above all, 1981 was the year when Glissant's sociopolitical study *Le Discours antillais* appeared, along with its fictional counterpart, *La Case du commandeur.*[5] Elaborating the cultural ideas mentioned above – Antillanité, the role of history in shaping national identity, the place of Creole – Glissant offers an overall analysis of the situation of Martinique at the start of the 1980s. The island's relationship to France is presented as a damaging one both psychologically and economically. Arguing against what he has described elsewhere as the Balkanization of the Caribbean,[6] he looks to Martinique's geographical neighbours to provide a fundamental dimension which France cannot: a common heritage, a sense of mutual recognition and a hope of shared psychological stability. Admitting the economic problems of the surrounding independent islands, he nevertheless asserts: '*Nous croyons à l'avenir des petits pays*' ('We believe in the future of small countries': *Discours antillais*, 178).

The book's central notion of a discourse has several ramifications. For example, the Caribbean love of rhetoric, so common a phenomenon in real life that it has inspired numerous literary imitators (one thinks of the lawyer Prolégomène in Orville's *Laisser brûler Laventurcia*, or Chamoiseau's magnificent Solibo), is taken to be a sign of alienation, an unconscious linguistic compensation for the absence of real power: '*Le délire verbal coutumier est substitutif du pouvoir économique néantisé*' ('The verbal delirium which is common here is a substitute for an economic power which is non-existent': 485). And so the manipulation of words, like the exploitation of women, is described as the response of an under-class to a situation of ongoing colonization. The deliberate French government policies (food subsidies or social security, for instance) which have turned that under-class into a 'nation' of unproductive consumers and inculcated in it a habit of dependency are condemned for their perpetuation of a passive slave mentality. Looking back on the lost chances for independence, Glissant sees Martinique as a country forever bypassed through its people's desire first to return to Africa, and then to accede to the wonders of metropolitan France.

But if the chance of independence, in 1981, no longer seemed to him to exist, Glissant advances the possibility of rewriting Martinican history from the point of view not of its overlords, but of its formerly silent majority. He contrasts the apparent continuity of the official periods of Martinique's past with its real discontinuity, the '*pans d'histoire*' ('pieces of history') which must have characterized the slave's life of arbitrary edicts imposed from without:

*Le pan d'histoire est subi, la période suppose un projet global vers lequel la communauté s'efforce... Le pan ne redevient période pour l'observateur qu'au moment où la communauté recompose pour elle-même un projet par quoi elle réintègre son passé historique. Pour nous, reconquérir le sens de notre histoire, c'est connaître le discontinu réel pour ne plus le subir passivement* (One is subjected to a piece of history; a period implies a global plan that the community strives to achieve... The piece does not become a period, for the observer, until the community constructs for itself a plan by means of which it may be reinstated in its historic past. For us, to reconquer the meaning of our history is to experience the discontinuity of reality so as no longer to endure it passively: 157).

*La Case du commandeur* is a further fictional illustration of Glissant's notion of history. In this novel he postulates that at the heart of folk consciousness there is an instinctive awareness of ancient deprivation and loss, a grieving sense of the truncations of history that have deprived West Indians of the dignity of knowing their ancestors. In a chain of episodes linking successive generations of the family of Marie Celat, he shows the depth of the wounds caused by slavery and the shattering of family structures; the failure of the effort to preserve collective memory, and the subsequent helpless striving towards an unattainable darkness and mystery, '*une Trace de nuit dans la nuit*', '*La Trace du Temps d'Avant*' ('a Trace of night in the night', 'The Trace of the Time Before': 231, 235).

This Trace is the primordial track, a leitmotif of Glissant's writing, which is called in *Le Discours antillais* '*le désiré historique*', '*le vertige du temps*' ('the historical object of desire', 'the vertigo of time': 147, 435). It represents the yearning dissatisfaction that springs from an absence of ancestry and history. In his view, it is the inescapable stance of New World writers (of the Caribbean, Latin America and the southern United States) faced with the vast unknowns of their countries' past. In Glissant's later poetry it appears as a '*passé farouche*' ('an intractable past': *Pays rêvé, pays réel*, Seuil, 1985, 85), provoking tension between the obsession with history on the one hand – '*Nous fêlons le pays d'avant dans l'entrave du pays-ci/ Nous l'amarrons à cette mangle qui feint mémoire*' ('We damage the earlier country in fettering it to this country/ We fasten it to this mangrove which feigns memory': 17) – and on the other, the need to learn to delight in the country to which the ancestors were forcibly transported:

*J'ai cette terre pour dictame au matin d'un village*
*Où un enfant tenait forêt et déhalait rivage*
*Ne soyez pas les mendiants de l'Univers*
*L'anse du morne ici recomposée nous donne*
*L'émail et l'ocre des savanes d'avant temps*

(I have this land as healing dittany in a morning village/ Where a
child held forests and hauled in shores/ Do not be the beggars of the
universe/ The bay of the hill reconstructed here gives us/ The enam-
elled brightness and the ochre of the savannahs before time began:
98).

The search for the ancestral track is a solitary, haunted occupation; an essential initiatory experience, yet one which must be tran-
scended so that the fragmented elements of Martinican society, '*ces
moi disjoints*' ('these disjointed "*I's*" ': *La Case du commandeur*,
239), can form the '*corps unique par quoi nous commencerions
d'entrer dans notre empan de terre*' (the 'single body which would
enable us to take possession of our span of land': 15).

Glissant's writing is difficult but always coherent, since always
devoted to the demonstration of his central preoccupations. His fifth
novel, *Mahagony* (Seuil, 1987), returns to some of the 'historical'
events touched on in his earlier elliptical chronicles of the Béluse and
Longoué families. *Malemort*'s technique of splicing past and present,
death and resurrection, is used in this story of repeated *marronnage*,
whose conclusion – a tasteful bungalow-style hotel is to be built on
the spot where maroons once died – points impassively to the phenomenon of collective indifference, the long process of memory loss
which, in obscuring the sites of former heroism, has bereft that heroism of honour. An interesting development in *Mahagony*, as in other
recent fiction, is the conscious insistence on the presence of the
author himself. Glissant employs his characters to define his purpose:

> *Un auteur accablé d'un avenir dont il avait mémoire me
> devait prendre pour type et modèle de ses explorations au
> maelström de notre temps passé* (An author overwhelmed
> by a future that he remembered was to take me as the type
> and model of his explorations within the maelstrom of our
> past: 21).

But also, disarmingly, he lets them send him up: '*Il n'est pas à l'aise
dans les éclaircies. Il préfère les grands tourments impénétrables*'
('He's not at his ease in the sunny intervals. He prefers great impenetrable torments': 239). There is a certain relaxation here of the tension and anguish formerly associated with the quest for history. Is it

Mathieu or his creator who hints at a transition from the too demanding realm of 'legend' (the world of *La Lézarde*) to the strange simplicities of survival? – '*La force qui nous tient, qui pousse Marie Celat à vivre malgré tout, nous choisissons pour le moment de ne pas essayer de la préciser*' ('As for the force that grips us, that incites Marie Celat to live in spite of everything, we choose for the moment not to try to define it': 227). A suggestion of faintly smiling acceptance softens this latest narrative from an *œuvre* which has now spanned many years and essayed many facets of Caribbean experience.

In the late 1980s and early 1990s, Glissant's most evident heirs have been his compatriots Patrick Chamoiseau and Raphaël Confiant. Their debt to him is, indeed, explicit in the essay *Eloge de la Créolité* ('In Praise of Creoleness': Gallimard, 1989) which they co-authored with Jean Bernabé. This witty, contentious, provocative work is sometimes slyly ungrateful to its mentors. '*Nous sommes à jamais fils d'Aimé Césaire*' ('We are forever Césaire's sons': 18) is soon followed by '*Il se peut même qu'elle [la Négritude] ait, quelque temps, aggravé notre instabilité identitaire*' ('It may even be that it [Négritude] increased, for a while, the difficulty of establishing our identity': 20); while '*Malemort... opéra le singulier dévoilement du réel antillais*' ('*Malemort...* brought us the remarkable revelation of Caribbean reality': 23) is preceded by a tongue-in-cheek reproach for Glissant's previous distance and obscurity: '*Nous tournâmes longtemps autour, porteurs du désarroi des chiens embarqués sur une yole*' ('We turned around him for a long time, as utterly confused as dogs carried aboard a skiff': 22–3). The authors' chief aim, however, is based on premises similar to those of the *Discours antillais*: cultural, political and economic dependence must be outstripped in order to establish a new vision of Caribbean identity. They distinguish their Créolité, primarily based upon cultural affinities within the franco-phone creole world (Haiti, Martinique, St Lucia, Dominica, Guadeloupe and French Guiana), from Glissant's 'geopolitical' Antillanité, but hope for an eventual loose federation of the Caribbean archipelago. It therefore follows that the de facto integration of French West Indians within the European Community is criti-cized as the latest in a series of politically imposed '*extériorités*'.

While Créolité encourages artists to write in Creole, it is much more than a linguistic project. It is a recognition of the islands' racial diversity; an effort to validate traditional oral culture; an affirmation of the importance of history which, while it downplays the notion of loss: '*les ancêtres naissent tous les jours*' ('ancestors are born every day': 36), still preaches, like Glissant, '*la mise à jour de la mémoire vraie*' ('bringing true memory up to date': 37). The concept of '*la littérature créole d'expression française*' ('Creole literature written in French': 47) is a key one, though the difficulty of defining this is evident in the kind of qualifications that the term generates: '*la créolité n'est pas monolingue*': '*garder une totale disponibilité vis-à-vis de tout l'éventail linguistique qu'offre la palette sociale*'; '*un usage fécond de l'interlecte peut constituer la voie d'accès à un ordre de réalité susceptible de conserver à notre créolité sa complexité fondamentale*' ('Creoleness is not monolingual'; 'remain completely open to the entire linguistic range offered by society as a whole'; 'a creative use of the interlect can provide the means of access to an order of reality capable of preserving the fundamental complexity of our Creoleness': 48–50). In fact, the subjectivity of deciding what constitutes 'Creole' literature is apparent in Chamoiseau's and Confiant's more recent *Lettres créoles* (Hatier, 1991). Here writers past and present are examined for evidence of their Creoleness – not according to criteria of birthplace, race, or choice to write in French or in Creole, but according to whether their work manifests the '*richesse éclatée, mais harmonieuse, d'une Diversalité*' ('bursting apart, yet harmonious richness of an essential diversity': 204) which is taken to be the hallmark of the Creole writer.

In the section of *Eloge de la Créolité* entitled 'La thématique de l'existence' ('Themes relating to existence'), the authors outline a programme that seems to spring from their admiration of Glissant's *Malemort*. The writer should speak with a collective voice, showing the true weight and substance of humble lives, the human worth of *djobeurs* and other forgotten heroes of the folk struggle for survival. Before the publication of either of their essays, Chamoiseau and Confiant were writing fiction in accordance with these theories. In 1986, Chamoiseau's *Chronique des sept misères* (Gallimard) celebrated a dying race of *djobeurs*, the freelance porters of the once flourishing Fort-de-France market which languished after World War II in the face of competition from subsidized produce imported from France. Here, as in his second novel *Solibo magnifique* (Gallimard, 1988), Chamoiseau's style has a strong oral quality, a sharp awareness of the reader as listener. Puns and exclamations, switches from the comic to the tragic mode, the accommodation of both the supernatural and the sardonic, together with a liberal peppering of Creole words and expressions, all contribute to an atmosphere evocative of the *conte*. The use of the *djobeurs* as collective narrator, and their fascination with ancestry, are in line with Créolité's aspiration to promote the '*mémoire vraie*' of the population. But underlying their surface humour is a mood of pessimism: as the market declines, their energy and zest for life no longer have a meaningful framework. The collapse of this microcosmic society into a '*survie collective et diffuse, sans rythme interne ni externe*' ('a diffuse sort of collective survival, with no inner or outer rhythm': 212) mirrors the dying folkways of creole culture.[7] The tenacity of that culture is, paradoxically, demonstrated with dazzling virtuosity in *Solibo magnifique*. Again Chamoiseau aims to depict '*la vibration d'un monde finissant*' ('the quivering of a world coming to its end': 212).

Fort-de-France is in an era of transition from the spoken to the written word, and Solibo the story-teller, unable either to understand this phenomenon or to resist it, sinks into depression. His mysterious death is finally explained as a choking from within caused by the pent-up words of many months that had been unable to find expression. The little group clustered around his body, whose concern for him is to lead them into a nightmarish entanglement with the law, are the last of his faithful followers. They are held together by many instinctive West Indian responses: their shared appreciation of the *conteur*, their readiness with the fitting anecdote that will honour his departure, their fear of the police and their respect for the supernatural. The unspoken tradition of the *veillée* inspires their tributes to the corpse on the savannah and later provides the only note of dignity in their interrogations. Amidst callous stupidity and grotesque horror, they ensure the continuing, lyrical presence of memory and human tenderness.

The novel is also a remarkable demonstration of the ways in which Creole, as language/culture, can become a dominant presence in a text ostensibly written in French. A great deal of the reader's pleasure stems from the sophisticated manipulation of the two languages and the author's numerous invented lexical variations. Bilingual puns (*chawa, kalieur, sousé, mofwaza*) and a host of multicultural jokes are important elements in the narrative, as is the tireless flow of metaphor that always derives from specifically Caribbean phenomena. With both fiction and language, the author pays homage to a fellow *marqueur de paroles* whose fabulous verbal energy, described with deceptive irreverence, was a '*vibrionnant enracinement dans un espace interlectal que je pensais être notre plus exacte réalité sociolinguistique*' ('something firmly rooted yet ever on the move within an interlectal space that I considered to be our most exact sociolinguistic reality': 44).[8]

*Texaco* (Gallimard, 1992), Chamoiseau's third and most complex novel, bears the characteristic imprint of his deft, exuberant word-play, fuelled by his intention to rescue the Creole past from its long neglect. History and legend are blended in an imaginative reconstruction of a period beginning two decades before the abolition of slavery in 1848, and ending in 1980. These years are recalled from the viewpoint of two central figures, the former slave Esternome and his daughter Marie-Sophie. In this narrative which strives to maintain the tone of oral story-telling, everything is made of the stuff of memories: Esternome's recollections of plantation life, his first heady and difficult months of freedom, the loss of his beloved when the town of Saint-Pierre was destroyed by volcanic eruption, how he moved to Fort-de-France and patched his life together; Marie-Sophie's recollections of her struggle to survive as a young domestic servant in the capital, her many unpredictable employers, her hazardous liaisons with various unreliable youths, and her gradual emergence as a *'femme-Matador'*, the defiant founder and focal point of Texaco, an irrepressible slum on a hillside above Fort-de-France. Through the voices of Esternome and Marie-Sophie, the past is retrieved with all its human gaps and omissions (Esternome, for example, misses the long-awaited declaration of the abolition of slavery because he and his girl-friend are sleeping late) and a picture is gradually built up of the aftermath of slavery, the exhilaration, terror and uncertainty of a destitute people attempting to invent a way of life after centuries of cultural loss.

The contrast between *l'En-ville* (the town) and the *Mornes* (the hills) highlights a tension within the moral structure of the novel. One of its implicit concerns is for the ways in which urbanization has stifled traditional creole life, a life associated with the hills, the maroons, the first freed slaves and their ability to draw on personal and natural resources. Marie-Sophie herself likes to see Texaco, perched on its slope, as an urban stronghold managing to prolong the folk wisdom of the old hill people, in contrast to the restlessness and confusion of many town-dwellers. But the tragic figure of the drifter who moves between Texaco and other unknown areas of *l'En-ville* comes to represent the slum community's inherent lacks: *'Le driveur, c'était notre désir de liberté dans l'être, notre manière de vivre les mondes en nous, notre nègre marron d'En-ville'* ('The drifter was our desire for freedom in our existence, our way of living out the worlds within us, our maroon from town': 394).

The opposition between town and hills is also relevant to the choice of an informal narrative mode. For Marie-Sophie, the act of writing down her memoirs seems like a betrayal of *la Parole* (the Word, the act of speech) – the privileged domain of the old oral culture, the maroon, the story-teller, her own father Esternome. This sense of conflict between the written and the spoken word is implied in other ways. Chamoiseau, present as a character in the novel, finds his own writing received less than enthusiastically by Marie-Sophie's literary friend Ti-Cirique, who also happens to be profoundly critical of Rabelais, that archetypal experimenter with words: *'il se méfiait des folies de la langue et de la démesure'* ('he distrusted [Rabelais'] linguistic madness and his excessiveness': 356). The implied comparison is apt: not only does Chamoiseau cajole the reader into crossing a number of linguistic frontiers between formal French and informal Creole, but he also displays total freedom in exploiting oral ambiguities. *'Sur la crête douloudouce des plaisirs'*, for instance (roughly, 'at the sweet-painful-sweet peak of pleasure': 78), plays on the equivocal sound of a half-finished *douce* (sweet) which unexpectedly seems to be turning into *douloureux* (painful), only to retrieve itself after two syllables and modulate into a *douce* – but, after this delay, a slyly qualified *douce*. Chamoiseau endows his invented Marie-Sophie with his own delight in the spoken word and in the wider cultural phenomenon of creoleness; she is the triggering device that releases her father's *Parole*, the remembered store of words from departed generations, and *'les bribes de nos histoires que le vent emportait comme ça, au fil des terres'* ('the scraps of our personal histories that the wind used to carry away just like that, drifting over the fields': 423).

Raphaël Confiant's early novels were the ultimate expression of Créolité: they were written in Creole. In recent years he has, like Chamoiseau, been experimenting with a form of literary French which is infused with Creole elements. Lexical variations (*ennuyance, foultitude, méprisation*) or survivals (*bréhaigne*) are the most noticeable Creole aspect of his style, whereas with Chamoiseau, Creole intonation and syntax are perhaps more immediately striking; but the involvement of both authors with the ideological function of language is everywhere evident. In his first novel in French, *Le Nègre et l'Amiral* (Grasset, 1988), Confiant uses the character of a renegade middle-class intellectual to highlight the role of Creole as social divider in Martinique, as well as to celebrate the pleasures of living and loving in *'une langue neuve, souple, serpentine, tout en étant conviviale et charnelle'* ('a new language, supple, serpentine, yet also inviting and sensual': 128).

Like other admirers of Glissant, Confiant writes about the experience of the group and seeks to capture a particular historical moment. *Le Nègre et l'Amiral* concerns life in Martinique during World War II, when the island, cut off from France and regarded as enemy territory by the United States, suffered severely from shortages of food and essential medical supplies. The multiple voices of the narrative show the hunger of the urban poor, the black marketeering of the élite, the army's raids on peasants for scarce foodstuffs, the displays of racial prejudice by French soldiers and sailors stationed in Martinique, and the patriotism of local youths who attempt to flee Admiral Robert's island so as to join De Gaulle. Two parallel experiences are chiefly chronicled: that of the intellectual in search of 'real life' among the slum-dwellers of Morne Pichevin (with occasional intellectual interludes such as the wartime visit of Lévi-Strauss and Breton to Martinique); and that of the amiable, unlucky Rigobert who is expelled from his glimpse of paradise in the archaic creole garden of Celle-qui-n'a-pas-son-pareil (the Incomparable One), and must in the end accept a sensible compromise back at Morne Pichevin.

There is a thread of folk magic running through this novel, with its fateful flight of steps, its dreams, superstitions and transformations, that is picked up much more strongly in Confiant's recent novel *Eau de Café* (Grasset, 1991). The supernatural is manifested here in ways reminiscent of Marvellous Realism: people double in size, statues provoke miracles, an incubus preys on the village maidens. The central character, Eau de Café, is a *séancière* who can tell the future through dreams. She is raped in her childhood by an old sorcerer and a curse is laid on any child she may bear. Her strange, sea-nurtured daughter Antilia, long lost and miraculously restored to her, ends her own life in the wild Atlantic waves. Mother and daughter are united by the recurrent motifs of death, sterility or failed maternity, which have also marked the lives of Eau-de-Café's mother and foster mother. Even the sea is infertile around the village of Grand-Anse, yielding corpses instead of fish. In this leisurely tale (the digression, typical of the folk tale, is characteristic of Confiant's manner, as of Chamoiseau's), the phenomenon of '*délire verbal*' is much in evidence, but it too is sterile. People talk to themselves, brooding on unfulfilled dreams or ancient wrongs; they talk to the narrator, withholding the truths he has come to seek; or else, like the changeling Antilia, they do not talk at all, but communicate indirectly with the world through solitary, wilful destructiveness. The way of life portrayed in the novel is itself a kind of abortion, of which the spiteful, unproductive sea is the image: the sea which accepts '*des fœtus qui s'ils avaient vécu auraient pu bailler le jour à quelque héros qui nous aurait arraché à la malemort*' ('foetuses which, had they survived, could have given life to some hero who would have snatched us away from *malemort* [a cruel, tragic death]': 322).

Chamoiseau and Confiant are heirs to Glissant's irony, to his vision of history and his Antillanité. Both, however, are evolving idiosyncratic types of Créolité compounded in varying degrees of irony and nostalgia, good humour and social protest, realism and the supernatural. Some of the uses of nostalgia are evident in their accounts of their separate childhoods, much more personal than anything Glissant has ever written, yet incorporating not only individual memoirs but also an important element of social history.[9] They represent the strongest new current in French West Indian literature; but they should not be viewed in isolation. Alongside them are other writers that have remained independent of formulated literary or social theory, yet who still strive, by different means, to convey to the reader their own perception of Caribbean reality.

## Notes

1 All translations by author.
2 For a version of Ti Jean's adventures closer to the original initiatory folk tale, see Ina Césaire's play *L'Enfant des passages* (Paris: Editions Caribéennes, 1987).
3 Xavier Orville, interview with Charles H. Rowell, *Callaloo* 12.1 (1989), pp. 164, 168.
4 Maryse Condé's views on pro-independence movements in Guadeloupe are expressed in an interview with Vèvè A. Clark, *Callaloo* 12.1 (1989), p. 106.
5 For a detailed discussion of *Le Discours antillais*, see J. Michael Dash's introduction to his translation of Glissant, *Caribbean Discourse* (Charlottesville: University Press of Virginia/Caraf Books, 1989).
6 Edouard Glissant, interview with Anne Fabre-Luce, *Quinzaine Littéraire* 351 (July 1–15, 1981), p. 7.
7 See Patrick Chamoiseau's discussion of the market as a socio-cultural force in his interview with Odile Broussillon and Michèle Desbordes, *Notes Bibliographiques Caraïbes* 48 (February 1988), pp. 9–22. On the socio-political structures underpinning the Creole world of *djobeurs* and storytellers, see Richard D. E. Burton, '*Débrouya pas peché*, or *Il y a toujours moyen de moyenner*: Patterns of Opposition in the Fiction of Patrick Chamoiseau', *Callaloo*, 16 (1993), pp. 466–81.
8 For a discussion of Chamoiseau's use of Creole and French in his first two novels, see M. C. Hazaël-Massieux, '*Chronique des sept misères*: une littérature en français régional pour les Antilles' and '*Solibo Magnifique*, le roman de la Parole', reprinted in *Antilla spécial* no. 11 (Dec. 88/Jan.89), pp. 13–21 and pp. 32–6.
9 See Patrick Chamoiseau, *Antan d'enfance* (Hatier, 1990) , and Raphaël Confiant, *Ravines du devant-jour* (Gallimard, 1993).

# Select bibliography

The following bibliography makes no claims to completeness. It consists entirely of secondary materials published principally since 1970 and excludes primary source material, including literary texts. Unless otherwise stated, works in French are published in Paris.

## I Reference

*Dictionnaire encyclopédique des Antilles et de la Guyane*, ed. Jack Corzani, Désormeaux: Fort-de-France, 1992, 6 vols.

*L'Historial Antillais*, Editions Dajani: Pointe-à-Pitre, 1981, 6 vols. (Hereafter referred to as *HA*).

## II General works on the French West Indies and on individual departments

Bangor, Henri, *La Guadeloupe*, 3 vols., L'Harmattan, 1987.

Blérald, Alain-Philippe, 'Guadeloupe-Martinique: a system of colonial domination in crisis', in *Crisis in the Caribbean*, (ed.) Fitzroy Ambursley and Robin Cohen, Heinemann: London, 1983.

Bonniol, Jean-Luc, 'La formation économique et sociale des Antilles', *HA*, 1, pp. 153–212.

Brossat, Alain and Maragnes, Daniel, *Les Antilles dans l'impasse?*, Editions Caribéennes, 1981.

Burton, Richard D.E., *Assimilation or Independence? Prospects for Martinique*, Occasional Monograph Series, 13, Centre for Developing-Area Studies, McGill University: Montreal, 1978.

—— 'Towards 1992: political-cultural assimilation and opposition in contemporary Martinique', *French Cultural Studies*, 3 (1992), pp. 61–86.

Chamoiseau, Patrick, *Martinique*, Hoa-Qui Editions, 1988.

Darsières, Camille, *Des origines de la nation martiniquaise*, Désormeaux: Pointe-à-Pitre, 1974.

Guillebaud, Jean-Claude, *Les Confettis de l'Empire: Martinique, Guadeloupe, Guyane française, la Réunion, etc.*, Seuil, 1976.

Hintjens, Helen M., 'France's Love children? The French overseas departments', in *The Political Economy of Small Tropical Islands. The Importance of Being Small*, (ed.) Helen M. Hintjens and Malyn D.D. Newitt, University of Exeter Press: Exeter, 1992, pp. 64–75.

—— 'France in the Caribbean', in *Europe and the Caribbean*, (ed.) Paul Sutton, Macmillan: London, 1991, pp. 37–70.

Jolivet, Marie-José, *La Question créole. Essai de sociologie sur la Guyane française*, Editions de l'Office de la Recherche Scientifique et Technique Outre-mer, 1982.

Lasserre, Guy, *La Guadeloupe, Etude géographique*, Union française d'impression: Bordeaux, 1961.

Suvélor, Roland, 'Regard critique sur la société antillaise', *HA*, 6, pp. 451–95.

Mam-Lam-Fouck, Serge, *La Guyane française du 17ᵉ siècle à 1960, de la colonisation à la départmentalisation: la formation de la société créole guyanaise*, Désormeaux: Pointe-à-Pitre, 1978.

Mouren-Lascaux, Patrice (pseud.), *La Guyane*, Karthala, 1990.

# III History

## 1 General works on French West Indian history

Achéen, René, 'Fondements historiques', in *Encyclopédie antillaise. Economie antillaise*, Désormeaux: Pointe-à-Pitre, 1973, pp. 141–203.

—— 'Pour une grammaire de l'histoire antillaise: tentative de définition. Martinique-Guadeloupe, années 1635–1946', *Les Temps modernes*, 441–442 (1983), pp. 1815–35.

Chauleau, Liliane, *Histoire antillaise. La Martinique et la Guadeloupe du 17ᵉ à la fin du 19ᵉ siècle*, Désormeaux: Pointe-à-Pitre, 1973.

De Lépine, Edouard, *Questions sur l'histoire antillaise*, Désormeaux: Fort-de-France, 1978.

Fredj, Jacques, 'Situation de l'histoire en Martinique', *Les Temps modernes*, 359 (1976), pp. 2138–58.

—— 'L'Assimilation dans l'histoire antillaise,' *Les Temps modernes*, 441–442 (1983), pp. 1836–52.

Jolivet, Marie-José, 'Migrations et histoire dans la Caraïbe française', *Cahiers ORSTOM*, 21, 1 (1985), pp. 99–113.

—— 'La Construction d'une mémoire historique à la Martinique: du schoelchérisme au marronnisme,' *Cahiers d'études africaines*, 107–108 (1987), pp. 287–309.

Price, Richard, 'An Absence of Ruins? Seeking Caribbean Historical Consciousness', *Caribbean Review*, 14, 3 (1985), pp. 24–9.

Suvélor, Roland, 'Elements historiques pour une approche socio-culturelle', *Les Temps modernes*, 441–442 (1983), pp. 2174–208.

## 2 Slavery in the French West Indies

Debbasch, Yvan, 'Le Marronnage. Essai sur la désertion de l'esclave antillais', *Année sociologique, 3ᵉ série*, 1961, pp. 1–112 and 1962, pp. 117–95.

Elizabeth, Léo, 'The French Antilles', in *Neither Slave Nor Free. The Freedmen of African Descent in the Slave Societies of the New World*, (ed.) David W. Cohen and Jack P. Greene, Johns Hopkins University Press: Baltimore, 1972, pp. 134–71.

Gautier, Arlette, *Les Soeurs de Solitude. La Condition féminine dans l'esclavage aux Antilles du 17ᵉ au 19ᵉ siècle*, Editions Caribéennes, 1985.

Gisler, Antoine, *L'Esclavage aux Antilles françaises (17ᵉ–19ᵉ siècle). Contribution au problème de l'esclavage*, Editions universitaires Fribourg: Fribourg, 1965.

Jarnard, Jean-Luc, 'Le Mode de production esclavagiste en Guadeloupe et en Martinique dans ses rapports avec le mouvement de la société française,' *Archipelago*, 1 (1982), pp. 57–93.

Schnakenbourg, Christian, *La Crise du système esclavagiste 1835–1847*, L'Harmattan, 1980.

Tardo-Dino, Frantz, *Le Collier de servitude. La condition sanitaire des esclaves aux Antilles françaises du 17ᵉ au 19ᵉ siècle*, Editions Caribéennes, 1985.

Tomich, Dale, *Slavery in the Circuit of Sugar: Martinique and the World Economy 1830 to 1848*, Johns Hopkins University Press: Baltimore, 1990.

# 3   The French revolution and the French West Indies

Abenon, Lucien, Cauna, Jacques and Chauleau, Liliane, *Antilles 1789. La Révolution aux Caraïbes*, Nathan, 1989.

Adelaïde-Merlande, Jacques, *Delgrès. La Guadeloupe en 1802*, Karthala, 1986.

Bangor, Henri, *La Révolution et l'esclavage à la Guadeloupe 1789–1802*, Messidor, 1989.

Benot, Yves, *La Révolution française et la fin des colonies*, Editions La Découverte, 1989.

Toumson, Roger (ed.), *La Période révolutionnaire aux Antilles*, Groupe de Recherche et d'Etude des Littératures et Civilisations de la Caraïbe et des Amériques Noires, Université des Antilles et de la Guyane: Martinique, no date (1987?).

# 4   Abolition and liberation (1848)

Césaire, Aimé, 'Victor Schoelcher et l'abolition de l'esclavage', in Victor Schoelcher, *Esclavage et colonisation*, (ed.) Emile Tersen, Presses universitaires de France, 1948, pp. 1–28.

De Lépine, Edouard, 'Sur l'abolition de l'esclavage à la Martinique: fausses querelles et vrais problèmes,' *Nouvelle revue des Antilles*, 2 (1988), pp. 7–30.

—— *22 mai 1848*, Centre Régional de Documentation Pédagogique des Antilles-Guyane: Fort-de-France, 1989.

Elisabeth, Léo, 'L'Abolition de l'esclavage à la Martinique', *Société d'Histoire de la Martinique*, 5, 1983.

Nicolas, Armand, *La Révolution antiesclavagiste de mai 1848 à la Martinique*, Imprimerie populaire: Fort-de-France, no date.

# 5   Nineteenth-century history

Achéen, René 'Conflits des institutions républicaines à la Martinique. Les Blancs Créoles et la question du pouvoir 1870–1885', *Cahiers du CERAG*, 30 (1976?), pp. 15–63.

Adelaïde, Jacques, 'Lutte de race ou lutte de classes à la Martinique dans la seconde moitié du 19ᵉ siècle', *Cahiers du Groupe Universitaire de Recherches Inter-caraïbes*, 8 (1969), pp. 4–24.

Boutin, Raymond, *Petit-Canal. Une commune de la Guadeloupe au 19ᵉ siècle*, L'Harmattan, 1983.

Burton, Richard D.E., 'Trois statues: le Conquistador, l'Impératrice et le Libérateur. Pour une sémiotique de l'histoire coloniale à la Martinique, *Carbet*, 11 (1991), pp. 147–64.

Chauleau, Liliane, *La Vie quotidienne aux Antilles françaises au temps de Victor Schoelcher (19ᵉ siècle)*, Hachette, 1979.

Mam-Lam-Fouck, Serge, *Histoire de la société guyanaise. Les années cruciales 1848–1946*, Editions Caribéennes, 1987.

Nicolas, Armand, *L'Insurrection du Sud à la Martinique (septembre 1870)*, Imprimerie populaire: Fort-de-France, 1971.

Pago, Gilbert, *L'Insurrection du Sud. Contribution à l'étude sociale de la Martinique, Cahiers du Groupe Universitaire de Recherches Inter-caraïbes*, 14, 1974.

Renard, Raymond, *La Martinique de 1848 à 1870, Cahiers du Groupe Universitaire de Recherches Inter-caraïbes*, 12, 1973.

Schmidt, Nelly, 'Formes de révoltes dans les colonies françaises des Caraïbes, 1848-années 1870. Repérages', in *Révolte et société. Histoire au présent*, Publications de la Sorbonne, 1989, II, pp. 149–56.

Thiébaut, Claude, *Guadeloupe 1899. Année de tous les dangers*, L'Harmattan, 1989.

# 6 Twentieth-century history

Alexandre, Rodolphe, *La Guyane sous Vichy*, Editions Caribéennes, 1988.

Ariès, Philippe, Dancy, Charles and Berté, Emile, *Catastrophe à la Martinique*, Herscher, 1981.

Burton, Richard D.E., 'Vichyisme et Vichyistes à la Martinique', *Cahiers du CERAG*, 34 (1978), pp. 1–101.

Celma, Cécile, 'La vie politique à la Martinique des années 1910 à 1939', *HA*, 5, pp. 31–59.

Chauvet, Camille, 'La Martinique au temps de l'Amiral Robert (1939–1944)', *HA*, 5, pp. 413–77.

De Lépine, Edouard, *La Crise de février 1935 à la Martinique*, L'Harmattan, 1980.

—— 'Le Parti Communiste et le mouvement ouvrier à la Martinique de 1945 à nos jours', *HA*, 6, pp. 181–295.

Farrugia, Laurent, 'La Guadeloupe de 1939 à 1945', *HA*, 5, pp. 363–411.

Mauvois, Georges B., *Louis des Etages (1873–1925). Itinéraire d'un homme politique martiniquais*, Karthala, 1990.

# IV  Social structure

## 1  Race and class

Giraud, Michel, 'Les Conflits raciaux considérés comme substitut à la lutte des classes aux Antilles', *Acoma*, 1 (1971), pp. 44–57.

—— *Races et classes à la Martinique. Les relations sociales entre enfants de différentes couleurs à l'école*, Editions Anthropos, 1979.

—— 'Crispation identitaire et antisémitisme en Martinique: le cas d'*Antilla*', *Traces*, 11 (1984), pp. 129–51.

—— 'Dialectique de la descendance et du phénotype dans la classification raciale mar-tiniquaise', *Etudes inter-ethniques*, 9 (1988–9), pp. 5–16.

Jamard, Jean-Luc, 'Réflexions sur la racialisation des rapports sociaux en Martinique', *Archipelago*, 3–4 (1983), pp. 47–81.

Leiris, Michel, *Contacts de civilisations en Martinique et en Guadeloupe*, UNESCO/Gallimard, 1955.

## 2   Ethnic minorities

Beaudoux Kovats, Edith, 'Les Blancs créoles: continuité ou changement?', *Les Temps modernes*, 441–442 (1983), pp. 1912–22.

Beaudoux Kovats, Edith and Benoist, Jean, 'Les Blancs créoles de la Martinique', in *L'Archipel inachevé*, Presses de l'Université de Montréal: Montreal, 1972, pp. 109–32.

Cardin, Jean-Luc, *L'Immigration chinoise à la Martinique*, L'Harmattan, 1990.

Hurault, Jean, *Les Noirs refugiés Boni de la Guyane française*, IFAN: Dakar, 1961.

—— *Les Indiens de Guyane: problèmes pratiques d'administration et de contacts de civilisation*, Nijhoff: The Hague, 1963.

—— *Africains de Guyane: la vie matérielle et l'art des Noirs Refugiés de Guyane*, Mouton: The Hague, 1970.

Hurbon, Laënnec, 'Racisme et sous-produit du racisme: immigrés haïtiens et domini-cains en Guadeloupe', *Les Temps modernes*, 441–442 (1983), pp. 1988–2003.

Jamard, Jean-Luc, 'Les Blancs créoles de la Martinique: minorité ethnique privilégiée et classe dominante?', *Information sur les sciences sociales*, 19, 1 (1980), pp. 167–97.

—— '"Les Békés sont des judokas ..."', *Les Temps modernes*, 441–442 (1983), pp. 1872–93.

## 3   Indianité

Achéen, René, 'Le Problème de l'immigration indienne devant l'opinion martini-quaise dans les années 1882–1885', *Cahiers du CERAG*, 27 (1972).

Horowitz, Michael M., 'The Worship of South Indian Deities in Martinique', *Ethnology*, 2, 3 (1963), pp. 339–46.

Horowitz, Michael M. and Klass, Morton, 'The Martiniquan East Indian Cult of Maldevidan', *Social and Economic Studies*, 10, 1 (1961), pp. 93–100.

'L'Inde en nous. Des Caraïbes aux Mascareignes': special number of *Carbet*, 9, December 1989.

Létang, Guy, 'Culte indien et évolution sociale en Martinique et en Guadeloupe', *Carbet*, 4, no date (1986?), pp. 36–47.

Moutoussamy, Ernest, *La Guadeloupe et son indianité*, Editions Caribéennes, 1987.

Singaravélou, *Les Indiens de la Guadeloupe*, Imprimerie Deniaud: Bordeaux, 1975.

—— 'L'apport culturel indien: le cas de la Guadeloupe', *HA*, 1, 290–303.

Sulty, Max and Nagapin, Jocelyn, *La Migration de l'hindouïsme vers les Antilles aux 19ᵉ siècle, après l'abolition de l'esclavage*, no publisher, no date (1990?).

# 4  Urbanism

Berthelot, Jack and Gaumé, Martine, *L'Habitat populaire aux Antilles*, Editions Perspectives Créoles: Pointe-à-Pitre, 1982.
'Habitat': special number of *Les Dossiers de l'outre-mer*, 78–79, 1985.
Laguerre, Michel S., *Urban Poverty in the Caribbean. French Martinique as a Social Laboratory*, Macmillan: London 1990.
Letchimy, Serge, 'Tradition et créativité: les mangroves urbaines de Fort-de-France', *Carbet*, 2 (1984), pp. 83–101.
—— *De l'habitat précaire à la ville: l'exemple martiniquais,* L'Harmattan, 1992.
Rolle, William, 'Rénovation urbaine et anomie communautaire', *Tyanaba*, 1 (1991), pp. 89–101.
Tanic, Max, 'Modes d'habiter dans un quartier populaire de Fort-de-France: l'expérience Texaco', *Carbet*, May 1985, pp. 49–61.
Torres, Gustavo (ed.), *La Volga-Plage, ou une ville dans la ville*, Région Martinique: Fort-de-France, 1991.

# 5  Crime

Ducosson, Dany, 'Adolescents des "ghettos" de Pointe-à-Pitre', *Les Temps modernes*, 449 (1983), pp. 1080–100.
Hospice, Marlène, *Pas de pitié pour Marny. Une affaire martiniquaise*, Désormeaux: Fort-de-France, 1984.
'Marge de la loi': special number of *CARE*, 8, May 1981.

# 6  Migration

Anselin, Alain, *L'Emigration antillaise en France*, Anthropos, 1979.
—— *L'Emigration antillaise en France. La troisième Ile*, Karthala, 1990.
'Blacks, Africains, Antillais, cultures noires en France', *Autrement* 49, 1983.
Constant, Fred, 'La Politique française de l'immigration antillaise de 1946 à 1987', *Revue européenne de migrations internatinales*, 3, 3 (1987), pp. 9–30.

# V  *Economy and politics*

## 1  General works on French West Indian economy

Blérald, Alain-Philippe, *Histoire économique de la Guadeloupe et de la Martinique du 17ᵉ siècle à nos jours*, Karthala, 1986.
Crusol, Jean, *Economies insulaires de la Caraïbe*, Editions Caribéennes, 1980.
—— *Changer la Martinique. Initiation à l'économie des Antilles*, Editions Caribéennes, 1986.
Démikas, Claude, 'L'Economie martiniquaise: croissance ou excroissance', *Carbet*, May 1985, pp. 70–87.
Eluther, Jean-Paul, *La Guadeloupe ambitieuse*, L'Harmattan, 1990.

Gaudi, Georges, 'L'agriculture à la Martinique après la départementalisation', *HA*, 6, pp. 361–435.

Lasserre, Guy, 'La petite propriété des Antilles dans la crise de l'économie de plantation', in *Etudes de géographic tropicale offertes à Pierre Gourou*, Mouton: The Hague, 1972, pp. 539–55.

Louis, Michel, 'Non-production et surconsommation: le cas martiniquais, *Archipelago*, 2 (1982), pp. 54–63.

Petitjean-Roget, Bernard, 'Situation économique des Antilles à la veille de la départementalisation: le cas de la Martinique', *HA*, 6, pp. 9–49.

—— 'Pour comprendre la situation économique des Antilles', *Les Temps modernes*, 441–442 (1983), pp. 1853–71.

Revert, Eugène, 'L'Economie martiniquaise pendant la guerre', *Cahiers du CERAG*, 33 (1977), pp. 4–11.

## 2   Social security

Eluther, Jean-Paul, 'L'Evolution des prestations familiales dans les départements d'outre-mer', *Revue juridique et politique*, 1981 (3), pp. 783–95.

Gautier, Arlette, 'Les Politiques familiales et démographiques dans les départements français d'outre-mer depuis 1946', *Cahiers des Sciences Humaines*, 24, 3 (1988), pp. 389–402.

Ouensanga, Louis, *Sécurité sociale et aide sociale aux Antilles*, Edouard Kolodziej, 1984.

## 3   General works on French West Indian politics

Armet, Auguste, 'Césaire et le Parti Progressiste Martiniquais: le nationalisme progressiste', *Nouvelle optique*, 1, 2 (1971), pp. 57–84.

Bébel-Gisler, Dany, *Le Défi culturel guadeloupéen. Devenir ce que nous sommes*, Editions Caribéennes, 1989.

Blérald, Alain-Philippe, *La Question nationale en Guadeloupe et en Martinique*, L'Harmattan, 1988.

Constant, Fred, *La Retraite aux flambeaux. Société et politique en Martinique*, Editions Caribéennes, 1988.

—— 'Les Usages politiques de la décentralisation dans les DOM. Le cas de la Martinique', *Cahiers de l'administration outre-mer*, 2 (1989), pp. 43–66.

Domi, Serge, Ebion, Monique and Fortuné, Fernand, 'Le citoyen manchot', *Carbet*, November 1983, pp. 101–12.

Fortier, Jean-Claude (ed.), *Questions sur l'administration des DOM. Décentraliser outre-mer?*, Economica/Presses universitaires d'Aix-Marseille, 1989.

Jacquemart, Sylvie, *La Question départementale outre-mer*, Presses universitaires de France, 1983.

Miles, William F.S., *Elections and Ethnicity in French Martinique. A Paradox in Paradise*, Praeger Special Studies: New York, 1986.

Ruprecht, Alvina, 'Radyo Tanbou: The Function of the Popular Media in Guadeloupe', in *Caribbean Popular Culture*, (ed.) John A. Lent, Bowling Green State University Press: Bowling Green, 1990, pp. 106–19.

Sablé, Victor, *La Transformation des Isles d'Amérique en départements français*, Larose, 1955.

William, Jean-Claude, 'Les origines de la loi de départmentalisation', *HA*, 6, pp. 50–61.

## 4 Europe and the European Community

Crusol, Jean, 'Bilan et perspectives de l'intégration des DOM à la Communauté économique européenne (1957–1992)', in Fortier, Jean-Claude (ed.), *Questions sur l'administration des DOM. Décentraliser outre-mer?* Economica/Presses universitaires d'Aix-Marseille: Paris/Aix-en-Provence, 1989, pp. 483–518.

Dupont, L., *Les Départements français d'Amérique: Guadeloupe, Guyane, Martinique face aux schémas d'intégration économique de la Caraïbe et de l'Amérique Latine*, L'Harmattan, 1988.

Moutoussamy, Ernest, *Un danger pour les DOM. L'intégration au marché unique européen de 1992*, L'Harmattan, 1988.

# VI Anthropology and psychology

## 1 General works of anthropology

Affergan, Francis, *Anthropologie à la Martinique*, Presses de la Fondation Nationale des Sciences Politiques, 1983.

Bébel-Gisler, Dany and Hurbon, Laënnec, *Cultures et pouvoir dans la Caraïbe*, L'Harmattan, 1976.

Benoist, Jean (ed.), *L'Archipel inachevé: culture et société aux Antilles françaises: travaux*, Presses de l'Université de Montréal: Montreal, 1972.

Horowitz, Michael M., *Morne-Paysan. Peasant Village in Martinique*, Holt, Rinehart and Winston: New York, 1967.

Levy, Joseph Josy, *Un village au bout du monde. Modernisation et structures villageoises aux Antilles françaises*, Presses de l'Université de Montréal: Montreal, 1976.

## 2 Religion and magic

Annezier, Jean-Claude, Bégot, Danielle and Manlius, Jack, 'L'univers magico-religieux: l'exemple de la Guadeloupe', *HA*, 1, pp. 459–78.

Amnet, Auguste, *Société et santé à la Martinique. Le Système et le masque*, Présence africaine, 1990.

Bougerol, Christiane, *La Médecine populaire à la Guadeloupe*, Karthala, 1983.

Henry-Valmore, Simonne, 'Une figure de l'imaginaire antillais: le quimboiseur', *Les Temps modernes*, 441–442 (1983), pp. 2090–107.

Henry-Valmore, Simonne, *Dieux en exil. Voyage dans la magie antillaise*, Gallimard, 1988.

Hurbon, Laënnec, 'Sectes religieuses, loi et transgression en Guadeloupe', *CARE* 8 (1981), pp. 79–102.

—— 'Les Témoins de Jéhovah en Guadeloupe', *Les Temps modernes*, 447 (1983), pp. 711–27.

—— 'Les Nouveaux Mouvements religieux dans la Caraïbe, (ed.) Laënnec Hurbon, Editions du CIDIHCA: Montreal, 1989, pp. 309–54.

Massé, Raymond, *Les Adventistes du Septième Jour aux Antilles françaises. Anthropologie d'une espérance millénariste*, Centre de Recherches Caraïbes, University of Montreal: Fonds Saint-Jacques (Martinique), 1978.

Revert, Eugène, *Magie antillaise*, Annuaire international des Français d'outre-mer, 1977.


## 3   Family studies

Bébel-Gisler, Dany, 'Nourrir ses enfants: une quête incessante depuis l'esclavage', in *Femmes, Livre d'or de la femme créole*, Raphy Diffusion, Pointe-à-Pitre, IV, pp. 87–114.

—— *Les Enfants de la Guadeloupe*, L'Harmattan, 1985.

Charbit, Yves, *Famille et nuptialité dans la Caraïbe*, Institut National d'Etudes Démographiques/Presses universitaires françaises, 1987.


## 4   Women in the French West Indies

Alibar, France and Lembeye-Boy, Pierrette, *Le Couteau seul. La condition féminine aux Antilles*, Editions Caribéennes, 2 vols., 1981–2.

'Antillaises': special number of *Nouvelles questions féministes*, 9–10, Spring 1985.

Beauvue-Fougeyrollas, Claudie, *Les Femmes antillaises*, L'Harmattan, 1979.

Bébel-Gisler, Dany, *Léonora, l'histoire enfouie de la Guadeloupe*, Seghers, 1985.

Celma, Cécile, 'Les Femmes au travail à la Martinique (17e–20e siècles): première approche', *Les Dossiers de l'outre-mer*, 82 (1986), pp. 24–31.

Dagenais, Huguette, 'L'Envers du mythe: la situation des femmes en Guadeloupe', *Nouvelles questions féministes*, 9–10 (1985), pp. 53–83.

—— 'Women in Guadeloupe: The Paradoxes of Reality', in *Women and Change in the Caribbean*, (ed.) Janet H. Momsen, Indiana University Press: Bloomington and James Currey: London, pp. 83–108.

Fanon, Frédérique, 'Les Femmes et la politique. La conquête de la citoyenneté, *Cahiers de l'administration outre-mer*, 2 (1989), pp. 7–14.

*Femmes, Livre d'or de la femme créole*, Raphy Diffusion: Pointe-à-Pitre, no date, 5 vols.

*Femmes de Martinique*, Annales du Centre Départemental de Documentation Pédagogique: Fort-de-France, 1975.

Martinel, Maryse, 'L'emploi des femmes à la Martinique', in *Femmes. Livre d'or de la femme créole*, Raphy Diffusion: Pointe-à-Pitre, no date, Vol. 4, pp. 177–89.

Naish, Julia, 'Désirade: a negative case', in *Women United, Women Divided. Cross-cultural Patterns on Female Solidarity*, (ed.) Patricia Caplan and Janet M. Bujra, Tavistock Publications: London, 1978, pp. 238–58.

Pépin, Ernest, 'La Femme antillaise et son corps', *Présence africaine*, 141 (1987), pp. 181–94.

Suvélor, Roland, 'La littérature et la femme aux Antilles', *Les Dossiers de l'outre-mer*, 82 (1986), pp. 37–44.

## 5 General works of pysychology

André, Jacques, *L'Inceste focal dans la famille noire antillaise. Crimes, conflits, structure*, Presses universitaires de France, 1987.

Dunis, Serge, '"Patate manman!"', *Tyanaba*, 2 (1992), pp. 119–26.

'Figures d'hommes': special number of *CARE*, 12, June 1985.

Gracchus, Fritz, *Les Lieux de la mère dans les sociétés afro-américaines*, Editions Caribéennes, 1986.

Lesne, Christian, *Cinq essais d'ethnopsychiatrie antillaise*, L'Harmattan, 1990.

Lirus, Julie, *Identité antillaise: contribution à la connaissance psychologique et anthropologique des Guadeloupéens et des Martiniquais*, Editions Caribéennes, 1979.

# *VII Language, literature and culture*

## 1 Creole and Créolité

Affergan, Francis, 'Langages d'acculturation et langages d'identité: le cas de la Martinique', *Etudes créoles*, 15, 2 (1992), pp. 56–62.

Bébel-Gisler, Dany, *La Langue créole force jugulée*, L'Harmattan, 1976.

—— 'L'Art de la parole dans la culture populaire caribéenne', in *Femmes. Livre d'or de la femme créole*, Raphy Diffusion: Pointe-à-Pitre, no date, Vol. 3, pp. 121–34.

Bernabé, Jean, *Fondal-natal. Grammaire basilectale approchée des créoles guadeloupéen et martiniquais*, 3 vols, L'Harmattan, 1983.

—— *Grammaire créole. Fondas kréyol-la*, L'Harmattan, 1987.

Bernabé, Jean, Chamoiseau, Patrick and Confiant, Raphaël, *Eloge de la Créolité*, Gallimard/Presses universitaires créoles, 1989.

Bernabé, Jean and Prudent, Lambert-Félix, 'La langue créole: sociogénèse des langues antillaises', *HA*, 1, pp. 319–46.

Césaire, Ina, 'L'idéologie de la débrouillardise dans les contes antillais', *Espace créole*, 3 (1978), pp. 41–8.

—— 'Littérature orale et contes', *HA*, 1, pp. 479–90.

—— 'La triade humaine dans le conte antillais', *Présence africaine*, 121–122 (1982), pp. 142–53.

Condé, Maryse, *La Civilisation du bossale. Réflexions sur la littérature orale de la Guadeloupe et de la Martinique*, L'Harmattan, 1978.

Crestor, Richard, *Annou palé kréyol. Cours de créole antillais*, Editions Richard Crestor: Martinique, 1987.

David, B. and Jardel, J.-P., *Les Proverbes créoles de la Martinique. Langage et société*, Cahiers d'Etudes Régionales Antilles-Guyane: Fort-de-France, no date.

Giraud, Michel, 'Les Conflits de langues aux Antilles. Fondements historiques et enjeux politiques, '*Etudes polémologiques*, 34 (1985), pp. 45–65.

Giraud, Michel and Jainard, Jean-Luc, 'Travail et servitude dans l'imaginaire antillais. Une littérature orale en question', *L'Homme*, 96 (1985), pp. 77–96.

Jolivet, Marie-José, 'Le Créole et l'idéologie du progrès. Le cas des Départements Français de la Caraïbe', *Culture*, 2, 1 (1982), pp. 43–52.

—— 'Culture et bourgeoisie créoles. A partir des cas comparés de la Guyane et de la Martinique', *Ethnologie Française*, 20, 1 (1990), pp. 49–61.

Ludwig, Ralph (ed.), *Les Créoles français entre l'oral et l'écrit*, Gunter Narr Verlag: Tübingen, 1989.

Ludwig, Ralph, Montbrand, Danièle, Poullet, Hector and Telchid, Sylviane, *Dictionnaire Créole-Français*, Servedit/Editions Jasor: Pointe-à-Pitre, 1990.

Prudent, Lambert-Félix, 'L'Emergence d'une littérature créole aux Antilles et en Guyane,' *Présence africaine*, 121–122 (1982), pp. 109–29.

—— 'La Langue créole aux Antilles et en Guyane', *Les Temps modernes*, 441–442 (1983), pp. 2072–89.

—— *Des baragouins à la langue antillaise*, Editions Caribéennes, 1980.

'Questions créoles et linguistique antillaise': special number of *Nouvelle revue des Antilles*, 3, 1990.

Relouzat, Raymond, *Le Référent ethno-culturel dans le conte créole*, L'Harmattan/ Presses universitaires créoles, 1989.

—— 'L'Indien médiateur: un conte martiniquais exemplaire', *Tyanaba*, 2 (1992), pp. 127–32.

Suvélor, Roland, 'Yé et les malédictions de la faim', *Acoma*, 3 (1972), pp. 52–70.

## 2 Education

Abou, Antoine, *L'Ecole dans la Guadeloupe coloniale*, Editions Caribéennes, 1988.

Giraud, Michel, Gani, Léon and Manesse, Danièle, *L'Ecole aux Antilles. Langues et échec scolaire*, Karthala, 1992.

Lucrèce, André, *Civilisés et énergumènes. De l'enseignement aux Antilles*, Editions Caribéennes/L'Harmattan, 1981.

## 3 Ideology

'L'Antillectuel': special number of *CARE*, 11, May 1984.

Blérald, Alain, *Négritude et politique aux Antilles*, Editions Caribéennes, 1981.

Burton, Richard D.E., 'Nationalist Ideologies in Contemporary Martinique', *Collected Seminar Papers 29: Caribbean Societies (I)*, Institute of Commonwealth Studies, University of London, 1982, pp. 78–92.

—— 'Between the Particular and the Universal: Dilemmas of the Martinican Intellectual', in *Intellectuals in the Twentieth-Century Caribbean*, (ed.) Alistair Hennessy, Vol. II: Unity and Variety: The Hispanic and Francophone Caribbean, Macmillan: London, 1992, pp. 186–210.

Dahomay, Jacky, 'Nouvelles questions sur le droit à la différence', *Chemins critiques*, 2, 1 (1991), pp. 91–113.

—— 'La philosophie politique moderne et la Caraïbe, *Chemins critiques*, 1, 2 (1989), pp. 7–29.

—— 'Habiter la créolité ou le heurt de l'universel', *Chemins critiques*, 1, 3 (1989), pp. 109–33.

Glissant, Edouard, *Le Discours antillais*, Seuil, 1981. (English translation *Caribbean Discourse. Selected Essays*, trans. J. Michael Dash, Caraf Books, University Press of Virginia: Charlottesville, VA., 1989).

—— *Poétique de la Relation*, Gallimard, 1990.

Lucrèce, André, 'Le Mouvement martiniquais de la Négritude. Essai d'analyse d'un discours idéologique', *Acoma*, 2 (1971), pp. 93–124.

Ménil, René, 'Notes sur le développement historique du Marxisme à la Martinique', *Action*, 13 (1967), 17–30, and 14–15 (1967), pp. 35–46.

Ménil, René, *Tracées. Identité, négritude, esthétique aux Antilles*, Robert Laffont, 1981.

# 4 Literature

André, Jacques, *Caraïbales. Etudes sur la littérature antillaise*, Editions Caribéennes, 1981.

Antoine, Régis, *Les Ecrivains français et les Antilles. Des premiers Pères Blancs aux Surréalistes noirs*, Maisonneuve et Larose, 1978.

—— *La Littérature franco-antillaise*, Karthala, 1992.

Burton, Richard D.E., 'Le Thème du regard dans la littérature antillaise', *Présence francophone*, 34 (1989), pp. 105–21.

Chamoiseau, Patrick and Confiant, Raphaël, *Lettres créoles. Tracées antillaises et continentales de la littérature 1635–1975*, Hatier, 1991.

Ormerod, Beverley, *An Introduction to the French Caribbean Novel*, Heinemann, 1985.

Rosello, Mireille, *Littérature et identité créole aux Antilles*, Karthala, 1992.

Toumson, Roger, *La Transgression des couleurs. Littérature et langage des Antilles (18ᵉ, 19ᵉ, 20ᵉ siècles)*, Editions Caribéennes, 2 vols, 1989.

# 5 Music and dance

Cally, Sully, *Musiques et danses afro-caraïbes: Martinique*, Sully-Cally/Lezin: Gros-Morne (Martinique), 1990.

Guilbault, Jocelyne, 'On Interpreting Popular Music: Zouk in the West Indies', in *Caribbean Popular Culture*, (ed.) John A. Lent, Bowling Green State Popular Press: Bowling Green, 1990, pp. 79–97.

Jallier, Maurice and Losen, Yollen, *Musique aux Antilles*, Editions Caribéennes, 1985.

Lafontaine, Marie-Céline, 'Musique et société aux Antilles', *Présence africaine*, 121–122 (1982), pp. 72–108.

—— 'Le Carnaval de l'"Autre": à propos d'"authenticité" en matière de musique guadeloupéenne: théories et réalités', *Les Temps modernes*, 441–442 (1983), pp. 2126–73.

*Les Instruments de la musique traditionnelle*, Bureau du Patrimoine du Conseil Régional de la Martinique: Fort-de-France, 1989.

Michalon, Josy, *Le Ladja. Origine et pratiques*, Editions Caribéennes, 1987.

Pierre-Charles, Livie, *Femmes et chansons*, Editions Louis Soulanges, 1975.

Rosemain, Jacqueline, *La Musique dans la société antillaise 1635–1902. Martinique, Guadeloupe*, L'Harmattan, 1986.

Schmidt, Nelly, 'Chansons des "nouveaux libres" 1848–1851', in *Itinéraires et contacts de culture, 8: Chansons d'Afrique et des Antilles*, L'Harmattan, 1988, pp. 107–33.

Uri, Alex and Françoise, *Musique et musiciens de la Guadeloupe. Le chant de Karukéra*, Région Guadeloupe, 1991.

# Index

Separate entries for Martinique, Guadeloupe and Guyane are given only when the department in question is treated in isolation.

# New World Studies

New World Studies publishes interdisciplinary research that seeks to redefine the cultural map of the Americas and to propose particularly stimulating points of departure for an emerging field. Encompassing the Caribbean as well as continental North, Central, and South America, the series books examine cultural processes within the hemisphere, taking into account the economic, demographic, and historical phenomena that shape them. Given the increasing diversity and richness of the linguistic and cultural traditions in the Americas, the need for research that privileges neither the English-speaking United States nor Spanish-speaking Latin America has never been greater. The series is designed to bring the best of this new research into an identifiable forum and to channel its results to the rapidly evolving audience for cultural studies.

SERIES EDITOR: A. James Arnold (University of Virginia).

ASSOCIATE EDITORS: J. Michael Dash (University of the West Indies, Mona), David T. Haberly (University of Virginia), and Roberto Márquez (Mt. Holyoke College). Consulting Editors: Antonio Benítez-Rojo (Amherst College), Joan Dayan (University of Arizona), Dell H. Hymes (University of Virginia), Vera M. Kutzinski (Yale University), Candace Slater (University of California, Berkeley), and Iris Zavala (University of Utrecht).